KIPLINGER'S
BUYING & SELLING

A HOME

By *The Staff* of
Kiplinger's Personal Finance Magazine

KIPLINGER BOOKS, Washington, D.C.

KIPLINGER BOOKS

Published by
The Kiplinger Washington Editors, Inc.
1729 H Street, N.W.
Washington, D.C. 20006

Library of Congress Cataloging-in-Publication Data

Kiplinger's buying & selling a home / by the staff of Kiplinger's
    personal finance magazine. — 4th ed.
    p. cm.
    Includes index.
  ISBN 0-938721-26-7 :$13.95
    1. House buying. 2. House selling. 3. Home ownership. 4. Real estate business. I.
Kiplinger's personal finance magazine. II. Title: Kiplinger's buying and selling a home.
HD1379.K52 1993
643'.12—dc20
        93-23777
        CIP

This publication is intended to provide guidance in regard to the subject matter covered.
It is sold with the understanding that the author and publisher are not herein engaged in
rendering legal, accounting, tax or other professional services. If such services are
required, professional assistance should be sought.

First printing. Printed in the United States of America.

Book and cover designed by S. Laird Jenkins Corp.

Contents

CONTENTS

Introduction

Housing markets are distinctly local and highly cyclical, so it is difficult to give guidance on home-ownership that suits all regions and all moments in time. The revisions that this book has gone through in 11 years illustrate the fickle nature of real estate counsel. With changing mortgage rates and economic conditions, preferences swung back and forth between adjustable mortgages and fixed-rate financing. When markets were slow, exotic new kinds of mortgages and seller-financing plans flourished, only to disappear when the selling climate improved.

At any particular time, market conditions vary greatly by region and kind of housing. In the mid '80s, for example, housing values were in the doldrums in many parts of the Middle West and the Oil Patch of Texas, Oklahoma and Louisiana. But the coastal regions, from New England and the Mid Atlantic to California and the Pacific Northwest, experienced jack-rabbit home appreciation through most of the decade. Then the tables were turned, when slow growth and then recession hit the once-hot regions. By 1990, housing prices were declining from unsustainable peaks in such cities as Boston, New York, Washington and Los Angeles, but values were rising in the agricultural Midwest and the industrial cities of the North Central states, where manufacturing was once again strong. And in 1992 and '93, nominal mortgage rates sank to their lowest levels in 20 years, boosting housing affordability, sales and home prices in many regions of the country.

Meanwhile, some interesting demographic trends are beginning to be felt in housing markets. During the 1970s and '80s, America built amazing numbers of small homes and condos for the first-time home buyers of the Baby Boom generations. But the generation that followed, born during the mid '60s through the early '70s, is much smaller. So when first-time buyers move up to larger homes, there is relatively less demand for the small townhouses and condos they are leaving behind. That means that prices will flatten for starter homes in many areas, improving affordability for young homebuyers. At the same time, there is strong demand for trade-up homes, as the Baby Boomers enter their highest-earning years. This also augers well for the value of vacation homes and retirement properties later in the '90s.

When home prices softened during the recession of '90–'91, forecasts of long, deep declines in real estate values began to appear in the popular press. We saw no basis for these projections, and we still feel that way today. Granted, home prices on a national basis will probably not see the rapid appreciation of the 1970s and '80s, but that doesn't mean residential real estate will become a bad deal.

We believe homeownership is returning to its traditional role in a family's finances. It won't be a hot speculative investment, but it will continue to be a good inflation hedge (matching or slightly exceeding the rate of inflation), an excellent tax shelter (just about the only one left), and a handy forced-savings plan, requiring you to add to your equity each time you write a mortgage check. And in case you forgot, an owned home will also be your shelter, some place you know you can stay, without worrying about rent hikes or termination of the lease.

How This Book Will Help You

Every chapter of *Kiplinger's Buying and Selling a Home* has been fully revised to reflect the various realities of today's housing and mortgage markets, as well as tax and real estate laws. While the book concentrates on single-family dwellings, it also covers what you need to know if your interest is in a condominium, cooperative, or even a mobile home.

The book is really three books in one: Part One,

for buyers; Part Two, for sellers; and Part Three, for residential investors. Whichever you are—buyer, seller, or both at once—carefully read the part addressed to the other party. You will gain insight into the concerns and strategies of all the major players in a transaction, and the knowledge will help you get a better deal for yourself.

Recognizing that the vast majority of real estate transactions are handled by brokers and agents who receive a commission on the sale, *Buying and Selling a Home* tells you the right way to select and deal with these professionals. The book also describes how buyers can often benefit from using a "buyer's broker," who is clearly working for the buyer, not the seller. And for homeowners who have the time and marketing flair to try their hand at selling without an agent, we give realistic, step-by-step advice on how to do it.

But *Buying and Selling a Home* offers much more than a comprehensive guide for buying or selling your primary home. It includes chapters on buying a vacation home and investing in residential real estate, fully covering what to look for when considering these properties and explaining the tax consequences that come with ownership.

The book also recognizes that your home is most likely your major investment. It will assist you in investing wisely, both in terms of choosing a house and financing it in a way that best meets your needs. *Buying and Selling a Home* will also help you safeguard your investment—and tells you how to use the equity you'll build up to relieve other financial concerns, from remodeling expenses to college tuition. Special solutions to problems senior citizens may face are also covered.

Inclusion of a score of work sheets and checklists and reference to many more resources will make your going easier.

This edition of *Kiplinger's Buying and Selling a Home* is the work of many talented people. The book's timeliness, accuracy and thoroughness is due to the efforts of Priscilla Thayer Brandon, chief of research for *Kiplinger's Personal Finance Magazine*. Kevin McCormally, senior editor of the magazine and author of *Kiplinger's Sure Ways to Cut Your Taxes*, provided new material on the tax angles of real estate. Rosemary Beales Neff, chief copy editor of the magazine, scrutinized the text, and Sarah Waters proofread the typeset pages. Patricia Mertz Esswein, managing editor of Kiplinger Books, squired the book through editing and design, with the advice of Kiplinger Books Director David Harrison and the support of Dianne Olsufka and Karmela Lejarde. Production Director Donald J. Fragale saw to its printing, and Publicity Director Jennifer Robinson spread the good word.

We hope that *Kiplinger's Buying and Selling a Home* helps guide you through the murky and often turbulent waters of real estate deals in America today—and tomorrow. Real estate has long been a core subject of *Kiplinger's Personal Finance Magazine*, the first magazine of personal finance guidance, so the subjects discussed here will be periodically updated there.

Don't hesitate to write us with your questions or comments. Your ideas will help us strengthen the book in future editions.

Knight A. Kiplinger
Editor in Chief, *Kiplinger's Personal Finance Magazine*

PART

ONE

For Buyers

To Buy or Not to Buy

Homeownership has long been regarded as one of the key elements of the American dream. The reasons for America's love affair with homeownership are many. Some are financial. Our tax code continues to subsidize heavily the ownership of homes, making it more attractive than renting for most people. Homeownership is also America's favorite forced-savings and investment plan, with an increasing share of the monthly mortgage payment going into the building of equity for future uses—another home, college expenses or retirement, for example. A home is truly the only investment you can live in, and over the past 40 years, it's an investment that's generally performed well, relative to alternative uses of money.

But much of the motivation behind homeownership is psychological. This country was founded on principles of individual destiny, personal control over one's life and surroundings, and freedom of individual expression. A home of one's own helps fulfill all those promises, making the owner free from rent hikes and landlord's whims, and free to live life as he or she wishes. A home can provide a sense of security and pride. A home gives a feeling of stability and commitment, not to mention autonomy and privacy. It is often the first step a person takes to put down roots in a community.

But like most freedoms, those that come with

The U.S. has one of the highest proportions of homeownership in the world, with more than six out of every ten families living in housing they own.

homeownership also carry heavy responsibilities—not only financial obligations but also the duties of maintenance, record keeping, and planning.

The Intangibles

It's no wonder that psychologists rank buying a home high on the list of stress-producing events. Not

Quality of Life

Before you take the plunge into homeownership, address questions like these:

What does being a homeowner mean to you?

_____

_____

To your spouse?

_____

_____

What do you really want in a home, and from a home?

_____

_____

If you have children or plan to someday, how will your choice of home affect them?
Your home determines where children will go to school and what facilities will be nearby for recreation, shopping and worship.

_____

_____

What about proximity and convenience for friends?
Your home's location or design can make it a favorite gathering place for your friends or extended family.

_____

_____

How will becoming a homeowner change you and the way you live?
You no doubt have heard stories about the totally unhandy new buyer who ends up renovating his or her home from top to bottom; the successful entrepreneur whose business began in a spare room or basement; or the irrepressible free spirit who is transformed into a model of financial responsibility by homeownership.

_____

_____

only is it the biggest purchase most people make in a lifetime, but also it forces a wholesale examination of goals, commitments and lifestyle. It's an emotional as well as a financial investment.

People buy homes for lots of different reasons. Before you dive into the search for a home, examine your motives, clarify your wants and needs, and focus your investigation.

With so much at stake, don't rush into the market without thoughtful preparation. If you join the ranks of buyers charging about for answers without knowing the right questions, you may—by luck—end up with a house you can live with. Then again, you may spend weeks, even months, looking at houses only to end up feeling thwarted and confused.

Before you dive into the search for a home, examine your motives, clarify your wants and needs, and focus your investigation.

Financial Benefits

Treating a home solely as an investment probably is impossible. Financial calculations alone don't give you the perspective you need for such a big decision. Still, a home is a major investment, and the financial aspects of homeownership should not be ignored.

Some key financial benefits of homeownership:

Budgetary Discipline

Accumulating the down payment on a home is often the goal that leads to a family's first real savings program. Later on, paying the mortgage is a strong inducement to creating and sticking with a budget. Depending on your personality and level of discretionary income, this form of enforced savings (and consequent equity buildup) can be an important factor in boosting family net worth. Stripped to its essentials, *equity* is the difference between what you would get if you sold your home and what you still owe. Equity includes the down payment, all payments against the principal balance and any appreciation in the market value of your home that occurs after you buy it.

The use of borrowed money enables you to profit from price increases on property you haven't yet paid for.

The Power of Leverage

Buying a home offers you the opportunity to magnify the purchasing power of your money through what is called leverage—the use of borrowed money to purchase an asset that is likely to appreciate, magnifying your profit.

Normally, you buy property—whether it's a home or a commercial building—with some of your own funds plus a long-term mortgage. That use of borrowed money enables you to profit from price increases on property you haven't yet paid for.

The larger your loan as a proportion of the home's value, the greater your leverage and potential gain. Say you purchase a $100,000 single-family house with no loan and sell it three years later for $125,000. The $25,000 gain represents a 25% return on your $100,000 outlay.

Suppose, on the other hand, that you had invested only $20,000 of your own money, and borrowed the other $80,000. When you sell (ignoring for the sake of simplicity the cost of the loan, tax angles, commissions and other costs) you'll have made $25,000 on your $20,000 investment, a spectacular 125% return over the three years of ownership.

Using maximum leverage—with a very small down payment and very large mortgage—isn't prudent or advantageous for everyone, but most first-time buyers will need all they can get just to open the door.

Appreciation

If your home is worth more when you sell it than when you bought it, that's appreciation. When you sell it you can use the profit as a springboard to a better home. Or you can tap the equity (appreciation buildup) to pay college tuition, to buy a vacation hideaway, to take a long-dreamed-of ocean cruise. For many people, the equity in their homes becomes a major source of retirement funds.

Tax Benefits

Homeowners benefit from the tax deductibility of mortgage interest and property taxes. When you sell, you can defer federal taxes on all profit if you buy another home of equal or greater value within two years. When you reach age 55, you can sell the home and keep up to $125,000 of profit completely free of tax.

The Risks and Hard Work of Homeownership

So far, it may sound as if there's no way to lose. But homeownership is not for everyone. There are risks—as well as burdens.

Financial Risks

The value of your home is not guaranteed to go up, and it could go down. The leverage that is so alluring when real estate values are on the rise can act to magnify losses as well as gains. For example, suppose you invest $20,000 in a home valued at $100,000 in a booming economy. Then recession hits your community, you lose your job and you're forced to sell for $80,000; the $20,000 loss wipes out 100% of your investment, and you'll probably have to dig into your pocket to cover commissions and other expenses. Real estate is not a liquid asset. You can lose if you have to sell in a hurry, because of a divorce or job loss, for example.

You lose, too, if you invest in a home money that could have been invested elsewhere for a better return. If alternative investments—such as stocks or bonds—are rising in value faster than homes in your area, you might do better, in the short run, as a renter/investor rather than a homeowner.

Even if you buy a home, you may want to hold back some of your cash to invest in income-producing assets rather than pour it all into your new home; this is espe-

The leverage that is so alluring when real estate values are on the rise can act to magnify losses as well as gains.

Figure on annual maintenance costs of 1% to 3% of the cost of your home, not counting major replacements such as the roof or furnace.

cially relevant for the trade-up home buyer who has substantial cash from the sale of the previous home.

Homes cost money to maintain. You have to be prepared to pay for routine maintenance (usually with time *and* money) and for the inevitable replacement of big-ticket items. Figure on annual maintenance costs of 1% to 3% of the cost of your home, not counting major replacements such as the roof or furnace.

Reduced Mobility

Homeowners have less freedom of movement; it's not easy to pack up and move for a change of scenery or a new job. And a hefty mortgage payment may make it hard to maintain savings and investment programs for retirement, vacations and other things.

Rent vs. Buy

In the short run, renting can make more financial sense than buying, in terms of how much shelter you can afford for a given price.

Rents tend to be an accurate reflection of the free-market pricing of housing simply as *shelter.* But the ownership cost of a house or condominium is a combination of both *shelter* value and *investment* expectation.

So at any given moment, you can usually rent an apartment or house for less than the monthly costs that a buyer of that property would pay to carry it through the early years of ownership.

This explains why many young people can't afford to own the very condominium that they've been renting with no financial strain, or why a young family might be able to rent a much fancier, more spacious house than they could buy.

That's the short-run picture, but the long-range view is different. Over time, rents tend to rise. But, if you have a fixed-rate mortgage, the basic cost of owning your own home—the monthly payment of principal and interest—stays the same. This relatively stable cost, combined with price appreciation, is what makes homeownership financially attractive in the long run.

Until the "long run" arrives, however, you may have to make some sacrifices as a homeowner. You may have to put up with less space if you have to pay more to own a small home than to rent a larger one. To find a house you can afford, you might have to move to a location farther from your job and favorite haunts; that means extra travel cost and possibly two cars when one used to suffice.

Buying a House With Others

The vast majority of houses are either owned solely by individuals or jointly by married couples.

But with the surge of alternative living arrangements in the 1970s came a new variety of ownership arrangements among unrelated individuals sharing the same principal residence or vacation home. Single people living as couples or in groups wanted the advantages of homeownership, too. Many lenders are still cool to such arrangements, but willing ones can be found.

There are proper ways to go about buying property jointly with relatives or unrelated friends, the two most usual being tenancy-in-common and partnership. A good real estate attorney can explain them to you (see also the discussion in Chapter 13 of how to take title).

Owning in a group or with an unmarried partner can create problems. When a tenancy-in-common ownership share changes hands, the lender may declare the loan due. The only recourse, if you don't want to sell the property, is to refinance.

Setting up a general partnership to own the place can head off many of those problems by anticipating and dealing with them in the partnership agreement. Use your lawyer to draw up the agreement (see the box on the following page).

A partnership may protect the existing mortgage when a new owner enters the picture, if the lender agrees that it is an interest in the partnership—not an interest in the property—that is being transferred.

Ideally, a general partnership should try to find a lender willing to limit each partner's liability on the loan to his or her respective percentage of ownership. Such agreements are unusual, however. Usually, each partner is responsible for 100% of the loan, so a lender could single out any partner to sue for the money if there's a default, instead of going through complicated foreclosure proceedings. Regardless of this protection, you'll want to be confident that each member of the buying group is financially responsible, creditworthy and stable in his or her career.

The legal and financial details associated with ownership by unrelated individuals are just the beginning of your consideration of this issue.

Just as important, perhaps more so, is compatibility of lifestyle and the prospects of a durable friendship

A Smart Contract for Partners

Make sure your partnership agreement addresses the following points:

- How ownership will be divided, which in turn determines who pays how much of the down payment, monthly payment, maintenance and repairs. The contract should also describe how any profits or losses from rent or sale of the place will be divided and how tax benefits will be distributed.

- How use of the house's space is to be divided.

- What constitutes a deciding vote, and under what circumstances such a vote is considered necessary.

- Which owner will act as managing partner and thus be responsible for signing checks and paying routine expenses.

- How much advance notice a withdrawing partner must give and how the buyout price will be set.

among all involved. As for investment value, keep in mind that partnership interests in a commonly owned house are not highly liquid. For any individual to get full value for his or her share, the whole group may have to sell.

There are a lot of obstacles to overcome in such an arrangement, but with careful planning and thoughtfulness among friends, it can work out well both socially and financially.

Assessing Your Resources

Prequalifying will give you a financial comfort zone within which to shop.

Once you have determined that you're serious about buying a home—but before you start looking at houses—gather the information you will need to present to lenders. Review your financial situation to determine what you can pay down and how large a monthly load you can carry.

When you've completed that task, visit with lenders to get your figures plugged into mortgage formulas that yield an affordable price range. This kind of preparation—called prequalifying—will give you a financial comfort zone within which to shop. You'll know what's easy, what's possible and what is out of the question.

Figure Your Net Worth

If you don't have a net-worth statement already, it's time to put one together. That inventory of your assets and liabilities will help you to determine the maximum down payment you can make. If money you will need is tied up in illiquid assets such as your current home, land or collectibles, you must allow yourself plenty of time either to sell or to borrow against them. You can use the accompanying work sheet to calculate your net worth.

How to Figure Your Net Worth

WHAT YOU OWN

Cash

	$ Amount
Cash on hand	_____
Checking accounts	_____
Savings accounts	_____
Money-market accounts	_____
Life insurance cash value	_____
Money owed you	_____

Marketable Securities

Stocks	_____
Bonds	_____
Government securities	_____
Mutual funds	_____
Other investments	_____

Personal Property (Resale Value)

Automobiles	_____
Household furnishings	_____
Art, antiques and other collectibles	_____
Clothing, furs	_____
Jewelry	_____
Recreation and hobby equipment	_____
Other possessions	_____

Real Estate (Appraised Value)

Homes	_____
Other properties	_____

Retirement Funds

Vested portion of company plans	_____
Vested benefits	_____
IRA or Keogh plans	_____
Annuities (surrender value)	_____

Other Assets

Equity in business	_____
Partnership interests	_____

Total Assets $_____

WHAT YOU OWE

Current Bills

	$ Amount
Rent	_____
Utilities	_____
Charge-account balances	_____
Credit card balances	_____
Insurance premiums	_____
Alimony or child support	_____
Other bills	_____

Taxes

Federal	_____
State	_____
Local	_____
Taxes on investments	_____
Other	_____

Mortgages

Homes	_____
Home equity	_____
Other properties	_____

Debts to Individuals _____

Loans

Auto	
Education	_____
Other	_____

Total Liabilities $_____

Total Assets $_____
Minus Total Liabilities –_____
Equals Your Net Worth $_____

The Down Payment

Now use the accompanying work sheet to find the maximum down payment you could make if you wanted to put all your liquid assets into the purchase of a new home. From your total *liquid* net worth (including the equity you'll get from the sale of your present home), subtract:

- savings for emergencies, educational expenses or retirement;

- settlement and moving costs;

- and cash you'll need to improve, decorate and furnish your new home.

The bottom line will be the sum that you *could* put down on the new house, if you wished to use it all. The more cash you pay up front, the less you will have to pay month by month on the mortgage, and the lower your total interest costs will be.

Figure Your Down Payment

	$ Amount
Net worth (total assets minus liabilities)	_____
Minus funds reserved for college expenses, savings, retirement, emergency needs, etc.	– _____
Minus cash needed to buy the new home	
Sales expenses for current home	– _____
Settlement expenses	– _____
Moving and relocating expenses	– _____
Immediate improvements to new home	– _____
Decorating, furnishing new home	– _____
Net Assets Available	$ _____
Plus gifts from parents, relatives	+ _____
Total Available Cash for Down Payment	$ _____

Conversely, the less you put down, the greater will be your leverage, tax deductions for mortgage interest, and available funds for other expenses, including decorating and furnishing. Also keep in mind that the money you hold back from your down payment, if invested wisely, might earn you more than the appreciation on your property will add to your equity.

As you figure the amount of your liquid assets, remember that you might not have to put the whole sum into the down payment. The minimum amount required will be determined by the type of loan, the lender and whether the mortgage will be sold in the secondary market.

Mortgage lenders, of course, prefer a big down payment to a minimal one. That tells the lender that the new homeowner has a major stake in the property and won't be tempted to default on the loan and walk away from the house. The larger the down payment, the less risk of foreclosure and the less chance the lender will suffer any financial loss on the property.

Help for Rural Buyers

••••••••••••••••••••••••••

The Farmers Home Administration (FmHA) also has a no-money-down program for moderate-income people seeking to buy in rural areas. For information, ask lenders or contact FmHA, Single Family Housing, Loan Processing, 14th and Independence St., S.W., Washington, D.C. 20250. Tell the FmHA where you want to buy a home, and it will give you names of prospective lenders.

In most cases you will need to pay at least 10% down on the purchase price of the property. If you plan to buy with a down payment of less than 20%, you will be expected to have a higher income, relative to total long-term debt, than someone putting down 20%.

If your calculations indicate that you can't put at least 10% down, here are some options:

- **Find out whether you are eligible for a loan** guaranteed by the Federal Housing Administration (FHA) or the Department of Veteran Affairs (VA), which require little or no down payment.

- **Look into the 3/2 Option loan.** The Federal National Mortgage Association (Fannie Mae) has developed a 3/2 Option loan to help first-time buyers. You may use a gift or unsecured loan for up to 2% of the down payment. The down payment must be at least 5%, and 3% of that must come from your own funds. (Fannie Mae promises to buy loans conforming to 3/2 Option loan criteria, thus removing the risk lenders would bear by holding them in their portfolios.)

- **Inquire about private mortgage insurance (PMI) to lower down-payment requirements.** (For a full discussion of PMI, see Chapter 11.)

- **Look into state and local programs for low- and moderate-income families and for first-time buyers.** You may be able to get a lower-rate mortgage with a small down-payment requirement. Check what's available through any lender or real estate agent, or through your state or local housing agency (see the accompanying box).

- **Consider buying a less expensive condo or house that needs fixing up.**

- **Use a lease-option contract,** which gives you the right to live in the house for a period of time *and* the right to buy the property for a specified price during an agreed-on period of time (see Chapter 17 for details).

- **Look for property whose seller is willing to act as the lender.** You don't have to meet institutional credit standards and may be able to work out a better deal.

- **Consider an equity-sharing purchase** with a relative who is willing to make the down payment (see Chapter 10).

- **Try to get help from family or friends.** As a rule, you'll be expected to make at least a 5% cash down payment in addition to any funds received as a gift toward the purchase price of the home.

A relative or friend may be willing to make you a "second-trust loan" (at a competitive market rate, not subsidized) to close the gap between the down payment and the mortgage. But such loans are not allowed by many lenders, and even if acceptable, the lender will scrutinize your finances carefully to make sure you can afford to carry both mortgages.

Most lenders will regard this loan as a gift and require you and the giver to sign a form saying the money is a gift that need not be repaid; if you and the giver want to treat the gift as a loan later—after the purchase— that's up to you. There may be gift tax and estate considerations involved, so consult an attorney.

> ## *For State Information*
> •
>
> Contact the National Council of State Housing Agencies (444 North Capitol St., N.W., Washington, D.C. 20001; 202-624-7710) to request the phone number for your state's housing agency.

- **Use a seven- to ten-year balloon loan.** This lets you make payments comparable to those for a much longer-term loan (see Chapter 10 for more information).

How Big a Loan?

How much you can borrow will depend on your income and the size of your down payment. Job stability, credit references, payment histories and other indications of creditworthiness also are factors. (The down payment required by a lender can be affected by whether the home you are buying is located in an area where prices are appreciating or depreciating. You may be permitted to buy a home with 5% down where prices are rising but be asked to put down 10% where prices are declining. Minimum down payments for adjustable-rate mortgages could be even higher.)

The less you pay down, the more closely your finances will be examined.

An old rule of thumb says you can qualify for a loan up to twice your family income. Using that outdated guideline, $50,000 of income should translate to a $100,000 mortgage. Sound too simple? It is. A family with $50,000 of annual earnings, three children, $5,000 in savings and a new car loan just won't stack up the same way with lenders as a childless couple with the same income, no debts and a $30,000 stock portfolio.

You'll get closer to reality by applying some of the same tools lenders use to evaluate the creditworthiness of prospective buyers. One common method is to apply a number of ratios to gross monthly income. For example, if you are making a 10% down payment, you may be allowed to devote up to 28% of gross (pretax) monthly income to housing expenses (including mortgage, property taxes, insurance, fees, utilities and maintenance). However, your combined housing expenses and installment-debt obligations may not exceed 33%.

If your down payment works out to 20% of the sales price, lenders will be more generous. Monthly payments and other housing expenses still can't exceed 28% of gross monthly income, but total monthly debt payments can go as high as 36%.

Prequalifying Yourself

Rules and formulas used to evaluate the creditworthiness of borrowers vary depending on the type of loan being sought. But whether you are seeking a conventional loan from a savings and loan or a government-backed (FHA or VA) loan from a mortgage company, the less you pay down, the more closely your finances will be examined. In the case of FHA and VA loans, the lender will want to know how many people you are supporting and how old they are. Government rules require lenders to estimate your living costs rather than take your word for it.

As you work through the work sheets in this chapter and examine your budget, try to assess the impact homeownership will have on your spending patterns. Will you take fewer vacations? Will you spend less on clothing? Will the cost of commuting to work rise or fall?

Most important, how much will your tax bill go down—and your monthly take-home pay rise—once you begin taking big deductions for mortgage interest, which constitutes most of your monthly mortgage expense early in the term of the loan? Study the next chapter carefully to get a full appreciation of the range and variety of tax breaks you will get from the purchase and ownership of your new home.

How Much Down, How Much Borrowed?

In deciding how much cash to put down, remember that getting settled in a new home always ends up costing more than you anticipate. Hold back some cash for furnishing and unexpected outlays. Add an extra cushion of cash if you're buying an older home that could surprise you with a plumbing or roofing expense.

Should you borrow as much as you can? When inflation runs as high as or higher than mortgage interest rates, and you are paying back what you borrowed with dollars that are steadily losing their purchasing power, the answer is easy: The bigger the mortgage the better. Many homeowners and speculators in single-family residences made a killing in the 1970s by making minuscule down payments and then trading up to larger (or more) houses as inflation made their equity grow enormously. During the 1980s, home

Figuring the What-Ifs

To help you calculate your monthly payments for hypothetical mortgages at various interest rates and terms, buy yourself a paperback book of mortgage amortization tables that will show the monthly principal and interest expense.

One widely available book is *Interest Amortization Tables,* by Jack Estes, published by McGraw-Hill Paperbacks.

If you have a personal computer, you can purchase software that will run amortization tables, and some real estate analysis programs will do much more. With either method, add in a monthly amount for your probable real estate taxes, homeowners insurance and utilities.

Loantech (P.O. Box 3635, Gaithersburg, Md. 20885) sells pocket-size mortgage slide charts for estimating maximum mortgage payments. It also sells, among other things, amortization schedules, a prequalifying service and adjustable-rate-mortgage analyses.

prices nationally rose an average of 10% per year. More recently, new home buyers haven't fared so well—according to one major mortgage-fund supplier, homes appreciated just one percentage point a year in 1990, '91 and '92.

Whether going for broke on a big mortgage will prove to have been a good financial strategy for the 1990s will be known only in retrospect. But one thing

How Much Can You Pay Monthly?

Annual Amount

INCOME

Add up the following:

Wages, salary, tips	$_____
Interest	_____
Dividends from stocks and mutual funds	_____
Bonuses	_____
Other Income	_____
Total Income	$_____

EXPENSES OTHER THAN HOUSING COSTS

Now, add up your expenses:

Income taxes	$_____
Social security taxes	_____
Other taxes	_____
Food	_____
Life, health, auto insurance	_____
Medical bills not covered by insurance	_____
Automotive loans	_____
Auto expenses (gas, repairs, other)	_____
Other transportation	_____
Other loans	_____

Annual Amount

EXPENSES, cont'd.

Credit card payments	_____
Child care	_____
Alimony or child support	_____
Education	_____
Clothing	_____
Home furnishings	_____
Recreation and entertainment	_____
Meals out	_____
Vacations	_____
Charity	_____
Miscellaneous	_____
Total Expenses	$_____

Now, write down the amount of your **Total Income** $_____

And from that, subtract your **Total Expenses**   –_____

To get your **Total Cash Flow or Discretionary Income** $_____

Divide that by 12 to get the **Maximum Available for Monthly Housing Expense** $_____

remains clear. Current tax law still stacks the deck in favor of the largest possible mortgage. Your original mortgage sets the cap for debt on which interest is deductible. (One exception lets you add to acquisition debt amounts you borrow—via refinancing or a second mortgage—for major home improvements. See Chapter 3.) If you make a large down payment but later need the cash, you can tap the money with a home-equity loan or refinance the house. But interest on home-equity loans over $100,000 isn't deductible.

Small down payments and big mortgages give you the power of leverage (see Chapter 1) as well as available cash for other investments.

For most first-time buyers, there's no point in weighing the trade-offs. Most will have to borrow to the hilt and scrape hard to come up with the minimum down payment. However, many so-called move-up buyers will come into a substantial sum of money when they sell their old home. Their decision will be tougher: whether to invest the cash in the new home and take out a small mortgage or to invest the money elsewhere and borrow a large amount.

Nationally, investment returns on single-family homes have been modest compared with returns on such financial investments as stocks and bonds. Home values in some areas will keep pace with inflation and in some areas may do significantly better. But don't expect a repeat of the late 1970s or the 1980s.

Before you buy, try to assess the future of the economy in your home area and the demand for homes of the type, location and price range of the one you want to own. For example, within a given metropolitan area, some neighborhoods may appreciate very well, while others stagnate. In some areas, luxury-priced houses will go up relatively more in value than starter houses; in others, just the opposite will occur.

If you have unusually good job security, you may want to gamble on a bigger mortgage than someone in a precarious field of work. Job security will affect the kind of mortgage you choose, too. If your job is safe in

Many move-up buyers will have to decide whether to invest the cash in the new home and take out a small mortgage or to invest the money elsewhere and borrow a large amount.

Debts and other obligations reduce the amount of cash you can spend on housing, so try to clear the decks as much as possible before applying for a loan.

high-inflation or recessionary times and your earnings will likely keep pace with the cost of living, you'll be more comfortable with an adjustable mortgage than someone who lost ground in the last period of high inflation and high interest rates.

Remember that home equity—unlike financial assets such as bonds, CDs and dividend-paying stocks—pays no current income, so be cautious about pouring all you have into a new home. For example, if the stock market is moving up, your cash will be tied up in a home that is not paying you any income and that may be appreciating less rapidly than good-quality stocks. If you put all your cash into your home and then need some money later, you can borrow it, but you'll be paying at least 1.5% to 2% over the prime lending rate for a home-equity loan, and usually more for a fixed-rate second mortgage.

Clean Up Your Credit Report

Even as you consider your strategy for buying a home, you should be paying attention to your current credit status. Any lender is going to scrutinize your monthly income and outgo at the time you apply for a mortgage. Debts and other obligations reduce the amount of cash you can spend on housing, so try to clear the decks as much as possible before applying for a loan. Pay off as many high-interest consumer loans as possible. If you are planning to buy a new car, boat or major furniture (paying by either cash or credit), postpone the purchases until after you've bought your home.

On the other hand, a good credit record requires that you have used credit in the past. Some cash-only buyers find themselves hampered by their own prudence when it comes time to buy a home. If you've been diligently saving for a down payment and haven't borrowed for a year or more, it's a good idea to create a record of credit activity during the year in which you plan to buy. Stick to small-ticket items, make one or two minimum payments promptly, then pay off the balance.

A Do-It-Yourself Credit Check

Federal law gives you the right to know what's in your credit files. Before you apply for a mortgage loan, find out whether anything in your record might present a problem. Order a report two or three months before making a loan application to give yourself plenty of time to iron out any wrinkles that you discover.

It's wise to check all three major credit bureaus—Equifax, Trans Union and TRW—for errors. TRW offers consumers one free report a year, but Equifax charges $8 and Trans Union charges $15—except where those charges exceed state caps: California ($8), Louisiana ($8), Maine ($2), Maryland ($5) and Vermont ($7.50). Call or write:

- **Equifax** (P.O. Box 740241, Atlanta, Ga. 30374-0241; 800-685-1111)

- **Trans Union** (P.O. Box 7000, North Olmstead, Ohio 44070; 312-408-1050)

- **TRW** (P.O. Box 2350, Chatsworth, Cal. 91313-2350; 800-392-1122

In most cases, you will need to write a letter including your full name, date of birth, names of current and past spouses, your social security number, and current and previous addresses going back five years. Your date of birth and a copy of your driver's license may also be required.

Mailing letters to all three credit bureaus can be a hassle. Credco Inc. (800-637-2422), a Carlsbad, Cal., credit-reporting company, sells a merged report that shows your combined credit history. At $24 the merged report costs about the same as getting separate reports directly from the big three.

If you discover an unfavorable report, now is the time to rectify the problem or seek settlement. A lender may view the problem more leniently if the record shows that the matter has been satisfactorily resolved.

If you've been tagged unfairly for non-payment or slow payment, write a well-documented letter setting forth your understanding of the facts, and file it with the appropriate credit bureaus. If you aren't sure which bureaus have a file on you, find out from the problem creditor.

Better still, get the problem resolved; then request, in writing, that the creditor inform all relevant reporting services that the problem has been fixed—with copies to you. This could take 30 to 90 days.

Errors generated by the credit bureau—such as mixed-up files—need to be corrected there. If using a complaint line or calling the local office doesn't help, write to the manager of consumer affairs. The bureau should accept documentation proving the account isn't yours.

If your problem remains unresolved, contact the U.S. Public Interest Research Group, 215 Pennsylvania Ave., S.E., Washington, D.C. 20003, or Bankcard Holders of America, 560 Herndon Parkway, Suite 120, Herndon, Va. 22070, for advice.

When you finally make a loan application, the lender will request a complete update on your file, and you may be charged $100 or so for this credit check. The lender will usually ask the credit agency to reverify your employer, salary, address and other information. Alert your employer's personnel office to the credit checker's call. If your credit application is turned down, you're entitled to know why.

Typically, your credit file will contain information covering the preceding three years. No adverse credit information, except bankruptcy, can be kept on file for more than seven years. Lenders look for these red flags: late payments, overextension, liens, garnishments and, the biggest flag of all, bankruptcy.

Prequalifying With a Lender

Now that you've gotten your financial affairs in order and checked out your credit record, the next step is a visit with a lender—mortgage company, savings and loan, bank or credit union—where you can translate all the data into hard facts about the upper price limit you can handle and the types of mortgages suited to your needs.

A real estate agent also can prequalify you. Some agents will do a professional job—one that will give you the same information you would get from a lender. Keep in mind, however, that the more costly the home you buy, the more an agent stands to earn in commission from the seller.

The prequalifying interview should be free. And you are not obliged to use the lender who conducts the interview. When you're ready to borrow, talk with several lenders. Bring tax returns, salary stubs and other financial data to the prequalifying interview—along with net worth and monthly cash flow work sheets you've prepared.

Kinds of Loans

Find out how much mortgage debt you can carry under the most commonly available mortgages.

"Conventional mortgages" are transactions between borrowers and institutions operating in the private sector of the economy. They are not insured or guaranteed by the government. Traditionally they feature set monthly payments, fixed interest rates, extended loan terms and full amortization.

Because the 30-year fixed-rate mortgage is still the benchmark against which other loans can be compared, find out what size conventional 30-year loan you can qualify for under the guidelines issued by secondary-market mortgage buyers such as the Federal National Mortgage Association (Fannie Mae) or the Federal Home Loan Mortgage Corporation (Freddie Mac). Because these institutions buy only loans that meet their criteria, such mortgages are often referred to as "conforming" loans.

Get information on a conforming 30-year fixed-rate mortgage, a one- and three-year adjustable-rate mortgage, and perhaps a 15-year fixed-rate loan as well. Knowing what you can afford to buy with these four mortgage types is a useful starting point.

For Additional Information

•••••••••••••••••••••••••••

A Guide to Homeownership is free from the Federal National Mortgage Association (Fannie Mae, Customer Education Group, 3900 Wisconsin Avenue, N.W., Washington, D.C. 20016-2899).

Affording Your First Home contains a review of fees first-time buyers face, a work sheet for determining how much they can afford to borrow, and an amortization table (HSH Associates, Dept. FTB, 1200 Route 23, Butler, N.J. 07405; $3).

If you're planning on an FHA-insured or VA-guaranteed mortgage, you may get a bigger loan. However, keep in mind that sellers in a hot market are usually not eager to do business with buyers using this type of financing. They may expect to have plenty of would-be buyers using conventional mortgages, so it's not uncommon for sellers to put the phrase "no FHA and no VA financing" right in the sales contract.

Due to the extra paperwork and appraisal delays these loans often entail, it may take longer to reach settlement, and some sellers won't put up with that. In addition, under VA financing, the buyer is permitted to pay no more than a 1% loan-origination fee (point), so if the lender is asking for more discount points, the seller will have to pay. For these reasons, it's a good idea to see whether you can manage a home purchase without resorting to an FHA or VA mortgage.

When interest rates are changing rapidly, shopping for a home can be frustrating. What you can afford may vary week to week. In such a market you can ask the institution prequalifying you to provide a computer list of the various size mortgages for which you qualify at the widely varying interest rates. Another option would be to figure it out yourself with a paperback book of amortization tables or real estate analysis software for your personal computer (see page 19).

Get Your Earnest Money Ready

Some people are short on liquid assets but have substantial equity in their homes. This could pose a problem when they have to write a check for earnest money to submit to a seller along with their purchase contract. Earnest money shows that you're a serious, qualified purchaser. (Of course, if the contract is not accepted or the deal later hits a snag through no fault of yours, you'll get the earnest money back, with interest if you specified in your offering contract that the money be held in an interest-bearing escrow account.)

If after assessing your resources you find that you'll be short on earnest money when it comes time to begin house hunting, consider getting a home-equity loan—a line of credit secured by the equity in your current house (see Chapters 3 and 15 for details). But don't succumb to the temptation to use your new equity credit line for unneeded things. As you prepare for the mortgage application process, you'll want to avoid adding to your current debt.

Home Sweet Tax Shelter

Your home—probably the biggest investment of your life—can be the best tax shelter you'll ever enjoy.

Uncle Sam is standing by to serve as a generous partner in your investment, ready to subsidize your mortgage payments while you're paying for your house and willing to turn a blind eye to profit you make when you sell it—so long as you buy another home that costs at least as much as the one you sell.

Given the favored status of homeownership in America, it is no surprise that deductions for mortgage interest and local property taxes have survived as others have gone the way of the dodo bird. Yes, there is a limit on mortgage-interest write-offs, but it kicks in only when mortgage debt exceeds $1 million. The mortgage-interest deduction can also be nicked by a restriction that applies to taxpayers whose adjusted gross income (AGI) exceeds $108,450 in 1993 ($105,250 in 1992). The same figure is used whether you file a joint, single or head-of-household return (see page 30). If you are married and file a separate return, the threshold is $54,225 in 1993. The law wipes out deductions equal to 3% of the amount by which AGI exceeds the threshold. If your 1992 AGI was $150,000, for example, the first $1,246 (3% of the $41,550 over the trigger point) of your deductions lost their tax-saving power.

It is impossible to say exactly how this will affect

Buying a home will cut your tax bill. But as veteran homeowners know, it will also complicate your tax life.

any specific taxpayer, since much depends on AGI and the makeup of your deductions. For that reason—and the fact that, despite the restriction, tax breaks for homeownership remain enormous—the discussion that follows generally assumes that all your mortgage interest will remain deductible.

Buying a home *will* cut your tax bill. But as veteran homeowners know, it will also complicate your tax life.

If you don't itemize deductions now, you're almost sure to begin once you buy a home. After all, the mortgage-interest portion of the first 12 monthly payments on a $100,000, 8%, 30-year mortgage is nearly $8,000. That's far more than the $6,200 standard deduction for 1993 for married couples filing jointly. You'll also get to deduct what you paid in state and local property taxes.

And once you begin itemizing, other expenses that are of no value to nonitemizers—such as state income taxes, charitable contributions and possibly medical bills—are transformed into tax-saving write-offs.

The mortgage-interest and property-tax deductions just scratch the surface of the tax benefits attached to homeownership. While becoming a homeowner doesn't demand that you memorize the tax law, you do need a general awareness of the rules to take advantage of them.

This chapter is designed as a primer for first-time buyers and a refresher for veteran homeowners in the process of moving. (For a discussion of the tax implications of selling a home, see Chapter 16.)

Powerful Tax Deductions

The opportunity to trade nondeductible rent payments for mostly deductible mortgage payments is a powerful lure enticing you from your rental abode into a home of your own.

Whether you are looking for a first home or planning to move up, the number crunching necessary to determine how much house you can afford demands two calculations: one for actual monthly outlays, the other for the true, after-tax cost.

In the early years of a home mortgage, nearly all of every monthly payment is interest. That's disappointing from one standpoint: It means you are paying off only a tiny bit of the loan principal. But it's great in terms of tax savings.

Look again at the $100,000, 30-year, 8% mortgage cited above. The monthly payment would be $734, and the table below shows the breakdown between principal repayment and deductible interest in various years.

In the first year, $7,970 of your $8,805 payment—or 91%—would be deductible as mortgage interest. Even in the tenth year, just over 81% of your payments would be deductible. In fact, only in the unlikely event that you live in the house for 22 years would the scales tip so that less than half of the total paid during the year would be tax-deductible.

Just what the deductions are worth to you depends, of course, on your tax bracket. If you are in the 28% bracket, every $1,000 of deductible interest and taxes translates to a $280 subsidy from Uncle Sam.

Deductible Interest

This table reflects the deductible interest on a $100,000, 30-year fixed-rate mortgage at 8%.

Year	Annual Payments	Principal	Interest
1	$ 8,805	$ 835	$ 7,970
2	8,805	905	7,900
3	8,805	980	7,825
4	8,805	1,061	7,744
5	8,805	1,149	7,656
10	8,805	1,712	7,093
15	8,805	2,551	6,254
20	8,805	3,800	5,005
25	8,805	5,662	3,143
30	8,805	8,435	370

In our $100,000 mortgage example, assume that in addition to the $734 monthly mortgage payment you pay $150 a month for local property taxes (which, most likely, your mortgage lender will collect, deposit into an escrow account and pay out as required). During the first 12 months, you pay a total of $10,605—that's about $884 a month.

But $9,770 is deductible. In the 28% bracket, that generates tax savings of $2735.60 and pulls the after-tax cost to $7,869.40, or about $656 a month.

The tax savings built into the home-buying equation is why you can afford to make higher mortgage payments than your current rent payments without squeezing your budget. As disgruntled renters often complain, there is no similar tax subsidy for tenants. For example, the after-tax cost of home payments of $1,000 a month are the equivalent of rent at $750 a month. Of course, owning the house could present you with repair bills a renter doesn't have to worry about, but on the other hand, as an owner you reap all the appreciation on the value of your home.

A Squeeze on Deductions

As mentioned, the tax law can restrict the deduction of mortgage interest for tax-payers whose 1993 adjusted gross income (AGI) exceeds $108,450. (AGI is basically your income before deductions and exemptions are subtracted.)

Although this take-away doesn't hit all deductions, mortgage interest and proper-ty taxes are among those threatened. But don't assume this diminishes the tax-saving power of a bigger mortgage or higher property-tax bill. Since the law sets a floor for itemized deductions—only those that exceed 3% of your adjusted gross income in excess of $108,450—it takes away the first dollars of your itemized deductions, not the last. Once your deductions pass the floor, every extra dollar of deductible expenses has full tax-saving power.

Even if your AGI makes you vulnerable to the squeeze, you'll probably get to deduct 100% of any increases in mortgage interest and property taxes that come with buying a more expensive home. Say, for example, that AGI of $150,000 costs you $1,246 (3% of the $41,550 over the 1993 trigger point) of your $30,000 of itemized deductions, so you deduct just $28,754. If buying a new home hiked your interest and property-tax expenses by $5,000, you'd get to add the full $5,000 to bring your itemized deductions up to $35,000. Only if your AGI rises would the amount of lost deductions increase.

Adjust Your Withholding

What good is the tax subsidy if you're worrying about coming up with the cash needed each month to make the mortgage payment? Fortunately, you don't have to wait until you file a tax return to cash in on the savings. As soon as you purchase your first home or buy a new house that carries higher deductible expenses, you can direct your employer to begin withholding less from your paychecks. If you are self-employed, it's likely you will be able to scale back your quarterly estimated tax payments beginning with the next one due. In either case, your cash flow can increase almost immediately to help cover the mortgage payments.

The revised W-4 form can be complicated, but basically, for each $2,500 of added itemized deductions, you earn one extra withholding allowance. And each allowance trims withholding from your paychecks, leaving you with more take-home pay to cover your mortgage. To reduce withholding, you must file a revised W-4 form with your employer. Get a copy of the form and its instructions from your personnel office or local Internal Revenue Service office.

Record Keeping

Buying a home may be your introduction to the endearing term "tax basis." That's the home's value for tax purposes. Keeping track of it is as demanding as it is important. The basis of your home is the figure you'll subtract from the amount you get when you sell the place, and the result determines whether you have a taxable profit that piques the interest of the IRS.

Although the basis of a home begins simply—as what it costs you to buy the house—it can change often before you sell. As discussed in Chapter 16, the basis of each home you own affects the basis of the next one you buy. You must keep track of all adjustments to the basis—for your entire homeowning career—to ensure you are not overtaxed.

Basically, for each $2,500 of added itemized deductions, you earn one extra withholding allowance. And each allowance trims withholding from your paychecks.

The tax basis of your home is the figure you'll subtract from the amount you get when you sell the place, and the result determines whether you have a taxable profit.

This record-keeping chore begins with sorting out the tax consequences of the closing costs you pay at settlement (discussed in Chapter 13). Although a few of these expenses may be deducted in the year of the purchase, most are considered part of the cost of acquiring the house so they're included in the basis. First, consider the deductible closing expenses because they have the most immediate financial impact.

Closing Costs

Points you pay to get a mortgage

A "point" is a fee—1% of the loan amount—that the mortgage lender charges up front. If the charge is for use of the borrowed money—as it is when the number of points charged affects the interest rate on the mortgage—rather than for loan-processing costs, the point is considered prepaid interest. As long as the home you build or buy is your principal residence, these points are fully deductible in the year paid.

Assume, for example, that to get a $100,000 mortgage you have to pay the lender three points, or 3% of the loan amount. You can write off that $3,000 on the tax return for the year of the purchase. The IRS even provides a special line for the deduction on Schedule A, in addition to space for deducting the interest paid on the mortgage. The deduction effectively serves as a rebate of part of the costs. In the 28% bracket, $3,000 in points translates into $840 in tax savings.

Until recently, points were often a controversial issue. In addition to the rule that, to be deductible, they had to be paid on a loan to buy your principal residence, an assortment of other rules had to be followed: Charging points had to be routine in your area; what you paid had to be in line with what other home buyers paid; you could use borrowed money to have the seller pay them for you; and on and on.

A standard piece of advice, in fact, was to write a separate check to pay the points, as proof that the expense wasn't rolled into the mortgage. That was critical because if the points were included in the mortgage amount you were using borrowed money and therefore were blocked from deducting the full expense right away. But a separate check is no longer necessary.

In 1992, the IRS decided to make things a lot easier. Officially, there's still a list of rules to be followed, but in practice only a couple of things matter.

- The charge must be based on a percentage of the loan amount and it must be clearly labeled on the settlement statement as *points, discount points* or *loan origination fee,* for example.

Proving Your Basis

Maintaining detailed records, beginning with the purchase of your first home, is the best way to ensure accuracy when computing its taxable basis. That's the determining factor in what you will owe in taxes when you sell this home and future homes. As you begin the running tab on your adjusted basis, add the items below to the purchase price.

Remember, starting to keep track now will be a lot easier than trying to reconstruct the basis later on.

- Appraisal and credit-report fees
- Attorney and notary fees
- Recording and title-examination fees
- State and county transfer taxes
- Property-inspection fees
- Title-insurance premiums
- Utility-connection charges
- Amounts owed by the seller that you agree to pay, such as part of the real estate agent's commission or back taxes and interest
- The cost of an option to purchase under a rent-with-option-to-buy arrangement
- Part of the rent payments made prior to closing may possibly be added to the basis if they were applied to the purchase price of the property.

- By closing, you must provide at least enough cash to cover the points. This can include your down payment, escrow deposits or earnest money.

If you make a $20,000 down payment, for example, you can actually roll points into the mortgage amount and still deduct the points in the year you buy the house. The IRS will assume that points were paid with part of the down payment, rather than with the money you borrowed. You'll get a statement from the lender (IRS Form 1098) showing how much you paid in points to buy your home.

When the house isn't your home

The right to deduct points fully in the year paid applies only to points paid on a mortgage to buy or improve your principal residence. Different rules apply to points charged for a mortgage used to buy a vacation home or rental property.

When points are not fully deductible in the year paid, the expense is deducted over the life of the loan. On a 30-year mortgage, for example, one-thirtieth of the points generally would be deducted each year. In the first year, though, an even smaller amount would be deductible, based on the month you bought the house.

An alternative method for figuring the annual deduction gives you somewhat higher write-offs in the early years of a mortgage. It's probably more trouble than it's worth because it involves finding what percentage of the total interest due on the loan is paid yearly and deducting that portion of the points in that year.

Whichever method you use, remember to claim this deduction each year. And, if you sell the house and pay off the mortgage early, any undeducted points are fully deductible in the year of the sale.

Prepaid interest and property-tax adjustments

If your settlement costs include reimbursing the seller for interest or taxes he or she paid in advance for a period you will actually own the house, you may deduct those amounts as though you paid the bills directly. Such adjustments ought to be spelled out on your settlement sheet.

If the seller made such payments and you do not reimburse him at settlement, the prepayments are considered built into the price you are paying for the house. In that case, you still write off the prepaid interest and taxes as itemized deductions on your return and reduce your basis the same amount.

Other closing costs and acquisition expenses are generally not deductible unless you qualify to write them off as job-related moving expenses, as discussed in Chapter 17. Instead, many such out-of-pocket costs are added to the purchase price to hike your tax basis. Since additions to basis don't produce immediate tax savings, you might be tempted to dismiss them. That would be a costly mistake. Eventually, you'll need to know the adjusted basis of your home, and the higher you can prove it to be, the better. The higher the basis when you sell, the smaller any potential taxable profit you have to report to the IRS.

Additions to basis don't produce immediate tax savings, but the higher the basis when you sell, the smaller any potential taxable profit you have to report to the IRS.

Other Tax Angles of Owning

It's easy to take advantage of the basic tax benefits—the write-offs for mortgage interest and property taxes. If your mortgage is held by a financial institution, you will receive a statement early each year showing how much deductible interest you shelled out in the previous year (the IRS gets a copy, too). The statement will also show how much you can deduct for property taxes if you make those payments through an escrow account handled by your lender. Otherwise, copies of tax bills and your canceled checks provide the information you need to claim that deduction.

Your tax situation is more complicated if your mortgage is held by an individual or you are buying with the help of some sort of "creative financing." The specifics of your arrangement dictate what part of your payments qualify as tax deductions.

Assume, for example, that in addition to a first mortgage at a bank, the seller holds a $10,000 second mortgage that calls for monthly interest-only payments for three years and then a balloon payoff of the entire principal. Assuming that the note was properly registered, all of your payments on it during the three years would be deductible as interest.

With a shared-appreciation mortgage (SAM), the home buyer gets a lower-than-market-rate loan in exchange for promising to share with the lender the future appreciation in the value of the house. As far as the IRS is concerned, the part of the appreciation that winds up in the lender's pocket is interest, too, and is deductible when paid. That can result in a huge interest deduction in the year a SAM-financed home is sold.

Say, for example, that a $125,000 home is purchased with a SAM that entitles the lender to 40% of the appreciation. If the home is sold three years later for $165,000, the borrower owes the lender $16,000 (40% of the $40,000 profit). In the year that sum is paid, the taxpayer can deduct the full $16,000 as mortgage interest, in addition to the interest portion of any regular monthly payments made before the sale.

What about a "zero-interest" deal involving seller financing at the best of all interest rates: 0%? Even if you find such a deal, the IRS does not believe such generosity exists. The law assumes that financing costs are built into the price of the home, so the buyer's basis is reduced by subtracting the value of interest-free financing from the purchase price.

The law also requires the seller to report as interest income each year an amount that reflects what would have been charged if the note carried a reasonable rate of interest. And the buyer can deduct as interest paid the amount the seller must claim as interest, even though the buyer doesn't actually make those payments. If you consider a zero-interest deal, be sure the price you pay reflects the tax consequences.

Special rules also apply to graduated-payment mortgages and other financing plans. The further you stray from conventional financing, the more need you have to consult with an attorney or accountant to discuss the many tax twists and turns involved in your home-buying pursuits.

Local Assessments

In addition to real estate taxes, it is not unusual for local governments to assess homeowners for services or benefits provided during the year. Such bills need to go in your home file because, depending on what the charge is for, the cost may be either a deductible expense or an addition to your basis.

In general, assessments for benefits that tend to increase the value of your property—sidewalks, for example—should be added to the basis of your property. Special charges for repairs or maintenance of local benefits, such as sewers or roads, however, can be deducted as additional local taxes. Fees for specific services, such as garbage collection, are not deductible and can't be added to the basis.

Improvements and Repairs

Monthly payments are just the beginning of the costs of owning a home. You can count on spending plenty over the years maintaining, repairing and improving your property. Here, too, Uncle Sam gets involved.

For tax purposes, work around the house is divided between projects considered *repairs* and those constituting capital *improvements* that enhance rather than just maintain the value of your home. The distinction is critical. While the cost of repairs and improvements are nondeductible personal expenses, improvement expenses add to your basis.

The idea here is that although you will use and enjoy the improvements, they also are likely to boost the amount a buyer will pay for the place. Since you add 100% of the cost of improvements to your basis, every $100 of such expenses will ultimately reduce by $100

In general, local assessments for benefits that tend to increase the value of your property—sidewalks, for example—should be added to the basis of your property.

the potentially taxable profit when you sell.

An improvement is anything that adds value to your home, prolongs its life or adapts it to new uses. There is no laundry list of what the IRS considers an improvement. However, the accompanying box provides a checklist of items and projects that can qualify.

Repairs, on the other hand, merely maintain the home's condition. Fixing a gutter or replacing a windowpane are repairs rather than improvements. In some cases, though, the cost of projects that ordinarily fall into the repair category—such as painting a room—can be added to basis if the work is done as part of an extensive remodeling or restoration of your home. Also, some major repairs—such as extensive patching of

Basis-Boosting Improvements

- **Addition or conversion of:** unfinished attic, basement or other space to living area

- **Air-conditioning:** a central system or window units that will be sold with the house

- **Heating and cooling:** attic fan, furnace, furnace humidifier, heat pump, radiators and radiator covers, thermostat, water heater, thermostat, water heater

- **Bathroom:** bathtub, faucets, Jacuzzi, medicine cabinets, mirrors, sauna, shower, shower enclosure, toilet, towel racks

- **Built-in bookcases**

- **Safety features:** burglar- and fire-alarm system, doorbell, intercom, smoke detector, telephone outlets

- **Electrical:** new or upgraded power lines, replacement of fuse box with circuit breakers, additional outlets or switches, floodlights

- **Fireplace:** including, chimney, mantel, built-in fireplace screen

- **Weatherproofing:** caulking, insulation, weather stripping

- **Kitchen:** dishwasher, freezer, refrigerator or stove sold with the house; countertops, cupboards, exhaust fan, garbage disposal

- **Landscaping:** shrubs, trees, underground sprinkler systems

- **Outdoors:** aluminum siding, barbecue pit, birdbath, carport, deck, fences and gates, garage, garage-door opener, gutters, hot tub, lamppost, new roof, paving and resurfacing of a driveway or sidewalks, porch, screen and storm doors, shed, skylight, swimming pool, termite-proofing, walls, waterproofing

- **Plumbing:** new pipes, septic system, solar-heating system, sump pump

- **Rooftop TV antenna and wiring**

- **Washer and dryer sold with the house**

- **Windows:** awnings, screens, shutters, storm windows, weather stripping

a roof—may qualify as basis-boosting improvements.

Keep detailed records of any work done around the house, including receipts for items that might qualify as improvements. The pack-rat habit can pay off handsomely for homeowners. It's better to save papers you might not need than to toss out evidence that could save you money. In addition to receipts and canceled checks, keep notes to remind yourself exactly what was done, when and by whom.

When toting up the cost of improvements, be sure to include any incidental costs. If you pay to have your lot surveyed as part of installing a fence, for example, the cost of the survey can be added to your basis. Although you can count what you paid workers you hired, you are not allowed to add anything for your own time and effort if you do the work yourself.

Home-Equity Loans

In 1986, Congress decided to outlaw the deduction of personal interest. That category included interest on car loans, credit card accounts, student loans, personal loans and almost every other kind of personal borrowing most taxpayers do—except for home mortgage interest.

By creating two classes of interest—some deductible and some not—Congress created immediate problems. How would one type be distinguished from another and, more important, how could the law discourage ever-ingenious taxpayers from rearranging their financial affairs to sidestep the intent of the law? For example, if you used a second mortgage on your home to buy a car, would the interest be deductible mortgage interest or nondeductible personal interest? To answer such questions, Congress divided debt secured by a home—including a second home—into two categories:

An improvement is anything that adds value to your home, prolongs its life or adapts it to new uses. Keep detailed records of any work done around the house, that might qualify.

Acquisition Debt

You can deduct all the interest you pay on up to $1 million of acquisition debt—money you borrow to buy, build or substantially improve your principal residence or a second home. For the interest to be deductible, the loan must be secured by the house.

Although $1 million is an enormous amount of mortgage debt, the amount on which you can deduct mortgage interest is likely to be far less. Your personal ceiling is set by the size of the original loans used to buy or build your first and second homes, plus amounts borrowed for major improvements. As you pay off those loans, the amount of tax-favored acquisition debt declines. (There is an exception to the general definition of acquisition debt. If on October 13, 1987, the mortgage debt on your principal home and a second home exceeded the amount borrowed to buy, build or substantially improve the homes, you can count that higher amount as acquisition indebtedness.)

Home-Equity Debt

This is the congressionally sanctioned end run around the loss of deductibility of interest on personal loans. In addition to deducting interest on acquisition debt, homeowners can deduct interest on up to $100,000 of home-equity debt. The interest on such borrowing is fully deductible—whether you tap your equity via refinancing, a second mortgage or a home-equity line of credit—as long as the loan is secured by your principal residence or second home.

The interest is deductible almost without regard to how the borrowed money is spent, but there are a couple of exceptions. If the borrowed money is used to invest in tax-exempt bonds or single-premium life insurance, the interest can't be deducted, no matter what kind of loan is involved. Also, if you are subject to the alternative minimum tax (AMT) discussed in Chapter 23, interest on home-equity debt is not deductible, unless the mortgage was taken out before July 1, 1982, and secured by a home used by you or a family member. Interest on acquisition debt is deductible for purposes of the AMT.

Another restriction—likely to come into play only if the value of your home plunges—blocks the deduction of interest on home-equity debt that exceeds the fair market value of the property. That is, home-equity debt is deductible only to the extent that it doesn't exceed fair market value when added to total acquisition debt.

Tax-Saving Opportunities

The special status of home-equity debt offers great tax-saving opportunities. To the extent that you can replace nondeductible personal borrowing with deductible home-equity borrowing, you can have the government help pay the interest on your debts. This makes home-equity lines of credit the debt of choice for millions of homeowners. These loans, secured by your home, offer a line of credit that you can tap simply by writing a check. In addition to preserving the deductibility of interest charged, these loans often carry lower interest rates than unsecured borrowing.

When you buy, the rules on acquisition indebtedness may encourage you to minimize your down payment. Remember that the size of your tax-favored debt is based on your original mortgage—not the price of the house.

The law can also encourage you to borrow rather than pay cash for home improvements. As long as the debt is secured by the home, money going toward an improvement counts as acquisition debt. The tax subsidy of the interest cost could make borrowing cheaper than pulling cash out of an investment to pay for the improvement.

It's important to keep reliable records of your borrowing to back up deductions you claim. If you use a home-equity line, distinguish between borrowing that pays for major home improvements and loans used for other purposes. The amount that goes for improvements is

To the extent that you can replace nondeductible personal borrowing with deductible home-equity borrowing, you can have the government help pay the interest on your debts.

added to your acquisition debt, rather than eating away at your $100,000 home-equity allowance. Also, if you use money borrowed through a home-equity line of credit or second mortgage for investment or business purposes, you can choose whether to treat the interest as home-equity interest or deduct it as investment or business interest. If, for example, you count it as investment interest—in which case certain restrictions apply—the borrowing would not reduce your $100,000 home-equity allowance.

Refinancing

When you refinance your mortgage—as millions of homeowners have done to take advantage of lower interest rates—there are tax angles to consider.

Points you pay to get the new mortgage are not fully deductible in the year paid, except to the extent that the funds are used for home improvements. Here's an example: A homeowner with a $100,000 mortgage refinances at $120,000 and uses $20,000 to add a sunroom. Assume that two points (2% of $120,000, or $2,400) were charged. Because one-sixth of the money went for a home improvement, one-sixth of the points, or $400, may be deducted in the year paid. The rest must be deducted evenly over the life of the loan. On a 30-year mortgage, that would basically mean one-thirtieth of the remaining $2,000, or $66.66, would be deducted each year. If the house is sold and the mortgage paid off before the end of the term, any remaining portion of the points could be deducted as interest at that time. (If the refinancing is part of the original purchase of your home—say you refinance to pay off a bridge loan or a short-term balloon note—the points can be fully deducted in the year paid.)

Refinancing can affect the tax status of the interest you pay on the mortgage. The amount of the new loan qualifying as acquisition debt is limited to the debt outstanding on the old loan, plus any part of the new money used for major improvements. This tale, too, is best told with an illustration:

Assume that several years ago you bought a $150,000 home with $30,000 down and a $120,000 mortgage. The debt is now paid down to $90,000 and you decide to refinance for $150,000. What's the tax status of the new loan?

Interest on $90,000—the remaining balance on the old loan—is sure to be deductible because that amount qualifies as acquisition indebtedness. The treatment of the other $60,000 depends on how the money is used.

Any part spent for major home improvements also earns the status of acquisition debt. Plunge $20,000 of the new loan into a swimming pool, for example, and your acquisition debt jumps from $90,000 to $110,000. Any part of the new loan that does not replace the old mortgage or pay for improvements—$40,000 in this example—is not acquisition debt.

That doesn't automatically mean you can't deduct the interest, however. Because the debt is secured by your home, the interest may be deducted as home-equity interest, subject to the $100,000 cap. If the extra funds are used in a business, the interest can be written off as a business expense. If you use the cash for an investment, the interest on that portion of the loan may be deductible as investment interest. If none of those options covers you, however, the interest would be nondeductible personal interest.

Another tax issue rising out of some refinancings is how to treat prepayment penalties. If the lender holding the original loan slaps you with a penalty for paying it off early, the amount is considered interest and is fully deductible in the year you pay it. But what if the lender is willing to cut the amount due to encourage you to pay off the mortgage early? That's not as unlikely as it may appear. In times of soaring interest rates, lenders sometimes offer sweet deals to get out of long-term loans at low, fixed interest rates. If you're on the receiving end of such an offer, beware. The amount of such a discount is considered taxable income to you.

Defining Your Housing Needs

If you don't decide what you like before wading into the market, someone out there will try to make up your mind for you.

Now that you know *how much* home you can afford, it's time to do some hard thinking about *what* kind of home you want and need. This chapter and the next two—dealing with location and kinds of housing—will help you narrow the choices.

Buying a piece of real estate is a science. Buying a home is an art. The science is getting the legal and financial parts right. The art is finding a property that you'll be happy living in.

You can hire all the help you need with the technical side. The nontechnical part is another matter. Only you know what you like.

Your best preparation for home buying is to clarify your needs, your financial ability, your preferences and your dislikes. The central questions: What kind of home do you want, and where do you want it? If you are sure about those things, you will be immune to pressure tactics and hype.

At any given time in a metropolitan area of a million inhabitants, thousands of residential properties are for sale. With a little thought you could categorize them a dozen or more ways: by price range, neighborhood, school district, new or resale homes, detached or townhouses, and so forth and eliminate ones that aren't right for you. Unfortunately you still would be left with several hundred potential homes. Start with the general—your price range and approximate location—and then move to the specific: neighborhood, age and type of home, and kind of ownership (traditional, condominium or co-op).

Shopping only within your chosen location can narrow down the range of properties to be inspected. Examining only selected properties within your price range should bring the operation within manageable proportions.

Knowing your financial limits is a good beginning. However, you probably will find ten or 15 entirely different sorts of homes within your price range. Decide now whether you want to be on the east or west side of town, whether you will accept a cookie-cutter housing development or will go to any length to avoid that, whether you can handle a "fixer-upper" or will need one requiring a minimum of maintenance. Otherwise, you're in for an emotional tug of war when you find the living room you want on the west side of town and the school district you want on the east side.

It can't be overstated: *Focus on the location and general quality of the property.* Don't go chasing an exact price or a particular feature, be it a deck, a high-efficiency furnace or a finished basement. Price can be worked out in negotiation with the seller (given the right general ballpark), and a good-quality home in a good location can be tailored to your specific needs later.

There are two phases to a house-hunting strategy. In the first, you get a feel for different areas and an idea about what's being offered at what price, and you draw up a list of specifications. In the second phase, you search for the house that meets all or most of those specifications.

Make a List of Needs and Wants

Most buyers are in search of something they cannot describe. They may be trying, often unknowingly,

Which Features Are Important to You?

Check off the features that you must have in your next home and those you'd like to have, by degree of priority.

	Musts	Wants (rank them)		
		High	Medium	Low
Commuting time				
Less than one hour	____	____	____	____
Less than half-hour	____	____	____	____
Setting				
Suburban	____	____	____	____
Urban	____	____	____	____
Rural	____	____	____	____
Specific neighborhood	____	____	____	____
Specific school district	____	____	____	____
Public transportation	____	____	____	____
Zoning laws				
(Allowing or prohibiting	____	____	____	____
on-street parking, pets,	____	____	____	____
in-law suites and so on)	____	____	____	____
Specific architectural style				
One story	____	____	____	____
Two stories	____	____	____	____
Split level	____	____	____	____
Yard	____	____	____	____
Specific number of				
bedrooms	____	____	____	____
Specific number of baths	____	____	____	____
Bath in master bedroom	____	____	____	____
Eat-in-kitchen	____	____	____	____
Separate dining room	____	____	____	____
Basement	____	____	____	____
Expandability	____	____	____	____
Fixer-upper	____	____	____	____
Energy efficiency	____	____	____	____
Fireplace	____	____	____	____
Garage	____	____	____	____
Other (specify below)	____	____	____	____

to replicate a childhood home, if it was a happy one. (If it wasn't happy, whatever stands out about that home goes on the buyer's negative list.) This doesn't mean that they are looking for the same red-brick house with privet hedge, but rather that they seek a feeling, an ambience. It could be a sense of spaciousness, warmth, airiness, the amount of daylight, the quality of the light, coziness, the abundance of nooks and crannies, a park-like backyard.

If you're looking for a home with the help of an experienced agent, he or she should be able to help you define your needs and wants. But, if you are too vague, a really good agent may decide not to waste time on you, and you could end up with someone who is more hindrance than help, someone with endless patience, but no direction.

Start your want list by recalling houses you have liked and jotting down their best features. You'll find further inspiration in the accompanying checklist. That list, combined with the price range you have already determined, will give you a sieve through which to sift the dozens of ads you will read in conducting your search. Keep in mind, though, that the final choice of a home almost always requires compromise.

Make a "Don't Want" List, Too

Say you have a well-defined want list, you screen ads closely, you carefully instruct every agent you work with, and you refuse to look at any property that doesn't have the requisite family room, master bath or whatever your firm requirements are. After weeks of looking, the seemingly perfect home shows up. It has every one of the items on your list.

First there is euphoria over finding all the desired features in one package. Then, to the bewilderment of the agent or the seller of this perfect home, you go silent. You may announce, "I need more time to think it over." That might mean hours, days, possibly even a week. At last your final answer is no.

Your wish list, combined with the price range you have already determined, will give you a sieve through which to sift the dozens of ads you will read.

Also consider things that other buyers might object to. Heavy traffic on the street might not bother you, but it could make resale tougher.

Why does the perfect home fail to win the only test that counts: whether, when it comes right down to it, you are willing to plunk down a deposit? The reason may be that you failed to identify your "don't wants."

Finding a home with all the desired features is only half the challenge. The property must also be free from objectionable features.

Objections, which constitute your don't-want list, are of two major types: personal prejudice and economic fear. And there's plenty of overlap between the two.

To avoid getting into a situation where you have to veto a house that has everything you say you want, do some systematic soul searching.

Go back through your past again, and this time think of all the homes you have not liked, whether you lived in them or merely visited them. Include the ones occupied by friends, acquaintances, family—all the houses and apartments that for one reason or another made a negative impression on you.

If they gave you a "I wouldn't want to live here" feeling, now is the time to identify what prompted that feeling for you. Make a list of the things you didn't like (see the accompanying box).

Also consider things that other buyers might object to. Heavy traffic on the street might not bother you, but it could make resale tougher.

Other buyers might also balk at buying your house if it's overimproved. A home may have great entertaining space, a swimming pool and extensive landscaping—all features that are normally attractive to upscale buyers. But if the house is the only upgraded home in an area of ordinary homes, it will not be attractive to the typical high-income buyer. That makes it an interesting white elephant, and it could be a terrific bargain for you if you can negotiate the price down to reflect the home's wrong location, but such bargains can be deceptive: sweet on the buying end and sour on the selling end.

After you have your list of things you don't want in a home, assign them weights. Decide which objections

Your List of Dislikes

Knowing what you don't want is as important to successful house-hunting as knowing what you do want. Use this check-list as a starting point for identifying your personal objections, and add to it.

- ❏ Windowless inside kitchens
- ❏ Windowless inside bathrooms
- ❏ Small bathrooms
- ❏ Northern exposures
- ❏ Too little daylight
- ❏ Frame construction
- ❏ Block construction
- ❏ Casement windows
- ❏ Dormers
- ❏ Fake brick siding
- ❏ Awkward floor plan
- ❏ Insufficient cupboard, closet or storage space
- ❏ House incongruous with its surroundings
- ❏ Too much of a child-rearing neighborhood
- ❏ Too much of a retirement neighborhood
- ❏ Scary neighborhood
- ❏ Restrictions of homeowners' association
- ❏ Tiny yard
- ❏ Too big of a yard to care for
- ❏ Too far out
- ❏ Too close to the road
- ❏ Proximity to a commercial zone
- ❏ Dead-end street
- ❏ Heavy traffic
- ❏ Street with no trees
- ❏ Street with overgrown trees, or
- ❏ Whatever else you can't live with:

_____

_____

_____

_____

Frequently, the person with the strongest objections is the silent partner of the team.

are negotiable and which aren't. You might, for example, accept a house with a western garden when you really wanted a southern one, but you would not take a heavily trafficked street, instead of a cul-de-sac.

If you are buying a home with a spouse or a partner, compare your don't-want lists. Frequently, the person with the strongest objections is the silent partner of the team. The more vocal one may take the lead in putting together the "want" list, but when it comes to crunch time, it is often the silent one who produces a veto, often for an objection not previously voiced—or even thought about.

Besides harming the house-hunting process, these out-of-the-blue vetoes can put terrific strains on a relationship. Agents, mortgage loan officers and escrow agents never cease to be amazed that a couple may know all about each other's tastes in food, vacations, cars, clothes and entertainment yet not be aware of strongly held prejudices and opinions about what makes a home. Since rental living is so often a matter of expediency or convenience, it doesn't offer a good comparison to home shopping with someone.

Objections are much more elusive than demands because they don't get thought about or talked about as much. But if you know yours, and know each one's relative importance, you will be ahead in your search for a home.

Choosing a Neighborhood

You've probably heard the old cliché that the three major determinants of housing value are 1) location, 2) location and 3) location. Like many clichés, it's basically true.

No single factor affects the value of a home as much as location. If you can't afford what you want *where* you want it, sacrifice something inside the house rather than sacrificing the location. You can add a second bathroom or install hardwood floors to bring a house up to your standards, but you can't improve the neighborhood single-handedly. Better to take one that needs work in a good neighborhood than to take one at the same price (or even a bit lower) that's all dolled up but in a marginal location.

What's more, price doesn't guarantee a fine location. Just because a builder puts a $300,000 house on a particular site doesn't mean the market will justify that price. Some builders can't resist gambling on a cheap piece of land, often to regret.

Obviously, everyone can't live behind the country club overlooking the seventh fairway—nor would many buyers want to. What's good about a location, like many other features of a home, depends on your own taste. Confirmed city dwellers won't be put off by a restaurant or corner deli on the block. But suburbanites might find the same low-key establishments intrusive.

When an agent rushes into the office with news of a hot new listing, the first question colleagues ask is not "How much?" or "How big?" but "Where?"

Looking at the Neighborhood

Much of the value of a home rests in its surrounding economic and social environment—its neighborhood. In general, the more defined a neighborhood, the more likely that homes there will maintain their value. You are looking for more than just a cluster of homogeneous properties. A few blocks of carefully tended homes otherwise surrounded by blight isn't a viable neighborhood. Typically, it takes at least a dozen blocks, marked off by recognizable boundaries, for a neighborhood to sustain its character. The boundary might be a park, a highway, a campus, a river, a county line, a string of stores—anything that interrupts the pattern. One highly visible boundary gives residents a sense of belonging within it. Several such dividing lines make the neighborhood identification even stronger.

In the 1970s and 1980s, city planners, developers and financiers redesigned single-family-lot subdivisions and replaced them with larger-scale planned unit developments, or PUDs. PUDs trade off mixed-use, higher-density plans for community designs that incorporate bands of open space separating neighborhoods from retail and commercial users.

Schools, religious centers and shopping centers are located within each community. The "new towns" of Columbia, Md., and Reston, Va., are large-scale models of the PUD concept.

Small towns and villages are the inspiration for one of the newest types of planned development—the village design. The idea is to integrate residential,

---

What Is Location, Anyhow?

• •

Depending on the market, "location" can be a city, a town or a county. Location also is a neighborhood. It may be a home on a particular plot of land. Consider all three levels of location in choosing your home.

- Pick a town or community with a character and style that match your own.
- Then, go and scout out the town's best neighborhood—within your price range.
- Finally, zero in on the best home on the best lot within that neighborhood.

---

retail, office and civic use of the land in a way that enhances a sense of community. Each development has a mixed-use core area that includes a major civic space and large, open public areas. There is a mix of residential designs—often on the same street—and roads and parks are laid out to encourage walking. Montgomery Village, N.J.; Seaside Village, in Tallahassee, Fla.; Mashpee Commons, in Cape Cod, Mass.; and Blount Springs, in Birmingham, Ala., are examples of such communities.

In addition to being located in the right neighborhood, a home must not clash with its surroundings. A poor fit imposes a harsh penalty on any home's value. Pick any million-dollar home in the poshest neighborhood of your city. Mentally move it to the worst slum you can imagine and guess what it would be worth.

Next pick a setting in between—say, a nice middle-class community. If you have an appraiser's eye for value, you will recognize that bringing that mansion from the slums where it is unsalable to a midway location won't restore even half its value. What's true for a transplanted mansion is just as true for a $250,000 house in a $70,000 neighborhood.

Be especially wary of the overimproved house in a neighborhood of lesser homes; even if you love it, it may be hard to find others who feel just as you do when the time comes to sell.

The Price of Caprice

Some homes command premium prices because of the special cachet of their neighborhoods. Even the plainest, smallest home on Beacon Hill in Boston, Nob Hill in San Francisco, Beverly Hills in Los Angeles or Georgetown in Washington, D.C., commands high prices on a per-square-foot basis. Professional appraisers call such premiums caprice value.

In any city, some neighborhoods enjoy inflated values because the "right" people live there. By comparison, other neighborhoods with strong schools or other

In addition to being located in the right neighborhood, a home must not clash with its surroundings. A poor fit imposes a harsh penalty on any home's value.

A buyer who is indifferent to fashion can find good values in neighborhoods that offer desirable amenities and services—and end up with a lot more house for the money.

highly desirable features may be undervalued because they aren't "in." A buyer who is indifferent to fashion can find good values in neighborhoods that offer desirable amenities and services—and end up with a lot more house for the money.

Deliberately choosing to pay caprice value can be a perfectly sound investment if social prestige is very important to you. If you want to buy a home with a socially desirable address, make sure the high price is in line with the market. Get a professional appraisal. Properties in prestige areas sometimes attract speculators who hope to make exorbitant profits off unwary buyers, especially wealthy newcomers from out of town. And not all residents of such neighborhoods are above doing a little "fishing" for gullible buyers. Go into it knowing why you're paying extra and comfortable with it.

Check It Out

If you're looking for a new home in an area where you already live, you'll have a good sense of the strengths and weaknesses of various parts of town, and you can do your neighborhood scouting on your own, without an agent. But if you're coming from out of town, you'll need help, especially if you're relocating on short notice.

Here are some tips if you're relocating:

- **Try to find acquaintances or friends of friends** in the area you're moving to, and get their opinions of neighborhoods.

- **If you're being relocated to a branch office of your current employer,** talk to your new colleagues and secure the services (at your employer's cost) of a relocation firm that works with real estate agents in your new area. Long-distance house-hunting is very difficult, and it can be smoothed by the services of professionals.

- **Try to schedule several lengthy house-hunting trips,** allowing enough time to drive around the whole area and get a feel for neighborhoods.

- **Don't overlook the obvious.** Make sure you choose a place you'll enjoy living in six months after moving in. If you like it, others will in the future when you're ready to sell.

- **The look and feel of a community** as you walk and drive around its neighborhoods can't be quantified, but it's important. Trees, shrubs, cul-de-sacs, curved streets and landscaping around small retail stores are good signs. But unless you already live there, you need to probe deeper.

- **Read up on the local politics and history.** It will offer possible clues to the future. The chamber of commerce, the town hall and the local library are other good sources for background. They also may have information on population and income trends. County and city governments also can provide critical information on taxes and zoning regulations.

- **Start your research by getting a detailed map.** It should indicate schools, fire departments, parks, lakes and shopping areas.

  Ask the local real estate board or title company for prices of homes in the desired neighborhoods and jot them down to give yourself a base for comparison shopping.

  Once you begin house-hunting, use the map to familiarize yourself with the area and to get a general feel for the proximity of individual homes to schools, stores and the like.

- **If time permits, attend a community meeting.** A political fundraiser, a PTA meeting, a zoning hearing or church or synagogue service will enable you to meet some of the residents.

- **Inquire about the quality of neighborhood schools,** even if you aren't a parent. Schools affect the taxes you pay on your property. And good schools increase property values for parents and nonparents alike. Parents may want to schedule a meeting with the neighborhood school's principal.

Questions to Ask About Schools

• •

- What schools are nearby?
- How many elementary schools are operating?
- What is the average class size in grades one through six?
- How do most children get to school?
- How do students in the town or county rate on standardized tests?
- What enrichment courses are offered?
- How are special needs met?
- Where do graduating high school seniors go to college?

- **Shop the stores.** Is parking adequate during hours of peak demand? Can you buy aspirin and sodas nearby, or will you have to hop in the car to meet unexpected family requests?

  Note the kind of stores and the quality of the merchandise. Merchants have to be responsive to subtle changes in the socioeconomic level of their patrons. They buy what they perceive their customers want. The range of products from staples to "luxury" items in a supermarket might tell you something about whether it's a neighborhood you'd feel comfortable in.

- **Do at least one rush-hour practice commute.** Make it on a weekday at the time you normally would be en route. Use the public transportation system if that would be your usual mode. How often do buses or subways run during morning and evening rush hours? What is the weekend and off-peak schedule? If you are depending on buses or trains to get to work or for other commuting, try to determine whether there are proposals to reroute or drop the line you would be using.

- **Consider your travel patterns.** Figure what roads you might travel to deliver children to day-care centers or school. Will it be convenient to stop after work to pick up groceries, or will buying bread and milk entail a lengthy side trip? Does the surrounding community offer recreation and entertainment that suits your interests, or will you face frequent long drives for a movie, concert or athletic event?

Weigh the Negatives

A town or neighborhood can decline, or take off toward renewal, before home-sales figures reflect it. Before you take a fancy to a home, rule out locations where negative factors outweigh positives.

Crime

Pass up casual conversations here and go to the police precinct station for records of robberies, break-ins, vandalism, assaults and drug-related problems. Is crime increasing, decreasing or staying about the same? Parents will want to know how safe their children will be going to and from school and playing in the neighborhood.

Traffic

Heavy traffic is a major drawback in any residential area. It generates noise and pollution. Of course, being on a busy street is less a problem for high-rise condo dwellers than for families in detached one- and two-story homes. Even so, a unit on the quiet side of the building certainly is more desirable than one where you can hear the steady roar of automobiles.

Visual "pollution"

Look for public-utility substations and transformers, radio or television broadcasting towers, gas stations, auto dealerships, salvage yards, overnight parking for commercial auto fleets, bus stops and ball fields where night games are played.

Pass up casual conversations here and go to the police precinct station. Is crime increasing, decreasing or staying about the same?

Full-blown blight is easy to spot. What you need to be alert to are the earliest signs of neglect or decay, and find out the reason for it.

Smells and sounds

Does the commuting pattern create air pollution or smog in the area? What about food-processing or chemical plants? Even something as delightful in small doses as the smell of bread wafting from a bakery is a nuisance when you can never escape it. Visit the area during the day and at night, and on weekdays as well as weekends. Does it lie in the flight pattern for airplanes? Is it too close to a bus stop, fire station or school?

Overcrowding

Are roads, parks, stores and pools too crowded? Are there too many cars parked on streets and in driveways? Is there any sign that homes are being used as rooming houses or broken into multiple units?

Full-blown blight is easy to spot. What you need to be alert to are the earliest signs of neglect or decay. A neighborhood that appears slightly down-at-the-heels may not reveal any other signs of decline...yet. Perhaps nothing is broken, littered or really shabby. You still should try to find out why the level of maintenance has slipped. Is the ratio of owners to renters shifting? Are such municipal services as sidewalk and road repairs being postponed or reduced?

How Is the Neighborhood Organized?

Once you find a home you like, give the land it sits on more than a perfunctory once-over. Step back and notice the overall pattern of blocks and streets in the neighborhood. Most subdivisions are laid out in blocks and lots. A section of land is blocked off and divided into lots. Use a map to determine the layout of the community that has piqued your interest. Common street patterns are described below and shown in the following illustration.

Common Street Patterns

Gridiron

Lots generally are rectangular, and homes face the street. In neighborhoods where lots are large, traffic is limited and back alleys are safe, the pattern works best. But such a layout can be monotonous, and the design doesn't provide open spaces and recreational areas.

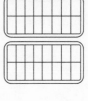

Curvilinear

When done well, this system is an improvement over the gridiron. Traffic patterns are improved by meshing major roads with secondary streets and cul-de-sacs. Small parks often are placed at intersections.

Loop streets

This pattern reduces the traffic on residential streets while still providing good access to the main highway. Compared with the gridiron system, fewer lots face busy roads, and there is more open space.

Radburn plan

Named after Radburn, N.J., where the plan originated, it clusters units into large cul-de-sac blocks. There is open space between each cluster, and pedestrians are well separated from auto traffic.

Cluster

This plan groups homes around cul-de-sacs. Street patterns are more varied, and there can be a dramatic increase in the amount of land available for recreation and other community uses.

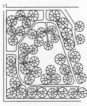

Examine the Lot

Give some thought to whether you will enjoy living on a lot before you fall in love with the house there. Your answer will depend, to some degree, on how you feel about the following:

- Do you spend a lot of time outdoors?

- How much privacy do you want?

- Will you maintain the grounds yourself, or will you hire someone for such routine chores as mowing the lawn and trimming hedges?

- Do you want to be involved with landscaping, or would you prefer an established yard with mature trees and shrubs?

Then, consider the physical dimensions and composition of the lot itself, including:

Shape

Look for a basically rectangular or square lot with adequate road frontage and enough land behind the house. Lots with unusual shapes can make it harder to sell your home.

Size

A lot that falls pretty much within the average for the neighborhood probably is the best bet. Bigger isn't necessarily better. Many couples don't have time for large-scale groundskeeping, and help is expensive and hard to find. Acreage that can't be subdivided can keep a property on the market.

Slope

The contour of a lot determines not only what was already built on it but also what could be added after you move in. A home built on a steep hillside may preclude the addition of two extra bedrooms that might be needed later by a growing family.

Drainage

Slope and the ability of the soil to absorb water combine to determine where and how fast water drains from the lot. Low areas that hold water can mean trouble inside and outside the house. Muddy spots are a nuisance, particularly just outside the back door. They may be only a symptom, however, of the real problem inside. A wet basement goes beyond the nuisance level. Drying it out permanently will likely be expensive. It may even be impossible.

Get a feel for a house's drainage problems by checking whether the building is on a rise or in a low spot, and simply asking yourself where rain is going to go after it falls on the roof. You want an obvious slope away from your foundation on all sides. If you are worried about what you see, go back for a look during and just after a hard rain. Also check local flood information—often available through mortgage lenders. You must get federal flood insurance through a commercial insurance agent if you live in a flood-prone area.

Soil composition

Look for a good layer of topsoil that will support a healthy lawn and border plantings. Is there an established vegetable or flower garden? An inexpensive soil analysis can provide you with answers about soil quality. Some lots are scraped bare in construction and may need extensive preparation for a top-notch garden. Soil composition also affects settling of a house. Unstable soil conditions can make settling a never-ending process, leading to cracked walls and other eyesores, even damaging foundations and other structural components in the home. Contaminated soil can raise health anxieties or even cause illness.

Many Kinds of Homes

The single-family detached house is the essence of homeownership, with all its joys and headaches. You get privacy—and the burden of upkeep.

Population density, topography, climate, history, and ethnic heritage all impact your choice of housing.

If you choose a particular school district in a small county, for example, you may rule out buying a condominium, townhouse or cooperative apartment. You'll have to buy the single-family detached dwelling best suited to your needs.

Thinking about a mobile home? Local zoning laws may dictate where you can live and limit your choices. Large metropolitan areas usually offer a mix of homes. But in expensive locales, the middle-budget home buyer may be forced to choose between a small, close-in condo and a detached home far from work.

Here's a brief rundown of the possibilities, with some pros and cons to jog your thinking:

Single-Family Detached Houses

The single-family detached house is the essence of homeownership, with all its joys and headaches. You have four walls to call your own, and often a yard or garden, too. These offer privacy, but they also present the burden of upkeep (painting, planting, mowing, snow removal, and so on) that would be less or nonexistent in a condominium, townhouse or apartment.

The big decision in detached housing is whether to buy an older home or something new.

The New House

Its Advantages

Predictable cost and low maintenance

Assuming competent design and craftsmanship in the new house (which is not always a good assumption today), the major mechanical systems—plumbing, wiring, heating and air-conditioning—as well as structural members should hold up for a long time after purchase. You can expect a minimum of repair and fix-up headaches, so the monthly mortgage payment and utilities should be the entire cost of maintaining the property into the near future.

Modernity

New homes may have the latest in floor-plan designs and kitchen and bathroom layouts, as well as adequate storage and closet space.

Economy in furnishing

Decorating costs can be reduced because many new homes come with wall-to-wall carpeting and window treatments, as well as more installed appliances and fixtures.

Energy efficiency

A new house ought to be well insulated and should come outfitted with storm windows. As a result, it should be less expensive to heat and cool than a comparable older home.

Recreational features

Community swimming pools, craft workshops and fully equipped gymnasiums often are found in large, new developments. Some even have tennis courts and bridle paths for residents' use.

Its Disadvantages

Location

Communities tend to grow from the center out, so new developments usually are located on the fringes of suburbia. That means a long commute to downtown, both for work and for outings to museums, restaurants and theaters.

Uneven quality

Shoddy construction is always a concern when buying a new home, because flaws can take time to show themselves. They may surface because a marginal builder has tried to cut too many corners, but they can turn up in houses built by large well-known firms, too.

The raw look

In all but the most carefully planned and expensive projects, developers tend to skimp on trees, foundation plantings and lawns. New developments can look downright barren. And, if you move in early on, substantial sections may still have to be built, graded and paved, so expect noise, dust, mud and a good deal of general nuisance.

Look-alikes

Brick chimney, stone chimney; white shutters, brown shutters; garage on the left, garage on the right—those may be your only choices among the houses in a new development. While some people might like the consistency such look-alikes give to the character of a development, others detest it, preferring instead to own a house with at least a few unique characteristics.

If the House Is Still on the Drawing Board

Buying a not-yet-built house isn't like buying an existing one—it's harder. You reap advantages similar to those you get buying a new house; ditto the disadvantages. But you can also tailor plans so you get your dream house.

Buy based on reputation.

The key point to remember: You're not buying a piece of land and a house; *you're buying a builder.* More to the point, you're buying a builder's reputation.

Make the usual checks with the Better Business Bureau and the local builders association. Look at the model homes, but keep in mind that you're looking at the builder's best effort, loaded with eye-catching "decorator options," such as molding, custom lighting and special finishes.

For a more realistic picture, go to a comparable subdivision also put up by the same builder. Walk around and visit with homeowners.

For a more realistic picture, go to a comparable subdivision also put up by the same builder. Walk through the neighborhood or attend a homeowner's association meeting, and visit with homeowners; ask what they think of the builder's quality and service. The latter is especially important because new houses routinely require follow-up repairs that are the builder's responsibility. You'll want to know:

- Did the builder respond to complaints?

- Were repairs well done?

- Did problems recur?

- Would they buy another home from this builder?

Ask owners how long it took to complete their home and whether it was delivered when promised. Ask the builder what happens to unsold homes. Houses that are discounted to sell quickly can affect the value of the entire subdivision.

Check out the neighborhood.

Once satisfied with the builder, look at the neighborhood. What will happen to those big fields to the west or that blank area to the south? Will it become home to more houses like yours? Or a gas station or factory? When it comes to information about future development, look beyond the sales agent for verification. Check the master plan filed with the local planning department. Visit other land-owning builders to find out what they have in store for nearby lots.

Time your offer.

Timing affects the price. You may find a slower market in fall and winter. You probably won't get a discount, but you may be able to negotiate for options like a deck or upgraded carpet. Consider at what point in the construction cycle to buy. Prices may be lower when you buy a house that's built early on. In booming markets, house prices can jump in $10,000 increments as development is completed. Buy too early, however, and you'll live in a construction site for several years. If you wait you may get further from the main road to the development. There's also less risk when you buy later. You can monitor the quality of houses and watch how the neighborhood shapes up.

Hammer out the contract.

You put a contract on a to-be-built house just as you would on an existing one, but you face many more decisions before you can sign on the dotted line. For starters, if the market is active, you may need to put a deposit on the lot immediately. Typically the deposit is 5%, but you may be able to bargain it down. Also, insert a clause in the contract to protect your right to regain the deposit if the deal falls through—because of financing, for example.

Sit down with the selling agent and hammer out the details. You pick the model and the options you want to add. If there is a model built, you can point to things you want. Otherwise, you'll be using illustrations, brochures and samples of materials.

Prepare to pay extra for everything—from kitchen

cabinets made of cherry rather than oak to better carpeting, humidifiers, intercoms, fireplaces, decks, and a finished basement. Consider how you'll pay for each option. If the cost is lumped into the mortgage, it's easier to afford but more expensive in the long run because it's amortized over two or three decades.

You may be told you must have certain things installed, even though you don't want them or don't like the quality. Carpet is a good example. Lenders may require carpeting before a house can be sold. Fine, but you think the basic carpeting stinks and don't like the optional colors any better. If you're told that the choices you see are the only ones available, keep pushing. Insist on getting something you want to live with, especially if your offer is not contingent on the sale of another house—a status that puts you in a powerful negotiating position. One solution is to draft a letter of agreement to the lender indicating you will place carpet of your choosing in the house within a specified time after the closing date.

In most states, contracts favor the builder. You probably won't be able to get the builder to guarantee delivery on a specified date. You can, however, add a clause to your contract demanding that your house be built to the quality standards of the model.

Study settlement details.

You'll be given a list of disclosures about the subdivision. It must include such information as the location of any airports within a given radius of the house.

You'll also get a copy of the development's homeowners association bylaws. As local governments have

---

An Extended Warranty?

• •

Find out whether the home will be covered by the Home Owners Warranty Corp. or another extended warranty plan. If so, check that your contract notes coverage. Such plans cover repairs for certain major construction defects and usually last for ten years. Builders pay the premiums for these plans, which remain in effect until expiration even if you sell the house (for more on this, see Chapter 9).

If you want a house with character, and perhaps even a history of its own, consider an older home. Middle-aged houses often reflect the love and care that have been lavished on them.

shifted the costs of maintaining services to residents, they have required new developments to assume more responsibility for road maintenance, garbage collection and recreation facilities. Homeowners associations may be relatively inactive, but they have power over how you live. They can assess you for emergency expenses and put a lien on your property if you don't pay your dues. Have an attorney review the bylaws as well as everything else in the contract—before you sign.

The Older House

Its Advantages

Location
An older home often is situated near work, schools, downtown shopping and public transportation.

Size
Many older houses have large rooms with high ceilings, or lots of rooms that can be remodeled to suit your needs. You often get many more square feet (and often cubic feet) for your money in an older home.

Individuality
If you want a house with character, and perhaps even a history of its own, consider an older home. Middle-aged houses often reflect the love and care that have been lavished on them through such owner-added touches as crown moldings, carved fireplace mantels and built-in bookcases.

Better construction
This is often, but not necessarily, true of older homes. It's something you have to check out case by case. If you want slate roofs, copper gutters and chimney flashing, hardwood floors, and plaster walls, you're more likely to find them in an older house than in a new house in the same price range.

Lower property taxes

Property taxes on an older home may be less than on a comparable new home. Even if they are higher, they are less likely to rise as rapidly as they might in a new community or development where streets, sewers, schools and public utilities have yet to be built.

Ambience

Mature trees and lawns and a variety of architectural styles, as well as a range of color and texture of materials, present a more varied environment.

Its Disadvantages

Functional inferiority

Unless an older house has been modernized, its floor plan and traffic flow may not suit modern living as well as those of a new home.

Unpredictable expenses

It may be love at first sight, but older homes can be costly to maintain and in need of renovation. Get estimates of such costs before you make a purchase offer, but don't be surprised if the eventual work ends up costing significantly more. In addition, it is difficult to predict exactly when such items as a roof, furnace or water heater will need replacing.

Remodeling costs

Major projects, such as kitchens and bathrooms, will have to be financed with a home-improvement loan, a home-equity loan or a second mortgage. These typically carry higher interest rates than first mortgages.

If you submit detailed plans and contractor bids for improvements that you intend to do immediately after settlement, your first-mortgage lender may accept a letter of agreement and give you enough to cover both purchase and renovations with one loan. More commonly, you'll take out temporary construction financing until the renovation is finished, at which point a new appraisal will be done and permanent financing, via a new first or second mortgage, is placed on the property.

Two programs, both somewhat limited by the number of lenders willing to be involved with loans involving more time and risk, may provide an alternative to the financing methods described above.

What Pays Off?

• •

The most popular remodeling projects—kitchens and baths—do the most to enhance your home's value. Depending on the housing market in your area, kitchens generally recoup from 40% to more than 100% of their cost when you sell. Bathrooms do just as well, with a second one adding more value than a third. Also offering good returns: upgrading to master suites and making renovations that blend the house and yard with larger windows or doors leading to decks and patios.

If payback is important, make sure the improvements you make don't put your house out of the neighborhood's price range. Your best bet is to keep styles conservative.

• **The Federal Housing Administration** offers a remodeling program that may meet your needs when you want to buy a home and then renovate it. Under this 203(k) program, you must spend at least $5,000 and meet other Housing and Urban Development (HUD) standards, but you will be allowed to borrow against the anticipated equity your remodeling will add to the home's market value. Once the loan is closed, the proceeds designated for improvements go into a rehabilitation escrow account, to be released as various stages of the rehabilitation are completed and inspected. For more information, contact an FHA-approved lender in your area.

• **HomeStyle, a new program offered by the Federal National Mortgage Association (Fannie Mae),** became available in 1993. You may be able to get remodeling money as a second mortgage or in combination with a loan to buy or refinance a home. A HomeStyle loan is intended to increase your borrowing power to the renovated value of your home, based on an appraisal of architectural plans. Under certain conditions, Fannie Mae may permit your total indebtedness on the property to go as high as 90% of its market value. It's not clear yet how many lenders will participate. In late 1992, when the HomeStyle program was announced, just two dozen lenders nationwide were involved.

For both of these arrangements, the lender will require blueprints and cost estimates in advance. That means buyers of houses needing renovation should get moving on design plans as soon as the purchase contract is accepted.

Condominium Ownership

The term *condominium* refers to a legal form of ownership, not a particular type of property. Under such a plan, the owners of individual dwelling units in a housing development also own undivided proportional interests in such common facilities as the grounds, hallways, elevators and recreation areas.

Condos give owners virtually the same financial advantages as single-family houses. The federal income-tax breaks are identical:

- Mortgage interest and property taxes on your home are deductible.

- You may be able to defer part or all of any profit made on the sale by buying another home.

- And when you are 55 or older, you may be able to exercise a once-in-a-lifetime right to exclude from income as much as $125,000 of gain on the sale or exchange of the condo unit.

On the downside, when the housing market goes into a tailspin, condo prices are usually the first to suffer and the last to recover.

Condos typically offer a trade-off: less cost for less

Condos give owners virtually the same financial advantages as single-family houses. The federal income-tax breaks are identical.

space. Instead of having your own backyard, you may share one with 200 or so other residents. In place of your own full basement or attic for storage, you get a storage bin in the basement. You may have to share coin-operated washers and dryers. And you can't keep a bike and workbench in your parking space.

On the other hand, less space is precisely what many buyers are looking for. They want the enjoyment of an indoor swimming pool an elevator ride away, or ready access to a tennis partner on Saturday mornings. They don't want to rake leaves and mow the lawn.

A condo—whether garden apartment, townhouse or high rise—locks you into community living. While cost may be your first priority, a condo's facilities and the lifestyle it mandates—particularly interaction with your fellow owners—should be ranked not too far behind. You may get a bargain on the place and still end up with buyer's remorse if neighbors are noisy or otherwise objectionable. You will be subject to rules adopted by other owners. Certain activities and hobbies may be restricted or even banned. Pets may be forbidden, especially cats and dogs.

Many Kinds of Condos
• •

Just about any kind of development you can think of comes in condominium form: converted older apartment houses, townhouse complexes, elegant old mansions divided into luxury apartments, commercial lofts and office buildings in busy downtown areas, apartments fitted into former schools or farm silos, and virtually self-contained villages of freestanding houses, complete with tennis courts, golf courses, pools and community houses.

Questions to Ask

Before you shop, learn as much about condominium ownership as possible. Line up a good lawyer who understands condos. Then investigate and question, question, question.

What's the area like?
You want your unit to be a good investment as well as a good place to live.

Generally, look for residential areas with good-quality apartment buildings and homes in the middle to upper price range. Assess convenience to public transportation, stores, schools, hospitals and parks.

Find out whether units have been appreciating. Compare recent selling prices with original purchase prices. How much of that appreciation occurred in the months or year after the development sold out? How much is occurring now? Information on sales is available from county land-transfer records.

Try to visualize what the neighborhood might look like in five, ten or 15 years. What are the zoning rules covering nearby unbuilt areas? Could the view be obstructed by a future high rise? Could a highway be constructed nearby?

Is it financially sound?

What debts does the condo association owe, and to whom? Are there adequate funds in reserve to handle routine maintenance as well as replacement of expensive items, such as boilers and roofs? Has the association tended to rely on special assessments for emergency needs?

Will you fit in?

Do you desire compatibility with other tenants, in terms of lifestyle, occupation, age or any other characteristic? How are problems resolved? Will you be expected to vote on every little detail—like what color to paint the halls—or will routine decisions be made by the elected board?

What's the vacancy rate in the region?

An oversupply of condo units in an area can depress prices generally. Too many vacant units in a particular building can not only depress prices but also, among other things, reduce the funds available to the condo association for maintenance and repairs and increase the pressure on the developer or current owners to rent rather than sell.

Do you desire compatibility with other tenants, in terms of lifestyle, occupation, age or any other characteristic?

How many units are rented?

Some units usually are rented out by investors, others by owners who have moved away temporarily. In resort areas, most of the units in a project may be on rental during the vacation season, but that's a special case. A high proportion of renters is undesirable, so much so that the FHA won't insure condo loans in projects with less than an 80% owner-occupancy rate. Renters, it's charged, are less concerned than owner-occupants with preserving the building and grounds, and investors are less likely than homeowners to upgrade and renovate their units.

Is there a heavy sales turnover?

You expect turnover in a resort project. But heavy turnover in a year-round residential community can create an uncomfortable feeling of impermanence; increase the wear-and-tear on elevators, hallways and other common elements; weaken security controls; and discourage compliance with rules.

Who owns the common facilities?

Developers sometimes hang on to such facilities—laundry room, parking areas, pool and other recreational facilities—for the income from rental fees. Avoid a project in which important amenities are not owned by the condominium owners. Otherwise, you become a captive user, exposed to uncontrollable fee increases and inconveniences.

Are the facilities adequate?

Inspect the pool, tennis courts, parking area and other facilities at times of peak usage. A pool that's big enough for a 200-unit building occupied mainly by working couples and singles could prove an overcrowded mess with the same number of apartments filled largely by families with small children. Free parking may be limited or unavailable. You may have to pay to use a party room or gym.

What are the restrictions?

There are sure to be some, so read the declaration or master deed, the bylaws and the house rules before you sign a contract. Ironically, you may find it best not to buy if the condo does not impose enough controls.

What happens if funds are stolen or mishandled?

Will you and other owners be adequately insured? Are funds in an insured account? If not, what would happen if investment losses occurred? Ask for evidence of liability insurance, property insurance and fidelity bond.

Where to Find the Answers

Answers to many of the important questions about condos can be found in the following documents, which you should examine before you buy a condo. Some states require developers to give potential buyers a prospectus with relevant facts about the offering. No matter how onerous the job, you and your lawyer should take the time to evaluate all this material before you buy. If your state doesn't require delivery of documents before you sign a contract, insist on your right to obtain and examine them.

Master deed

Also called an enabling declaration, a plan of condominium ownership or a declaration of conditions, covenants and restrictions, the master deed is the key document. When recorded, it legally establishes the project as a condominium. Among other things, the master deed authorizes residents to form an operating association and describes individual units and commonly owned areas.

Bylaws

These spell out the association's authority and responsibilities, authorize the making of a budget and the collection of various charges, and prescribe parliamentary procedures. They may empower the

If your state doesn't require delivery of condo documents before you sign a contract, insist on your right to obtain and examine them.

association to hire professional managers or contain other special provisions. If the condo master deed doesn't do so, the bylaws may set forth insurance requirements and authorize imposing liens against property owners who fail to pay monthly charges.

House rules

These state what owners can and can't do. Restrictions on pets, children, decorations, use of facilities and such are among them. House rules may be incorporated in the bylaws or set out in a separate document.

Sales contract or purchase agreement

While basically similar to other real estate contracts, there are a couple of differences. When you sign a condo contract, you probably acknowledge receipt of the other documents just described. The contract may provide for a cooling-off period during which you can back out. If not, insert a clause to that effect.

Likewise, make sure the contract sets out when and how you'll get out of the deal if you fail to get the financing you want.

If the project isn't yet completed, ask for written assurance that it will be—and as promised.

Ensure your right to an inspection prior to settlement, and make sure your deposit is placed in an escrow account.

Other papers

No less important, these could include a copy of the operating budget, a schedule of current and proposed assessments, a financial statement for the owners' association, any leases or contracts, a plan or drawing of the project and your unit, and an engineer's report if one was done.

Determine how much money has been set aside for emergency outlays. (The board should set owners' condo fees high enough to create a reserve fund for replacements and major repairs.) Ask the board treasurer for copies of recent budget reports, and obtain an engineer's summary of the physical condition of the building, including projections for major repairs.

Find out what assessments have been made during the past five years in addition to the regular condo fee. While some associations deliberately choose to operate with minimal reserves, relying instead on special assessments, good management is generally associated with a healthy reserve.

Getting to Know Them

If you've never lived in a condo, you may be astonished to discover just how much power is held by the board of directors. As mentioned, the board has the power to put a lien on your unit if you don't pay your monthly fee or are late with the money for a special assessment. It may have license to spend tens of thousands of dollars on a repair or improvement without the prior approval of other owners.

Elected by condo owners, the board is much like a miniature government with ultimate authority to run the condominium even if it turns day-to-day operating details over to a resident manager or outside management company.

Request information on the background of each member, and attend at least one board meeting. If you are serious about condo ownership, plan on participating in a certain amount of organizational activity just to protect your interests.

Financing

You may be asked to make a larger down payment on a condo than on a comparable single-family property. But otherwise, getting a mortgage for a condo is no different from getting one on a single-family house.

Lenders may be reluctant to give you a loan if you plan to put down less than 10%, and FHA-insured mortgages are not available to prospective owners of condo projects less than a year old.

If you are serious about condo ownership, plan on participating in a certain amount of organizational activity just to protect your interests.

Cooperative Apartments

The "stockholder in 202-F" may sound like someone with a seat on a securities exchange, but if you live in a cooperative apartment, that's how you might describe your neighbor.

Unlike condominium ownership, which gives you title to a particular unit and an undivided interest in the common areas, buying a co-op entitles you to a share in a corporation. Stock ownership or certificate membership in the corporation, in turn, gives you the right to live in a particular unit. You become a tenant-stockholder. Typically, the corporation owns and manages the co-op, pays the property taxes, and finances the project with a "blanket" mortgage.

In most states your collateral is considered personal property rather than real property. However, if your cooperative complies with certain Internal Revenue Code requirements, that portion of your assessment going to pay real estate taxes and interest on any blanket mortgage may be tax-deductible on your personal income taxes, along with interest on any share loan.

Because a tenant is a fellow shareholder in the whole building, current co-op tenants tend to be choosy about prospective owners. It's common for a co-op board to interview prospects and require them to submit personal references as well as financial statements. Most co-op boards zealously protect the lifestyle of their tenant-stockholders, going so far as to reject those they believe could be noisy, reclusive, sloppy or inclined to throw large, boisterous parties. But they can go only so far. Boards are prohibited by federal law and many state statutes from rejecting or discouraging a prospective buyer on the basis of race, gender, creed or national origin.

Financing a Co-op

Unlike the collateral (property) that secures a traditional mortgage, collateral for a "share loan" includes stock in a corporation. In the past, before a lender could make individual share loans, it had to determine the value of the stock by assessing the legal structure, financial stability and physical condition of the co-op. In addition, because there was no secondary market for such loans before 1984, banks couldn't sell the ones they made. The practical result? It was nearly impossible back then to get a co-op loan. Prospective owners had to pay cash or take out personal loans with high interest rates. With the exception of a few co-ops sponsored by state housing agencies, this financing fact restricted most ownership to those in the upper income brackets.

Then, in 1984, the Federal National Mortgage Association (Fannie Mae) began buying qualified co-op share loans. That same year, the National Cooperative Bank (NCB) was formed to act as lender to co-ops that met its own or Fannie Mae's underwriting and legal standards—among them are such things as structural soundness, restricted commercial use, fiscally responsible operating budget and appropriate management.

Today, the NCB, through its affiliate, NCB Savings Bank, is the largest single share-loan originator. Once a co-op becomes a "participating" project by meeting NCB/Fannie Mae standards, you can apply for a share loan from NCB Savings Bank. The NCB usually works through a local lender or processing agent. Check with the cooperative's office to find out where to call for an application and interview.

Share loans are secured by the stock and occupancy rights of co-op ownership, with terms similar to those

---

For More Co-op Information

- You can get a free brochure, *A Consumer Guide to Financing a Cooperative Unit Using Share Loan Financing,* by writing NCB Savings Bank, 139 High St., Hillsboro, Ohio 45133, or by calling 800-322-1251.

- If a cooperative you are considering isn't affiliated with the NCB, it will have to get approval before it can offer loans for tenant-stockholders through the bank. Have a co-op official send a letter of inquiry to: Project Approvals, NCB, 1401 Eye Street, N.W., Suite 700, Washington, D.C. 20005.

of mortgage loans. While they're still not quite as common as mortgages on a single-family houses, share loans are a boon to co-ops. They carry interest rates about one-quarter percentage point higher than the going rate on conventional mortgages. Closing costs, however, are usually less.

Share-loan and co-op documents of projects meeting NCB/Fannie Mae legal requirements must include various legal safeguards to protect the interests of the tenant-stockholders, the corporation and the lender.

Required Reading

The following are common cooperative documents you need to study before you buy:

Articles of incorporation
A cooperative is incorporated under state law and the corporation's purpose, powers and obligations are described in the Articles of Incorporation.

Bylaws
These spell out the duties and responsibilities of shareholders, officers and directors.

Stock, shares or membership certificates
Shares or membership certificates are your proof of ownership in the corporation.

Proprietary lease or occupancy agreement
The lease sets up the terms and conditions by which you occupy your co-op unit. It obligates you to pay your pro rata share of the corporation's expenses, including real estate taxes, operating costs and debt. Rules on using your unit, subleasing and maintenance also are found in the agreement.

Recognition agreement
A share-loan lender and the co-op corporation enter into this agreement in order to document the

lender's rights as well as the corporation's responsibilities and obligations to the lender. A corporation may enter into recognition agreements with more than one lender.

Security agreement

In this document, the share-loan borrower assigns the proprietary lease (or occupancy agreement) and pledges his or her stock, shares or membership certificate to the lender in return for a loan.

The Right Questions

Is it financially sound?

Is there adequate income in the co-op to meet expenses? Income has three primary sources: tenant/ stockholders, commercial use—for example, rental income from parking, and interest or dividends earned on reserve funds. Expenses include debt repayment, real estate and income taxes, building maintenance and operations, and reserve fund payins for replacements and capital improvements.

A cooperative financed with an FHA-insured blanket mortgage is required to have reserve funds that meet the agency's criteria. Besides collecting money for taxes and debt, adequate sums must be set aside to replace structural elements and major components, such as heating, cooling, plumbing and electrical systems. In addition, a general operating reserve must be established for other contingencies and for resale problems. These reserves are established under the co-op's regulatory agreements, and documents should be available to prospective owners.

NCB/Fannie Mae's project-approval standards give lenders the tools they need to evaluate co-op pro-

Co-op Associations

• **The National Association of Housing Cooperatives,** 1614 King St., Alexandria, Va. 22314, can provide a list of publications.

• **The National Cooperative Business Association,** 1401 New York Ave., N.W., Suite 1100, Washington, D.C. 20005.

jects. Typically, they require, among other things, that each project have an adequate cash flow and that monthly assessments be structured to handle operating expenses and build sufficient reserves.

Age and condition of the building?

The answer to that sets the stage for the kind of financial experience you'll have once you're a tenant-stockholder. Is there an engineering report on the condition of the property? If you discover the galvanized plumbing in the building is nearing the end of its anticipated 40-year life span, you know it will have to be replaced, not repaired. How does the board plan to pay for the job? From the reserve fund? With a special assessment? By refinancing the mortgage?

How will you fit in?

How old is the average shareowner? What is the financial status and philosophy of the majority? Up-and-coming professionals in their early forties may have a very different money-management philosophy than retired or soon-to-be retired people. Likewise, if you can afford to buy into a particular cooperative only by living in the smallest unit, you may be at odds with affluent neighbors who insist on a uniformed doorman—regardless of cost.

Composition of the board and its financial philosophy?

Is there some consensus among board members on how to conduct the corporation's affairs? Do their views on important issues reflect those of other tenant-stockholders? Do they jibe with yours?

Are you prepared to participate in cooperative living?

Many of the problems of condo and cooperative living are similar. How willing are you to be involved in meetings and group efforts?

How many units are rented?

What do the bylaws permit? Conceivably, a majority

of a co-op's units could be occupied by tenants or "nominees" of partnerships, trusts, estates and corporations rather than by shareowners who have joined together as "cooperative homeowners." If a building is dominated by tenants rather than owners, it changes the nature of cooperative living. It also may have tax and resale consequences for individual tenant-stockholders.

May you sublet your apartment?

Some cooperatives forbid it. Others allow it but may impose a one-time sublet fee or an additional monthly maintenance surcharge.

Mobile Homes

Despite their name, most mobile homes aren't all that mobile. Nine out of ten stay on their original sites. This fact, plus changes in design and construction over the years, means you hear the term "manufactured home" used as often as the familiar term "mobile home." Built in factories and assembled in the plant or on site, manufactured homes make ownership possible for many families and individuals who would otherwise be priced out of the home market. On a per-square-foot basis, manufactured homes cost about a third as much to build as site-built homes.

Rent or Buy the Land?

Before you buy, decide whether you will place the home on land you own or on land you rent or lease. The decision is important because if you later regret your choice of a homesite, the only practical solution may be to sell. It also has tax implications.

The majority of buyers put their manufactured homes on land they own. Your best approach is to select a lot *before* you buy the home. While zoning restrictions that keep manufactured homes out of residential neighborhoods still exist in some areas, 19 states have passed legislation that prevents such zoning dis-

On a per-square-foot basis, manufactured homes cost about a third as much to build as do site-built homes.

There are numerous well-designed, attractive subdivisions to choose from; you may be able to find land in a ready-made community.

crimination. Check local zoning ordinances before making plans to situate your new home.

There are numerous well-designed, attractive subdivisions to choose from; you may be able to find land in a ready-made community, complete with swimming pool, recreation center and nearby schools and shopping. A good subdivision developer can help you select a lot suited to the home you have in mind.

If you plan to rent the land on which your home will be situated, be prepared to have certain activities controlled by mobile-home park management on the one hand and by a group of neighbors on the other. If you move into an established community, you will rent a piece of property and have your home installed at your expense. A lease may or may not be involved. There are generally rules and regulations, and you should ask for them in writing. In most cases you will rent your space from month to month or year to year, but longer-term leases are now offered in many states.

In a new development, the management may also be the dealer, and you can get into the park only by buying a home from the dealer. This arrangement isn't entirely self-serving. It allows management to enforce strict standards for homes that go into the park. When you select a lot, you also pick a home from among models approved by the management. You will be shown a complete catalog and price information, and in some developments management will encourage you to go to the factory to custom-design your model.

New developments and those still under construction are often promoted on the basis of nonexistent amenities such as swimming pools, shuffleboard courts and recreation halls. Once settled in, you may discover—to your dismay—that the landlord lets the pool wait while funds and space are devoted to developing homesites. What's more, you may have been required to pay an entrance fee of several hundred dollars—a practice now banned in some states.

Keep in mind that leasing land rather than buying puts you in a vulnerable situation. You will own a valuable piece of property located on someone else's land. In a dispute with the landowner you may have no recourse but to sell or move. Moving even a single-section home is costly. Including necessary dismantling and reassembly, you can pay thousands of dollars to move a luxury multisection home less than 50 miles. Because of the expense and damage that can result from vibration and road shock, you could be forced to sell, possibly at a loss, and be faced with the prospect of buying another home elsewhere.

Questions of Quality

You might pay around $20,000 for a single-section unit, $37,000 for a multisection. Those were average prices for new single- and multisection units in early 1993. The purchase price usually includes some furniture, major appliances, draperies, carpeting and delivery from the manufacturer to a homesite.

Selecting a Home Site

Whether you intend to buy or rent a home site, here are some considerations:

Visit several developments. Stay a few days if you can, to sample the neighborhood and meet residents.

Familiarize yourself with each community's rules and regulations. In condominium developments, for example, residents own part of the common facilities plus their own units and lots.

Try to determine how much turnover there is and how most residents view their community. Is your lifestyle compatible with that of your potential neighbors?

Check on security, fire protection and trash collection.

Remember that the complexion of a rental park can change much more rapidly than that of a community of landowners. As a tenant, there may be little you can do if a park is sold or if the management becomes lax.

Study the purchase contract or lease, bylaws, rules and regulations, and all other pertinent documents.

Do not commit yourself to a lot or a home until you've consulted with an attorney.

Don't sign anything you don't understand.

"Single section" or "single-wide" units may give you up to 1,000 square feet of living space. You can join two or more single-sections together to form a multisection home. At first glance, the most luxurious multisection models—featuring wood siding, pitched roofs, cathedral ceilings, fireplaces, bay windows, drywall interiors, and the like—can be hard to distinguish from their conventional site-built counterparts.

What's required

Manufactured homes are not subject to local building codes. Units built after June 14, 1976, are covered by the National Mobile Home Construction and Safety Standards Act and must display a permanent label saying that the manufacturer has conformed with the standards.

The standards do not apply to units made before then, nor to multifamily mobiles or special units for the handicapped. The Department of Housing and Urban

Quality in Manufactured Homes

Signs of good construction include:

- a floor that is level and firm;

- windows and doors that open and close smoothly;

- walls that do not give excessively when pushed;

- a firm ceiling;

- a chassis with two parallel steel I-beams 10 to 12 inches high that are reinforced over the axle area;

- and three axles if the unit is 60 feet long or more.

Also, look for a 2- by 4-inch aluminum label—located at the outside rear of each section—indicating that the home conforms with Department of Housing and Urban Development (HUD) standards. The plate gives:

- the name and address of the home's manufacturer,

- serial number,

- model and date of manufacture,

- the wind and snow loads for which the unit is designed, as well as

- other key information.

The home should come with important information relating to appliance operation and efficiency.

Development (HUD) has overall responsibility for enforcement, but inspections are conducted by approved state or private agencies.

In 1992, Hurricane Andrew destroyed thousands of homes in south Florida, including about 9,000 manufactured homes. HUD has proposed interim standards for builders focused on improving the ability of manufactured homes to withstand high winds. Once in place, the upgraded standards would apply to all manufactured homes being built. Until then, the manufactured housing industry has voluntarily agreed to build homes sold in the Southeast and Gulf Coast areas to the same wind-safety standards required of site-built homes. (The Southern Building Code 91 for site-built homes is being reviewed in light of Hurricane Andrew's destruction.) If you buy a manufactured home that you plan to locate on the southeastern coast or near the Gulf of Mexico, get written verification from the manufacturer that the home was built to the industry's higher voluntary standard rather than the current HUD standard.

Single-section mobile homes are more prone to wind damage from hurricanes, tornadoes and severe thunderstorms than site-built homes—even when properly tied down. Multisection units are more stable than single-section, particularly when properly tied or attached to a permanent foundation. A significant number of structural problems have been traced to improper installation of units on their sites, which HUD does not regulate. For that reason, installation should be done only by trained personnel.

States set their own standards and regulations governing proper installation. Check with your local building inspection offices (or your state's Manufactured Housing Association) on details and procedures to ensure that your home is properly installed.

Financing the Purchase

You should be able to finance your home with a mortgage if the unit is permanently set up on land you

A significant number of structural problems have been traced to improper installation of units on their sites. Installation should be done only by trained personnel.

own or are buying along with the unit in what is known as a single real estate transaction. The Federal National Mortgage Association (Fannie Mae) and the Federal Home Loan Mortgage Corp. (Freddie Mac) buy qualified mobile-home loans originated by banks, savings and loans, and mortgage bankers.

Manufactured houses are eligible for government-backed FHA and VA loans. In California, you may be able to title your manufactured home as real estate even if you don't own the land on which it is installed. Some lenders in that state have made mortgage loans on such homes when the borrower has had a long-term lease on the land.

But most manufactured homes are financed like motor vehicles—with personal property, or so-called chattel, loans—and mobile home dealers and park and subdivision developers still arrange most financing.

More About Manufactured Homes

See the following two sources:

The Manufactured Housing Directory (Meetings + Plus, P.O. Box 1981, Palm Springs, Cal. 92263; $49.95). The latest edition lists, among other things:

- names, addresses and phone numbers of the lending institutions providing manufactured home/land financing;

- names, addresses and phone numbers of major lenders offering VA and/or FHA financing;

- names, addresses and phone numbers of housing and finance agencies in the federal government;

- information about manufactured-housing appraisal services;

- names and locations of the various state and national manufactured-housing trade associations.

How to Buy a Manufactured Home, by the Manufactured Housing Institute, in cooperation with the Federal Trade Commission's Office of Consumer and Business Education (Consumer Information Center, Department 427Y, Pueblo, Colo. 81009; 50 cents), includes:

- information on warranties and other consumer protections;

- home selection and placement;

- site preparation;

- transportation and installation;

- and home inspection.

Most lenders will want a minimum down payment of 10% and will have loan terms ranging from 15 to 25 years. Interest rates are higher than on real estate loans—as much as two or thee percentage points—and payback periods shorter than on FHA, VA or Freddie Mac- or Fannie Mae-qualified loans.

Interest on debt you take on to buy or renovate a manufactured home (or home and land together) is fully deductible for federal tax purposes, so long as it is secured by the house and you use the house as your principal residence or as your second home.

When you find a unit you like and know how much you want to borrow, ask lenders about rates and terms. A few phone calls could save you big bucks.

Check Your Warranties

• •

Once you've bought your unit, you may get warranties from the retailer, transporter, installer and appliance manufacturer. Note what each warranty covers and doesn't cover. How long does each last? Who will actually do any necessary work under the warranty? And where will it be done?

Mobile-home loans are subject to the federal Truth in Lending law—and if land is involved, the Real Estate Settlement Procedures Act (RESPA)—which means you must be informed in writing of the finance cost expressed as an annual percentage rate (APR). If you're quoted an unusually low figure, it's probably an "add-on" or "discount" rate, neither of which reflects the true cost. Always insist on being told the APR, and have the APR inserted in any purchase contract. With add-on loans, interest is added to the amount borrowed before payments begin. If an interest-rebate formula called the rule of 78s is used on prepayment or refinancing, you could actually owe more than you borrowed even after making payments for several years.

Two FHA programs are available for financing mobile homes. FHA Title I insures loans of up to $40,500 for terms of up to 20 years if the home meets HUD standards. FHA Title II covers homes on permanent foundations sold with the land as real estate. In general, loans insured under this program may go as high as $54,000—in some expensive areas the limit can be up to $151,725—with a maximum 20-year term for single-section units and a maximum 25-year term for multisections.

The VA guarantee for mobiles is $20,000 or 40% of the loan, whichever is smaller. (This means you can finance a house and lot costing much more than that.) A 5% down payment will be required. Loan terms are just over 20 years for single-wide units, just over 23 for double-wides and just over 25 for double-wides and lot.

House-Hunting Strategies

Once you've gone through the steps outlined in previous chapters—assessing your resources, prequalifying for a mortgage, defining needs and wants—you're ready for serious house hunting.

Adapt your strategy to the mood and economic realities in your targeted location and price range. The housing market depends on the economy—local, regional and national. But within the best and worst markets, there are recurring seasonal differences. Try to shop when other buyers aren't out in force.

Across the country, demand surges in April and May. It's understandable that sellers generally don't feel pressured then to cut a deal right away. Some will feel differently by June; more will be eager to sell by the time the late-summer doldrums hit.

September, October and November generally usher in a brisker pace. But from Thanksgiving through the winter, holiday activities and cold weather combine to slow activity. Buyers should find sellers more interested in dealing—an advantage offset by the smaller number of houses for sale.

Naturally, the seasonal ebb and flow of market activity varies. Ski areas and beach resorts have their own market cycles, as do other specialized markets and different climatic regions. A seven-year analysis of prices and sales activity in Texas, for example, showed

Adapt your strategy to the mood and economic realities in your targeted location and price range.

When things are cold for sellers, time is on your side. You can be more deliberate and drive a harder bargain.

that July, August and September were the best months for selling a home in that state; by contrast, the first quarter—January, February and March—was usually a buyer's market. Learn the local pattern and, if possible, use it to your advantage.

The Buyer's Market

In a buyer's market, there are lots of houses for sale relative to the number of serious lookers. Houses sit on the market, and sellers often cut asking prices and even assist buyers with cut-rate financing.

When things are cold for sellers, time is on your side. You can be more deliberate and drive a harder bargain. You can get a house appraised before you submit an offer and ask the seller to pay all or part of the cost. You can spend more time checking out comparable properties. You can even load your offer with contingency clauses that help you—inspection, financing at a specified interest rate, seller's help with mortgage points, even the condition that you be able to sell your current home before closing on this purchase—and still get it accepted.

In a buyer's market, a diligent house hunter can do reasonably well without a real estate agent. You generally don't have access to new listings in the local multiple listing service (MLS) computer (the real estate trade's clearinghouse of properties for sale), but you might not miss much. Most houses will remain on the market long enough to be advertised and shown, many more than once.

The Seller's Market

When asking prices are firm or rising and new listings are snapped up as soon as they show up in the MLS, it's a seller's market. You'll notice more sale-by-owner properties, too. In a sizzling market, good houses are often sold before being advertised or keyed into the MLS computer. Often within hours, multiple contracts are submitted on the same property, and buyers vie with each other by bidding more than the asking price.

If you want to buy in this climate, be ready—financially and emotionally—to move fast when you spot something that meets your needs.

Sellers won't pay much attention to timid or unprepared buyers or those who load their offering contract with lots of protective contingencies. The would-be buyer who must have the contract reviewed by a not-yet-selected attorney and the buyer with insufficient earnest money who wants the seller to take a personal note for a few days won't get serious consideration from owners of desirable properties.

Have an attorney and home inspector on standby. If you haven't selected them, do so now. Get names from friends, lenders, a title company and real estate agents. If you are buying a condominium, co-op or farm, find a lawyer and inspector who specialize in such transactions.

Save time by becoming familiar with the contract you intend to use. Have contingencies you plan to insert drawn up by your attorney in advance, but remember, a "clean" contract—one not littered with lots of escape clauses—will be treated with more respect by the seller.

Financial Readiness

Be prepared to write a check for the earnest money—this usually accompanies your offer as evidence of your intentions, good faith, and ability to close the deal. If necessary, cash in certificates of deposit and stocks and move the money to your checking or money-market account. Consider establishing a home-equity line of credit on your current home well before you begin looking for your next home (see the discussions of home-equity loans in Chapters 3 and 15).

In a hot market, one thing that could set your

If you want to buy in a seller's market, be ready—financially and emotionally—to move fast when you spot something that meets your needs.

offer above other bids would be your ability to go to settlement fast. Prequalifying with one or more likely lenders can give you bargaining leverage with an eager seller. But don't promise what you can't deliver. Mortgage commitment times have declined with technological advances, but the system still tends to bog down whenever sudden demand for new financing or refinancing spikes. You may be able to arrange a speedier mortgage commitment, cutting the time between application to approval from weeks to days, but it's likely to cost you more in points or fees.

The Search for Houses

In a hot seller's market, use every tool at your disposal to spot good prospects. It is not enough to watch the newspapers every day for advertisements of houses just put on the market or to wait around for weekend open houses. Many fine offerings will be sold by word of mouth, without ever being advertised in the paper or entered in a multiple listing service.

Some of these unpublicized sales will be "by owner," with no agent involved. Others will be transactions started and completed within one real estate firm, where one agent's new listing is sold to a buyer assisted by another agent in the same office.

For these reasons, use the scouting services of at least one aggressive, experienced agent who knows your targeted neighborhood. In some cases, it may be useful to have several agents in different firms helping you simultaneously. (But keep in mind that when agents are competing to sell you a home, they are under tremendous pressure to get you to buy. Helping you find the best property may take second priority.)

Use your own energy and ingenuity. Ask friends who live in or near your ideal neighborhood to let you know if they hear anything that suggests a house might be coming on the market soon. It could be news of a company move, a split marriage, retirement or the death of an elderly person living alone.

Cold-calling on your own

Smart house hunters will approach the owners of houses they admire, even if the house is not for sale. They do this by driving through the target neighborhood and jotting down the addresses of houses they like the look of, then using a criss-cross directory (available at many public libraries) or public land records at the courthouse to determine the owner's name and phone number. A note or phone call sometimes yields the information that the owner is, indeed, contemplating putting it on the market. Sometimes the owner has never thought of selling but is surprised to hear what his house might be worth; suddenly, you've got an interested seller.

More Than One Way

As ghoulish as it may sound, some house hunters watch the obituaries and look up the address of the deceased to see where he or she lived; after a suitable period of time, they write or phone an heir listed in the story and inquire respectfully whether the house will be for sale.

If you're looking at houses with an agent, he or she can make this "cold" contact for you and work with both interested parties to make a deal, earning a commission in the process (see page 108 in this chapter for tips on handling the "sale by owner" purchase). Go solo, though, and you'll have to do that yourself, and much more. For one, you have to know the comparables—the selling prices and descriptions of similar homes that recently changed hands in the neighborhood where you are looking. You can get a ballpark idea by attending open houses in the area. But check asking prices against actual sale prices in local newspapers or at the county courthouse.

Suppose one of your contacts does show an interest in selling to you—what then?

- **Once you agree to talk business, do it in writing,** even if you're sitting across the table from each other.

- **Start with things the seller wants to know,** such as

If the owner has no idea what the house is worth or how to conduct negotiations, you may be wise to advise the owner to ask an agent to represent him.

how financially qualified you are, how much earnest money you'd be willing to offer, and when you could go to settlement.

• **Keep the offering price off center stage** until you can get agreement on as many other contract details as possible.

• **If the owner is interested but unprepared** and leaning towards calling an agent for advice, ask for the chance to tour the house, obtain an appraisal and make an offer.

• **Point out that a private transaction, without an agent's commission, could net substantially more.** Savings could be split in some proportion between you, benefiting both.

• **You could also suggest sharing the cost of a professional appraisal**—for the owner's protection and your own—in order to get negotiations under way.

If that approach doesn't work, perhaps the owner has no idea what the house is worth or how to conduct negotiations. At that point, you may be wise to advise the owner to ask an agent to represent him. If he does so, here's your strategy: Suggest the seller add a clause to the listing contract specifying that he may, for a specified period of time, sell to you and you alone (you must be named in the listing contract) without paying a commission. The unsure seller gets the advice and counsel he needs and the possibility of an immediate sale. The agent gets the possibility of a listing and a commission if the deal with you falls through. If the deal does go through, you benefit from a seller who is better prepared to work with you—and you get the house you want.

Shopping With a Real Estate Agent

Most people don't venture into the housing market without the help of an agent scouting out new listings, accompanying them on tours of open houses and offering advice.

By and large, house hunting on your own puts you at a disadvantage. Unless you're very knowledgeable about the market in a given area, you will miss the help and access to the MLS computer listings of houses for sale that an agent can supply.

Since most houses for sale are listed with realty agents, when you call to inquire about an advertised house or go to an open house, you are going to encounter agents at every turn. If you identify yourself by name—for example, by signing the registry book at an open house—you'll soon start getting calls from agents offering to help you find your dream house. At this point, it's "choose or be chosen." If you want help, take the initiative and do the selecting by contacting agents with proven reputations in the neighborhoods and price range in which you're looking. If you don't, be firm and avoid entanglements until you're ready.

How Agents Work

There are two basic roles in the real estate business: broker and agent (or sales associate). A broker is licensed by the state to conduct a real estate business and to negotiate transactions for a fee. An agent is a broker's representative and is usually an independent contractor rather than an employee. He or she is permitted to sell real estate under the supervision of a licensed broker. Both brokers and their representatives are properly called agents because they act as agents for their clients.

Contrary to public impression, not all brokers and agents are Realtors. A Realtor (capital *R*—it's a trade name) and a Realtor Associate (who works for a Realtor) are members of the National Association of Realtors, a trade and lobby organization.

Since most real estate agents are compensated by sellers through a commission based on the sales price of the house, why would an agent who didn't make a listing want to help you find and buy a home listed by another agent? Because the sales commission is split between the seller's listing broker and the so-called selling broker who brings in the buyer. The brokers in turn pay their respective agents a portion of their proceeds. Real estate agents make money from finding both houses to sell and people to buy them, so a well-qualified, serious house hunter represents a paycheck to the agent—but only if the sale goes through. Unless "your" agent submits a successful offer, there will be no compensation for all the hours spent accompanying you through houses.

Unless you hire your own agent (a so-called buyer's broker; see page 102), an agent always works for a seller and is paid by a seller. This is true even when an agent spends hours and hours working with you, the buyer. It is true even if "your" agent has never met the owners of the home you ultimately buy. For both buyers and agents, this awkward situation is a gamble. The agent gambles that in return for his time you will be loyal enough to buy a home through him. You gamble that your loyalty will reward you with service and produce a suitable property.

How to Pick an Agent

If location, location, location are the watchwords for picking a property, experience, experience, experi-

---

Who Works for Whom?

• •

Most states and the District of Columbia require agents to disclose the legal and financial arrangements they make with the sellers, for whom they work, to buyers they help. Even so, unwary buyers continue telling agents too much about their strategies and intentions—all of which agents are duty-bound to tell sellers.

ence are the watchwords for picking an agent.

Too many buyers don't pick their agent—they acquire one at an open house or by responding by telephone to an advertisement. Many select one who is a friend, relative or neighbor. You could be lucky; such an agent may turn out to be skilled, experienced and resourceful. On the other hand, you could end up with an amateur.

- **Obtain the names of brokers and agents active in the area where you want to buy.** The classified ads are a good place to start. Brokers with agents that list and sell homes in a particular neighborhood will advertise regularly. Ask friends, associates, lenders and attorneys for recommendations. And by all means, consider using a buyer's broker, who will be paid by you (see the full discussion that begins on page 102).

- **Check the broker's reputation in the community.** In the case of an agent, find out who his or her managing broker is, then check out the broker's reputation and that of the firm. Ask the local real estate board or state real estate commission whether there have been complaints or problems reported. Talk to clients they've worked with in the past.

- **Call two or three recommended brokerage firms.** Talk to the managing broker. Let her know what kind of buyer you are, what kind of house you're looking for and the general price range you are working with.

    If this is your first foray into the housing market, you may want an agent who is intuitive and patient. If you're a much-transferred corporate executive, you may want an agent who specializes in listing exclusive homes.

    Once you've chatted with the managing broker, ask for the names of two agents she thinks could best meet your needs.

If this is your first foray into the housing market, you may want an agent who is intuitive and patient.

- **Interview the agents,** using the accompanying work sheet as a guide.

- **Select one or two finalists.** If you conducted phone interviews initially, arrange to meet each of them face to face in their offices. If you conducted interviews in person, have follow-up phone conversations. Be candid about the degree of service you're expecting and whether you'll be looking at houses with other agents.

    Use the work sheets in Chapter 4 to develop must-have, would-like, and don't-want lists. Use these to give agents a sense of how much deviation from the ideal you'll tolerate and in what areas. Will you want them to screen new listings or show you everything remotely similar to your target house?

What's the Protocol for Working With an Agent?

If an agent takes you to a house and tours it with you the first time you see it, you should submit your contract offer through him or her. If you don't, that agent may still be entitled to a share of the sales commission from the seller should you buy the house.

On the other hand, if an agent merely mentions that a particular house is for sale, but you first tour it by yourself or with another agent, the first agent will probably not have any claim to part of the commission. That's why agents don't give house hunters the address of a listing when they call. Instead, an agent will offer to pick you up and drive you to the house for a tour.

Should you ever use more than one agent to help you with a house hunt? Yes, if the house you're looking for is very unusual in some way and you don't want to risk missing the few possible listings, or to extend your reach in a hot market—when houses move very quickly, you may need more eyes and ears and scouring energy than one agent can supply. Good listings are often sold within one firm, with the seller's commission being

Prospective Agent's Profile

Name of firm _____

Phone number _____

Managing broker _____

Recommended agent _____

Number of years selling real estate full-time _____

Names of previous firms _____

Continuing Education
☐ GRI (Graduate, Realtors Institute)
☐ CRS (Certified Residential Specialist)
☐ CRB (Certified Real Estate Broker)
☐ CRE (Counselor of Real Estate)
☐ Other _____

Number of listings _____
(acquired in the past year and comparable to the house you want)

What does the agent know about your targeted community?

_____

In general, what services will the agent and firm provide?

_____

How will disputes be handled?

_____

During your meeting, does the agent pay attention to your

concerns? _____

Would you enjoy working with this person? _____

Miscellaneous notes _____

_____

_____

shared by the listing agent and a colleague in the same firm who brought in the buyer. Since the listing won't show up in the MLS computer, if you don't have a relationship with an agent at that firm, you wouldn't ever hear about the house in time to see it or bid on it.

If you intend to work with more than one agent, tell each one you'll reward hustle by accompanying him or her immediately to see the new listing—providing that agent is the first one to call and tell you about it. Then remain loyal to that agent for all dealings relating to that particular house.

Pretty soon, you'll start getting calls from several agents within minutes or hours of each other, each trying to be the first to tell you that something good has just shown up in the MLS computer or, even better, that a new listing has just come into the firm and won't go into the computer for another 24 hours—a typical period after which the firm is obligated to enter the new listing for other agents to see. (Privacy-minded sellers may ask their agent to keep the listing unadvertised and strictly "in house" for a while, with no notice to the MLS computer.)

The Smart Approach

Savvy buyers keep their lips zipped when it comes to strategy and price bids. They study the art of real estate negotiation to better represent themselves, and they retain an impartial attorney to review the contract and settlement papers.

Using a Buyer's Broker

The special fiduciary relationship between seller and agent should cause buyers to wonder whether they can trust the agent who is helping them find a house. How can an agent who is going to be paid by the seller, and whose pay will be based on how *high* the sales price is, negotiate in the your best interest? This concern about conflict of interest in residential real estate sales—dual agency, as it is called—is why buyer brokerage is a growing business.

To command an agent's undivided loyalties, hire

your own. When you do that, you enter into a "single agency" relationship with an agent; it becomes your responsibility, not the seller's, to arrange compensation. Some buyer's brokers are paid by the hour, others with a set-in-advance fee. Ideally, this fee should not be tied to the selling price of the house.

There are three or four advantages you get when your agent really works for you:

- **You expand your options.** A buyer's broker can help you buy a property not currently being listed for sale—without seeking to get the owner to list it.

- **You get help negotiating the deal.** A broker you employ and pay is obligated to help you find a home that meets your needs, at the best possible price and terms. Your agent can openly suggest a smaller down payment, different financing terms, use of a contract that meets your needs and an opening offer far below the list price.

- **You know who to trust.** Since your agent's fee is no longer tied to the selling price of properties you are considering, a major conflict of interest is eliminated. Confused representation, in which "your" agent is actually a subagent of the seller's broker, is gone. Now one broker represents you, the purchaser, and another represents the seller.

- **You can also remain anonymous** if it suits your purposes. A buyer's broker can act as an agent for an undisclosed principal.

Unfortunately, things rarely stay so neat and clean. Some agents who call themselves buyer's brokers engage in such activities as fee splitting. In this case, your agent will be paid by the seller. Since compensation is tied to the sale price of the home, it raises the very conflict-of-interest issue most buyers were seeking to avoid by hiring a buyer's broker. If you use an agent

A broker you employ and pay is obligated to help you find a home that meets your needs, at the best possible price and terms.

operating this way, hash out and address your concerns in writing in any contract you sign.

Pick the Right Firm

Before you sign a contract, check the reputation and experience of the firm and agent. Does the firm handle sales and buyer's brokerage under the same roof? How does it avoid conflict of interest? What are the firm's disclosure rules? Once you're satisfied, set up a meeting with the broker to discuss your needs. You

Finding a Buyer's Broker

Ask your local board of Realtors and large real estate firms for names of buyer's brokers. Professors of real estate at local colleges and universities may also be willing to help you.

The Buyer's Broker Registry, part of a larger directory entitled *Who's Who in Creative Real Estate, Inc.,* lists about 400 buyer's brokers (Buyer's Broker Registry, P.O. Box 23275, Ventura, Cal. 93002; 800-729-5147). The directory gives advice on using buyer's brokerage and employing a broker.

The brokers listed submitted two completed buyer's brokerage transactions to the company for its review and finished a qualifying course on buyer's brokerage. In addition, all listed brokers agree to work for, and be paid by, only one party in a real estate transaction, and to abide by other professional real estate practices.

Copies of the directory are available for $10. You can get the names of three registered buyer's brokers in your state or region by sending a request to Buyer's Broker Registry, along with a cover letter

mentioning this Kiplinger book; additional names are available for $1.00 each.

Who's Who in Creative Real Estate also publishes a booklet, *What Is Single Agency?* (available for $10), which discusses in detail the concept of single agency.

Single Agency Realty Association Inc. (SARA) (P.O. Box 1791, Rockville, Md. 20849; 301-353-1191) will also help you locate an agent who can represent you. Send a self-addressed, stamped, business-size envelope along with your request. SARA will send you a brochure describing single agency and how you can protect yourself when buying or selling a home.

Two regional brokerage sources are:

- **Buyer's Agent,** 2014 Exeter Rd., Germantown, Tennessee. 38138 (800-766-8728).

- **Real Estate Buyer's Agent Council,** P.O. Box 2096, St. Louis, Missouri 63158 (314-776-6224).

The Agreement Contract

Use this work sheet when interviewing a prospective buyer's broker. The compensation plan you agree on with him or her should be spelled out in the brokerage contract.

What kinds of services and advice will the broker provide?

_____

Will you pay the agent: ❑ an hourly rate ❑ a set fee
❑ or a percentage of the purchase price?

Will there be an incentive commission? This applies if the agent negotiates a price lower than the asking price—say, 10% of the savings.
❑ Yes ❑ No   Comments_____

_____

Will you pay an initial retainer? ❑ Yes   ❑ No
If yes, will it be applied against the total fee due?
❑ Yes ❑ No   If yes, how much?_____

Is there a minimum fee?
❑ Yes ❑ No   If yes, how much?_____

Is there a cap on total cost? This is especially important if you are paying by the hour.
❑ Yes ❑ No   If yes, how much?_____

How will conflicts of interest be handled?

_____

What will happen if you buy a property shortly after the brokerage agreement ends? Will the broker get a commission? If so, under what conditions?

_____

How will disagreements be handled? For example, both parties could agree to submit to binding arbitration, using a neutral third party.

_____

When you buy a house with a buyer's broker, the seller's agent should be willing to cut the 6% sales commission.

shouldn't have to pay for this initial consultation. Before they'll start work, some buyer's brokers may require a nonrefundable fee, which will vary depending on the difficulty of the search and the overall compensation plan.

Who Pays Whom?

When you buy a house with a buyer's broker, the seller's agent should be willing to cut the 6% sales commission. If the total cost of two separate fees—one paid by you to your buyer's broker and one paid by the seller to the listing broker—is held to an amount equivalent to the 6% commission the seller expects to pay anyway, your agent should have no difficulty persuading a seller to accept your offer.

Here's an example: Say the owner lists her property for $104,000 and agrees to pay a 6% commission. If the house sells for $100,000, and commission is $6,000, the seller will get $94,000. In a conventional transaction, the $6,000 commission would be divided between the listing broker and the cooperating or selling broker, with each getting 3%.

Now suppose the owner receives an offer from a buyer represented by his own agent. The owner is told that the purchaser will pay his own agent and she accepts an offer of $97,000 for her home. Result: The seller still nets $94,000—after paying $3,000 to the listing broker. The listing broker goes along with the deal because he gets the 3% commission he was likely to earn anyway. The buyer pays $97,000 plus $3,000 to his agent, for a total of $100,000.

Alternatively, the buyer could offer a higher price to the seller—say, $100,000—and stipulate in his offering contract that the seller will pay the buyer's agent and his own listing agent. The buyer could specify the amount to be paid to his agent. The seller could net $94,000 (after splitting $6,000 between the brokers).

You can ask your lender to fold your buyer's broker fee into the mortgage loan; most lenders will agree to this. However, lenders making loans guaranteed by the VA are not permitted to do so.

Decoding the Classified Ads

Whatever kind of market you're hunting in, get acquainted with the classified real estate ads. They can help you get a feel for various neighborhoods. A few weeks of discriminating reading will give you an indication of price ranges and acquaint you with brokerage firms concentrating their efforts in a particular area. Ads can also uncover homes being sold by owners and builders as well as the weekend array of open houses.

The classified section is particularly useful in a slow market. You could keep current on new offerings, price reductions and published sales prices. If you know how long a property has been advertised, what its starting price was and how many real estate firms have offered it, you have an advantage when you're negotiating an offer.

A successful ad tries to entice you to a property. It tells you only about features that might attract you. It withholds details that might discourage you. Before you start calling agents to inquire about an advertised property, make a standard checklist of wants and don't-wants. Have it handy when you call and cut through the ad's smoke screen with a few key questions. That way, you'll avoid a long conversation about how you could buy the property with seller financing, only to realize that you hung up without learning how many bedrooms it had.

After a while, you get the hang of real-estatese with all those cryptic abbreviations like "2b, 1ba, lctm, owc, q.pos." You'll decode it as: two bedrooms, one bath, low cash to mortgage, owner will carry mortgage, quick possession.

You'll also get acquainted with all the clever euphemisms that agents use in their ads. "Handyman's special" and "lots of potential" often mean the house is falling in. "Just awaits your loving touch" means a total redecorating is needed. "Charming dollhouse" means the rooms are tiny. "Convenient to everything" can signal a busy corner near the bus route. "Low upkeep" might mean it has no yard at all. And so on, limited only by the agent's gift for poetic license.

Don't overlook new developments and apartment condominium conversions. You won't be pointed to these properties by most agents, unless they specialize in condos or the builder has promised to compensate agents for bringing buyers in.

Condos and cooperatives will usually be listed in the same classified section as detached houses but under their own listings. The new-house market tends to be advertised separately from the classifieds, in large display ads in newspapers' weekend real estate sections.

Looking From Long Distance

• •

If you're looking for a home in a distant area, subscribe to the local newspapers and get a detailed map of the vicinity, showing neighborhood names. Use these sources to get an arms-length sense of the market before you make your first visit.

Handling the "Sale by Owner"

Don't overlook the "sale by owner" ads in the classifieds. They could result in sticky, awkward negotiations, but good deals are to be had if you are determined and knowledgeable, and get the advice of a good attorney. You could hire an agent to negotiate on your behalf.

If you stumble on the perfect for-sale-by-owner house while working with an agent you haven't hired, you have some options:

- **You could abandon your agent and deal directly with the seller, with no compensation to the agent.** After all, the agent knew all along that he or she would get paid only if you bought a listed house you first saw with the agent; that's the risk of the business.

- **You could deal directly with the seller but pay the agent a modest fee for the time and effort expended on you.** But you're not legally obligated to do so.

- **You could try to persuade the seller to accept your agent and pay the agent a 3% commission** (or a sum you can agree on). The agent would then help the seller with negotiations and mortgage arrangements, and work to get you both to settlement without a hitch. The agent could end up getting the same commission (some part of the 3%, shared with the broker's firm) he or she would have earned from a regular listing.

    Why would a seller agree to this? After all, hasn't he listed the house himself, arranged for advertising, prepared fact sheets and held open houses at least partly to avoid paying someone a 6% commission? His reaction to your suggestion will likely depend heavily on how much he needs a willing buyer. An eager seller might be willing to pay "your" agent 3%, getting some service for the price.

    In fact, many "sale by owner" sellers put the phrase "brokers welcome at 3%" in their ads. They don't want to pay a full commission, but they don't want agents to boycott their property, either.

    If the seller refuses to consider compensating the agent, you're left with options one or two.

Many "sale by owner" sellers put the phrase "brokers welcome at 3%" in their ads. They don't want to pay a full commission, but they don't want agents to boycott their property, either.

Touring the House

If you have the luxury of deliberation, make several visits to any house you're seriously considering. If things are so frenzied that you're likely to lose out if you follow that route, get the most out of every minute you're in the house. Consider yourself a reporter and detective, there to gather as much information as possible about the house and the sellers.

You probably know your wants and don't-wants list well enough that you won't need to take a checklist with you, but by all means take a notepad and tape measure. At most open houses you'll find an information sheet about the house. The most complete spell out such things as square footage of lot and house, room sizes, property taxes, average monthly utility bills, and the ages of appliances and major mechanical systems, as well as the number of bedrooms and baths, and other basic data.

If, at first glance, this looks like a house you'll want to pursue, sketch out floor plans on your first visit; they'll help you envision the house hours or days later.

You'll want a professional inspection made later if you decide to buy, but you can make some tentative judgments on your own:

- Take a close look at the furnace, electrical box (fuses or circuit breakers?) and appliances. Do they appear to be in good shape?

- How about the roof, gutters and exterior finish?

- Does the house have storm windows, or will you have to add them at your own cost?

- If the floor plan doesn't suit you, can you rearrange space or add on?

- Are you looking at older houses with the intention of remodeling or expanding? If so, have an architect or contractor standing by to accompany you on a second visit. The judgment of these professionals on the ease and probable cost of renovation should play a major role in how much you offer.

Scope Out the Sellers

Find out as much as possible about the sellers, starting with the first visit. Everything you learn will make you a better informed, and therefore more capable, negotiator should you decide to make an offer.

Conversely, don't give away strategic information

to the seller or the seller's agent or broker. You are at a disadvantage if the seller discovers you've sold your current home and are anxious to find a replacement. The same is true if you have a soon-to-expire lease or are shopping from out of town.

It's hard not to be forthcoming in a pleasant conversation, but resist showing your hand. Put on your best poker face and give noncommittal answers.

If you would rather remain anonymous until your offer is presented, don't give your name to agents at open houses and don't sign visitor registers. And ask the agent who is helping you look to refrain from identifying you to sellers until an offer is submitted.

Seller motivation will determine how the house is priced to sell in the first place and how receptive to price cutting the seller may be later on. But the seller, and the seller's agent and subagents, may be coy or less than candid because everything you learn will make you a tougher adversary in the negotiation that follows. Try to ferret out answers to the questions in the following box. If you can, talk with the seller's neighbors in a nonthreatening way that doesn't invade their personal privacy. You might ask whether any houses have been sold in the neighborhood recently, and so forth. Then, try to steer the conversation toward the sellers and the house you want to buy.

What Sellers Must Tell You

Sellers and their agents are required by law to warn buyers of "material" defects in a property that would not be apparent during a routine inspection. Each state puts a different twist on the definition of *material,* but generally it means physical defects that would change your assessment of the property's value. Bad septic systems, cracked foundations or leaky basements are obvious material defects.

Sellers should tell you about known structural deficiencies or building-code violations. A homeowner selling a house in the middle of a long, dry summer

Don't give away strategic information to the seller or the seller's agent or broker. Put on your best poker face and give noncommittal answers.

What You Need to Know About Your Sellers

Here are some things you'll want to know about sellers whose home you're interested in:

Are the sellers truly "motivated," as the agents say, or are they just trying to find out how much they could get for their house?

_____

Are they scheduled to go to settlement on a new house?

☐ Yes ☐ No   Comments _____

_____

Why are they selling?

☐ A job transfer   ☐ Divorce
☐ Retirement   ☐ Financial setback
☐ Need for more (or less) space   ☐ Health problem
☐ Children off at college   ☐ Death of spouse
☐ Dissatisfaction with the house or neighborhood

How long have the sellers lived here? _____
(You can learn this, and also how much they paid for the house, from public land records.)

When do they want to settle? Date_____

Comments _____

_____

Do the sellers need to stay in the house after settlement?

☐ Yes ☐ No   If yes, for how long?_____

Would they consider helping you with the purchase—by taking back a second trust, for example?

☐ Yes ☐ No   Comments _____

_____

_____

_____

could be held responsible later by the courts if he or she doesn't tell prospective buyers that the basement usually leaks in the spring. That's a hidden defect even a responsible buyer could not discover. And sellers can probably be held responsible for defects that are covered up. Say the walls of a basement showed water damage and the seller covered them with paneling prior to putting the house up for sale. Sellers in states that still subscribe to the "buyer beware" philosophy may have less liability for easily detectable defects—so-called patent defects—unless they make misleading comments about them.

But the trend—in recent court cases, new state statutes and pressure from the National Association of Realtors—is to hold home sellers to tougher standards. In more than two dozen states, written seller-disclosure forms are now voluntary, although some real estate firms won't show a home without one. Sellers in California must complete them; sellers in Maine are bound to do so only when an agent is involved in the sale. The California disclosure law requires sellers to provide a prospective buyer with a statement indicating, among other things, known defects or malfunctions in walls, ceilings, floors, insulation, windows, foundations, electrical and plumbing systems, and other structural components.

An agent can't know everything about a particular property, of course. But honest ones should tell you about problems they're aware of, and agents can be held accountable for giving buyers misinformation about things they should have known.

The trend is to hold home sellers to tougher standards. In more than two dozen states, written seller-disclosure forms are now voluntary.

If You Encounter Discrimination

Members of racial and ethnic minority groups often encounter overt or subtle discrimination when they go looking for a home to buy. A black family may be steered away from a neighborhood because "you probably can't afford to buy there." A seller may refuse to sell her home to an Hispanic family because she believes her neighbor would be angry. A Jewish home buyer may be told that an owner "just took the house off the market," when in fact it's still available. A borrower may be turned down because "we don't make loans under $50,000."

Discrimination may be wrong, but it's not always illegal. The federal Fair Housing Law (Title VIII of the Civil Rights Act of 1968, as amended in 1974 and 1989) broadly prohibits discrimination in the rental, sale and financing of housing.

However, the law has a big loophole: It doesn't cover private individuals who own no more than three single-family dwellings, providing: 1) a broker is not involved in the sale or rental; 2) there is no discriminatory advertising; and 3) the owner has not sold more than one house (in which he or she was not the most recent resident) during any two-year period.

Real estate professionals—who handle the bulk of the nation's housing transactions—*are* covered. Agents and mortgage lenders may not:

- refuse to sell, rent, deal or negotiate with you because of your race, color, religion, sex or national origin, or because you are disabled or have children under 18 in your family.

- deny that housing is available for inspection, sale or rent when it really is available.

- persuade owners to sell or rent their homes by telling them that minority groups are moving into the neighborhood—a practice called blockbusting.

- set different terms or conditions for mortgage financing based on race, creed, religion, sex, national origin, disability or pregnancy.

For More Information

• •

The Fair Housing Information Clearinghouse (FHIC, P.O Box 6091, Rockville, Md. 20850; 800-343-3442) has free consumer publications explaining your rights as a home buyer.

What You Can Do

If you suspect discrimination by a real estate agent or a seller using an agent, keep a record of meetings and phone calls. Note the person's name, title (if you know it), meeting place, date and time. Write down what happened and what was said. Save all receipts, applications, business cards and other such documents.

Then confront the person and demand an explanation. If you don't get a satisfactory answer and your suspicions persist, write a letter about the agent to the agent's employer-broker and send a similar letter to the local board of Realtors. Complain in writing to the fair-housing enforcement agency in the city, county or state where you are house hunting (see the accompanying box). The state or local agency is required to begin proceedings within 30 days and proceed with "reasonable promptness." Complaints can also be taken directly to a U.S. District Court or state or local court within 180 days of the alleged discriminatory act.

Help From HUD

• •

If you think you've been discriminated against, you can write to the Fair Housing Division, U.S. Department of Housing and Urban Development (HUD), 451 7th St., S.W., Washington, D.C. 20410-5500.

You can also call HUD's toll-free number for advice: 800-669-9777.

HUD may intervene directly or refer the matter to a state or local agency that administers a law comparable to the federal statute.

Making an Offer

No two "comps" will be exactly alike, but they should be similar enough to serve as a useful tool in setting an offering price.

You know what you can afford. Now decide just what you're willing to pay for the home you want. There are several ways to do this; some are more realistic in slow markets, but all require you to gather certain information.

Get an analysis of comparable properties from your assisting agent. There should be several on the list. No two will be exactly alike, of course, but they should be similar enough to serve as a useful tool in setting an offering price. Look at sale dates. Under normal conditions, a comparable should have sold no more than six months earlier. Note locations. A similar home in a different neighborhood may not be comparable at all. An identical house on a prime lot may be worth a lot more. Compare the features of each property. Comparables should be roughly the same age and condition. Elements such as lot size, number of rooms and baths, and total living space should be close.

Finally, scrutinize terms and conditions. Properties sold with seller financing, for example, can't be readily compared with those sold using conventional 30-year mortgages. A sale in which the seller took back a second mortgage at a below-market interest rate was really one in which the price was cut. You'll have to discount the price to use it for comparative purposes.

Getting an Appraisal

If you know the neighborhood, have studied sale prices of comparable homes and have an adequate sense of your seller's motivations, you may be comfortable making an offer. But if you aren't—and if time permits—consider an appraisal.

Appraisals don't come cheap, but weigh the cost against the possibility of paying thousands too much. A purchase offer much higher than the appraised value could force you to come up with a bigger down payment or cancel the deal. And later on, if appreciation doesn't bridge the gap between what you paid and what you sell for, the difference comes out of your pocket.

When might shelling out for an appraisal be wise? When you're from out of town. When a property is unusual in a way that makes finding good comparable properties difficult. Or when a house has been for sale much longer than others in its price range. In fact, any circumstance that makes putting a value on a home hard makes it a candidate.

If you opt for an appraisal, find out what it will cost and how long it will take. Demand for appraisals from home buyers and refinancers, combined with newly implemented licensing requirements, could leave you waiting too long for a valuation. In a few states where demand has been heated, appraisers have set up what is called tiered pricing. Under this system, buyers pay the normal $250 to $350 if they can wait four to five weeks. They pay $400 to $450 for a two- to three-week turnaround or $500 for a one-week response.

Finding an Appraiser

Pick a licensed appraiser who specializes in residential properties. (Unlicensed appraisers may be allowed to evaluate residential property worth less than $100,000 or do appraisals that don't fall under federal purview, such as estates and property tax-appeals. But 21 states and the District of Columbia have decided to

Any circumstance that makes putting a value on a home hard makes it a candidate for an appraisal.

Appraisers are not infallible. They can be inexperienced or incompetent, or too eager to please lenders.

apply the licensing requirements to any real estate transaction. Regardless of requirements in place in your state, use only a licensed appraiser.

Licensed appraisers have passed a written examination, completed required educational courses, and been judged to have enough hands-on experience to perform the job. They have also agreed to comply with certain professional and ethical standards.

Ask local mortgage lenders for names of appraisers they use on a regular basis. Check the status of their licenses, work experience, training, credentials and education. Appraiser organizations, in which appraisers claim membership, should be able to tell you whether an individual is a member in good standing and has the credentials claimed. They may also be willing to give you names of other licensed members working in your area, so long as you don't ask them to recommend anyone—something they can't do.

A big drawback to getting an appraisal before you apply for a loan is that you're going to be required to pay for a lender-ordered appraisal before your mortgage can be approved, anyway. That's the major incentive for picking an appraiser from your prospective lender's approved list—you may not have to pay twice for the same service. If you have no idea at this point who might become your lender—and if paying for two appraisals strikes you as unreasonable—consider hiring an experienced local real estate agent, one not connected with the property in any way, for advice.

Appraisers are not infallible. They can be inexperienced or incompetent, or too eager to please lenders. In the past, "independent" appraisers have been pressured to fudge the numbers so appraised values are the same as full contract offering prices. Appraisers hired by a bank or savings and loan have sometimes been unable to resist pressures exerted by the institution's loan production department. Lenders anxious to make loans have been known to reward malleable appraisers with repeat business. As states implement federally mandated licensing, these concerns should fade.

When and What Kind?

Whatever the state licensing procedures or lender appraising standards, your essential dilemma remains the same. Unless you get an appraisal *before* you submit an offer, your may offer too much.

The appraisal should show how the appraiser arrived at the value, pictures of the house and street, a map locating the site, and possibly a floor plan. One common appraisal is written up on a standard Fannie Mae form and, depending on where the property is located, costs from $200 to $350.

You don't need a full narrative report, which could run to over a hundred pages. Such extended reports are sometimes required for court testimony or to settle an estate, but rarely for routine home purchases.

Also, don't ask for a Fannie Mae appraisal if you intend to buy a home with VA- or FHA-backed financing. And don't order one written to VA or FHA specifications when you'll be seeking a conventional loan. Such a move precludes the possibility that a lender could be persuaded to accept the appraisal you ordered and paid for. Keep in mind, too, that sellers amenable to buyers wishing to use VA or FHA financing may have obtained conditional commitments or certificates of reasonable value from the VA or FHA, thus eliminating any reason for you to order your own. As we went to press, Fannie Mae, Freddie Mac, the FHA and the VA were testing a Uniform Residential Appraisal Report. It should become the standard appraisal form sometime in 1993.

Whether you get an early appraisal or not, request a copy of the lender-ordered one. Do this in writing when you apply for a loan.

Establish Your Priorities

Price is always important, but it may not be the primary factor. Rank the elements of a deal according to your own wants and needs: price, financing, date of possession, extras. Put your priorities down on paper. They will be an important tool in evaluating any counteroffer you receive from the seller.

Consider how you might accommodate the seller—at the right price. For example, suppose the owner doesn't want to repaint before moving. What price reduction or added feature would make that hassle tolerable for you?

Need Seller Financing?

Seller financing was common in the late 1970s and early '80s, when market mortgage rates were high and sellers had to help buyers if they wanted to make deals at all. (When they did, they usually took back paper carrying interest rates below the going market rates.) But as rates dropped in the mid- '80s, seller financing evaporated. Now, as we approach the mid-'90s, seller financing is back. This time around, the forces driving it are different. Mortgage rates are low. But many buyers fail to meet the stiff down-payment and loan-qualifying hurdles imposed by commercial mortgage lenders. Hardest hit are first-time buyers, the self-employed, those who need to spend more than a third of their monthly income for housing, and families with heavy credit card and car-payment obligations. Sellers, on the other hand, have begun to realize they can get a better return by holding mortgage paper on the homes they sell than by putting their cash in certificates of deposits or money-market funds. With lenders disqualifying so many would-be buyers, a seller who can carry financing automatically expands the number of prospects willing to buy his or her home. Add to this the possibility of deferring taxes on the gain and you have thousands of sellers taking a serious look at this kind of financing.

If your down payment and first mortgage won't be enough to swing the deal, you'll need seller financing.

Because seller-assisted financing would tie you and the seller together long past the purchase transaction, it's only natural for him to take a strong interest in your financial resources, job stability and personal life. Be prepared to supply considerable detail; as your prospective creditor, he's entitled to know.

Your need for seller financing greatly reduces your ability to negotiate the purchase price of the house. Concentrate your efforts on the other terms of your offer. The seller will demand a price high enough to compensate for the risk of becoming a lender and accepting installment payments rather than up-front cash at closing.

If you think you'll need seller financing, turn to the discussion of "creative financing" in Chapter 10. Bone up on the details before you make an offer.

Your need for seller financing greatly reduces your ability to negotiate the purchase price of the house. Concentrate your efforts on the other terms of your offer.

Hire Your Own Representative

This is a good time to get expert help, if you haven't already done so. A buyer's broker or a real estate lawyer you pay will represent your interests, deciphering the contract form, suggesting contingency clauses and negotiating with the seller or seller's agent.

Get names of experienced lawyers from friends, associates, bankers, title insurance officers and the local bar association. When interviewing, ask for an advance estimate of the fee. Find out what role he or she usually plays, and determine the charge for reviewing a contract, for being present at settlement, and so on. Do you expect more?

Do you want assistance in drawing up a contract? During negotiations? Now is the time to get this settled.

Hone Negotiating Skills

Buyers often are seriously handicapped by their lack of negotiating experience. Many don't realize they can bargain on every element of the deal, and agents don't always tell them. Don't forget that *you* initiate the bargaining when you make an offer to the seller.

Negotiation

If you're going to be doing your own negotiating, *Successful Real Estate Negotiation,* by Peter G. Miller and Douglas M. Bregman (Harper & Row), addresses the art of negotiation from your perspective.

Remember, good negotiating has more to do with knowing exactly what you want from a deal than it does with playing the role of tough bargainer.

Keep a log of the negotiating process, using the accompanying work sheet. Make note of repairs and replacements that are needed or soon will be. Write down the negative features of the property.

Put It in Writing

Do your negotiating in writing. Don't reveal your strategy, and don't make oral offers.

You want to buy the house, but you don't want to hand over your money until you're sure the seller is legally capable of conveying a good title and meeting other conditions. The seller, in turn, doesn't want to deliver the deed until you've paid for the property. Now what? You (or your representative) present the seller with a written contract setting out the commitments and promises that you and the seller need to agree on and fulfill in order to make the sale. A well-drawn contract should protect all parties.

A written purchase offer can bind both you and the seller. Whether it is called a contract-to-purchase, an offer, binder, or earnest-money agreement, and even if it spells out only the terms of the sale, you can be held to your offer once it is signed by the seller.

The first contract you submit should be comprehensive; everything of any importance should be written into it. Once it's accepted by the seller, it may be too late to add or change anything. Your contract should include, among other things, the offering price, down payment, legal description of the property, method of conveying the title, fees to be paid and who will pay them, amount of deposit, conditions under which the seller and buyer can void the contract, the settlement date, financing arrangements, and a list of appliances, furnishings and other items being sold with the home.

You can have your attorney or buyer's agent draw

A Scratch Sheet for Negotiation

Address of Property _____

_____

Name of seller _____

Asking price _____

Amount of your offer _____

Payment of mortgage points ❑ You pay ❑ Seller pays

Amount of earnest money deposit _____

Settlement date _____

Items that convey (appliances, lighting fixtures, window treatments, and so on) _____

_____

_____

Necessary repairs or replacements _____

_____

Other contingencies _____

_____

Property's negative features _____

_____

_____

Notes on comparable properties _____

_____

_____

_____

Offer what you think the house is worth. If the owner is offended, so be it.

up a purchase contract. Naturally, a contract used by a real estate agent acting on behalf of the seller is written to meet the needs of sellers, not buyers. It may lack important clauses and contingencies that protect you, such as a requirement that your offer be accepted within a specified time or become void, or a statement that the contract becomes binding on you only after it has been reviewed by your attorney and after a professional home inspection satisfactory to you has been completed.

If you are working with an agent who is acting as subagent to the listing broker, you probably will be asked to use the firm's preprinted contract form. Although you are under no obligation to do so, you can start there and then amend and modify it to meet your objectives. Contingencies typed or written in the margins or on the back of preprinted forms should be initialed by you before the contract is submitted to the seller. The same goes for other changes to the body of the contract.

The Opening Bid

Whether you should go ahead and make your highest bid right away or send up a trial balloon in the form of a lower offer depends on how fair the asking price is, how many buyers you may be competing with and what other enticements desired by the seller you can offer.

Asking prices often have a good bit of padding built in. You shouldn't offer the asking price, or something close to it, just because that's what the owner wants. Offer what you think the house is worth. If the owner is offended, so be it. You'll find out in a counteroffer or by the lack of any kind of response within the time limit specified in your contract. Occasionally, a house may be priced below market value because of owner ignorance or a desire to sell fast. Should you be the first to spot this, here's the rub: In a hot market, you could offer full price and still find yourself outsmarted by the savvy buyer who offered slightly more than the full price.

Whatever your strategy, don't signal future intentions either by word or gesture. If, during contract presentation, the seller should ask the agent whether you might go higher or make a bigger down payment, the agent will be obliged to reveal everything he or she knows. Unless your agent signed a buyer representation agreement, he or she will get paid only if you buy this house. "Your" agent wants to get the deal closed, and "your" agent owes primary allegiance to the seller. This person can't fully represent your interests in negotiations with the seller.

A Smart Buyer's Purchase Contract

Your purchase offer goes beyond the offering bid into every detail and aspect of the sale. It should state the date and amount of deposit, and name you as buyer and the property owner as seller. It should give the total purchase price and full legal description and street address of the property you are offering to buy. The contract should name lawyers, brokers and others involved in the sale, and set out the terms and conditions of their compensation. It should describe the options available to both buyer and seller should either party default. Beyond elements basic to any contract, your offer should contain important protective and escape clauses making the entire agreement subject to, or contingent on, their fulfillment.

Here are some key "subject to" clauses and useful contingencies to be considered for insertion. This list isn't complete; it doesn't take the place of a review by your attorney and consultation with your buyer's broker prior to signing.

Earnest Money Deposit

With the exception of court-ordered sales, you are not required by law to make a deposit of a certain size, or any deposit at all. Nevertheless, most sellers tend to measure the seriousness of a buyer's intention by the size of the deposit. A seller could refuse to consider an offer not coupled with a reasonable deposit. Conversely, a large earnest-money check just might swing a deal in your favor.

Most real estate agents expect to carry an earnest-money check with them when they go to present a contract to a seller. You will be asked to make it out to the firm or to the managing broker. Add the words "trustee" or "fiduciary agent" after the name on the check as further protection. Never make out a deposit check to a seller.

Find out whether the broker routinely deposits earnest money in a trust account or with a neutral third party, such as a title company, escrow service or attorney acting as an escrow agent. If not, insert that requirement in the contract. Are you putting up a large earnest-money payment? Then stipulate that it be held in an interest-bearing account and that interest earned will be redited to your side of the ledger at settlement. Your contract should require all money to be handled in escrow. Private individuals are not answerable to any regulatory authority on how they handle funds while a deal is pending. If it goes sour, you might have to sue to get your money back.

Don't allow your deposit to be tied up too long. Unless you have plenty of cash, you will need it to make a bid on another property if this sale doesn't make it through.

If you don't want your check deposited until the contract has been accepted, write this into the contract. (On the other hand, if a seller balks because he has qualms about your creditworthiness, you could offer to let him have it deposited in escrow to assure him that it will clear.)

Obligate the seller and his agent to return your earnest money within a specified number of days after your offer expires or is withdrawn. Set out other conditions that would require it to be returned.

Deed and Title Condition

Your offer should state the type of deed and condition of title you will accept from the seller. If customary in your area, the contract could obligate the seller to pay for the lender's title insurance policy and possibly to provide you with an owner's policy for the amount of the sale price. (And even if it doesn't, consider the policy cost a negotiating point.) Your contract should also make clear what actions the seller must take to deliver a good title by settlement, and what recourse you have should that not occur. (Chapter 12 discusses getting a good title at length.)

Financing

The contract should be subject to your getting satisfactory mortgage financing—satisfactory to *you*. Make your offer contingent on getting a written loan commitment within a specified time and at terms agreeable to you. State the maximum interest rate and number of discount points you would be willing to pay. Put that way, should you fail to get the desired financing, you will be released from the contract and your deposit will be returned.

Set out how discount points, appraisal fee and other expenses involved with financing your purchase are to be apportioned between you and the seller. These are typically negotiated through counteroffers and counter-counteroffers.

If you're told it's customary for buyers to pay all points (one point equals 1% of the mortgage), don't assume that's so. In many areas and in certain market climates it's just as customary for sellers to help the buyer by paying a point or so. The point is, what do you want to pay? What can you afford? What could the seller offer that would make it worthwhile for you to back down and pay the point?

Making the contract contingent on financing is important from another perspective, too. Once an offer

If you're told it's customary for buyers to pay all points (one point equals 1% of the mortgage), don't assume that's so.

with this type of clause is accepted, the owner must take the property off the market to give you time to shop for a mortgage.

If you went through a prequalifying process, you know what size loan and interest rate you are eligible for. Don't put down unrealistic numbers—a below-market interest rate or a loan bigger than you could get. Such tactics justifiably raise suspicions and make your offer unattractive.

Seller Financing

The terms and conditions of any seller financing should be fully and exactly set out in the contract.

Settlement Date and Possession

The sale should be made subject to a settlement date and a possession date—when you will be entitled to take physical possession of your new home.

Settlement usually correlates with the length of time required for a title search and mortgage approval—typically 45 days to 60 days. In busy markets lenders and appraisers get backed up, so allow yourself enough time. This is particularly important if you plan to sell your current home and bring cash from that settlement to the closing on your new one. If settlement comes too soon, you could be faced with having to ask for an extension.

Possession usually occurs immediately after settlement. If you need to move in prior to closing, or if the seller needs to remain after closing, the preferred procedure is to arrange for a separate rental agreement between you. Such agreements can have horrendous legal and tax consequences, so all documents should be prepared or reviewed by your attorney before you accept them.

Settlement Agent

It's usually your privilege to select or approve the attorney or title company who will perform settlement services. Name them in your offer or state your right to do so. Pick a skilled neutral party to ensure that all contract requirements are met before money is disbursed.

Prorating

The contract should state that property taxes (among other things) will be prorated to the closing date. Prorating is a method of equitably dividing continuing expenses, such as mortgage interest, property taxes and insurance, between buyer and seller. Government-backed loans and conventional mortgages may not prorate the same way, but in general it works like this: In January, Mr. Owner pays the annual premium on his homeowners insurance policy. He then puts his house on the market and sells it; he and the buyer agree to settle at midyear. What happens to the insurance coverage paid for but not used? In many cases, the purchaser "buys" the remaining coverage from the owner by arrangement with the insurer. Payment is made at settlement.

Sale of Current Residence

If your purchase of this house is contingent on the sale of another, this should be carefully stated. It should be clear to all parties exactly what the "sale" of your current home means. Does that mean an acceptable contract in the eyes of the seller? Or one acceptable to you? Sellers are wary of such a contingency and a contract containing it may be far less desirable than others.

Response Time Limit

Your contract should require the seller to accept the offer *in writing* within a certain time—such as 48

Sellers are wary of buyers whose offers are contingent upon the sale of their own homes. Such contracts may be far less desirable than others to sellers.

Failure to state a time limit invites having your contract "shopped"—used to stimulate slower-moving buyers to top your offer.

hours—or the offer will be void. How long you give depends on market activity in general and likely buyer interest in that home in particular. Failure to state a time limit invites having your contract "shopped." That means that the seller or agent may use your offer to stimulate slower-moving buyers to get a move on and top your offer.

You are free to withdraw and cancel an offer at any time before the seller has accepted it and you have received notice of that acceptance in accordance with the terms set out in the contract.

The phrase "time is of the essence" should be included to emphasize the time limit on the offer and the closing date. Although this does not prevent you or the seller from obtaining a mutually agreed-on extension, it precludes it from being available unilaterally on demand.

Home Inspection

This contingency clause gives you the right to have the property inspected and to withdraw your offer if the inspection report isn't satisfactory to you for any reason. It may also allow for price adjustments to pay for any necessary repairs. Accept no exceptions. You don't want to end up in the same boat some Arkansas buyers did not long ago: Their contracts excluded the foundations, floors, walls, ceilings, roofs, fireplaces and chimneys! And in at least one state, real estate agents were pushing for a contract that would let buyers cancel only when the inspection report uncovers substantial structural or mechanical problems.

The critical portion of a typical inspection clause reads: "This contract is contingent on a property inspection report which, in the sole judgment of the purchaser, is deemed satisfactory." Such a contingency clause leaves you with an escape hatch as big as the house itself. Consequently, most real estate contracts allow the seller to determine how long you can take to get the job done and by whom. Typically, the seller allows no fewer than three and no more than ten days, and specifies "a recognized professional."

Insert language to the effect that should the home inspector not be able to examine the roof, you retain the right to obtain an inspection satisfactory to you from a qualified roofing professional prior to releasing the inspection contingency. In some areas of the country, it is customary for the seller to pay for a roof warranty, which is usually good for 90 days.

Under normal circumstances, you will pay for the inspection. Since sellers often worry that buyers will raise issues about the condition of the house at settlement, savvy ones demand a copy of the inspection report as part of the deal.

If necessary, offset the negative impact of your inspection contingency with a larger earnest-money deposit, or some other bargaining chip that will impress the seller with your interest in the property.

If you haven't lined up an inspector or are uncertain about how to find one, see Chapter 9.

Environmental Tests

You may want to include a clause requiring that the property be tested for radon by a company approved by the state's radiation-control or radiological-health office, or a clause that requires testing for lead paint, asbestos, or ureaformaldehyde insulation.

Connecticut, Florida, Indiana, Massachusetts, Montana, New Hampshire, New Jersey and Virginia have placed some form of environmental-disclosure requirement on home sellers. Sellers generally must spell out what they know or what they don't know about their property.

Borrowers using FHA mortgages to buy homes built before 1978 are required to read and sign a lead-based-paint disclosure notice before they sign a sales contract. (HUD lenders are not to process loan requests until they have evidence that buyers have signed this document. Lacking proof, they will return the sales contract for reexecution—presumably after the buyer signs off on the warning.) Homeowners in Massachusetts and Virginia must tell prospective buyers about the risks posed by lead paint regardless of the type of financing they choose (see Chapter 17 for information about what sellers should disclose).

Termite Inspection

Many contracts require the seller to order and pay for a termite inspection. If yours doesn't, insert language to that effect. Be sure you can void the deal or negotiate with the seller for extermination and repairs if termites, or damage, are found.

What Goes With the House

Specify what furnishings—such as curtains, rugs, chandelier, and so on—are included in the sale. You may assume the seller will leave major appliances, built-in bookcases, sheds, wall-to-wall carpeting, fences and outside lighting, but such an assumption would be unwise. Customary practices vary; the more specific your contract, the fewer opportunities for later dispute.

Condition of House at Settlement

Specify what must be in demonstrable working order at the time of settlement, as verified during a walk-through of the premises a day or so before settlement. Include electrical, plumbing and mechanical systems, such as furnaces, air-conditioners, toilets, as well as appliances. This is no guarantee that these things will continue working after you buy the house—just that they were functioning properly when you took title. It may be impossible to test the air-conditioning during the winter, so allow for a test to be done as soon as the temperature permits.

If there are exceptions—such as appliances being

conveyed to you "as is," with no guarantee made as to working order—describe them in the contract.

As for cleanliness, note that the house should be left empty of all stored objects and debris (including things in the attic, basement and garage) and handed over in "broom-clean" condition.

Other Conditions

The list could go on, but every additional condition runs the risk of making your offer more complicated and less appealing.

Presentation and Counteroffer

At this point, your offer—signed and with all clauses initialed—is presented to the seller, either by you, your representative (buyer's agent or attorney), the seller's agent or the agent who has been assisting you all along.

Bolster the appeal of your offer by providing a financial statement as evidence of creditworthiness. In the eyes of the seller, your ability to get a loan and get to settlement is as important as the terms of the contract. You will require the seller to take the property off the market while you arrange financing, so his confidence in your financial strength will play a big role in weighing your contract against a rival bid.

Your financial statement doesn't have to have a lot of detail, but it should include information about employment, current homeownership, and other basics. If you have prequalified for a mortgage sufficient to swing this deal, point that out when you provide the information needed to verify your claim.

Once the seller accepts your offer as set out in the contract by signing within the acceptance date specified, the offer becomes binding on both parties, subject to removal of specific contingencies. Rejection of even the smallest provision in your offer is a rejection of the

If you have prequalified for a mortgage sufficient to swing this deal, point that out when you provide the information needed to verify your claim.

entire thing. If the seller wishes to negotiate, he or she will present you with a counteroffer.

The Counteroffer(s)

The counteroffer typically takes one of three forms: a fresh purchase contract identical to your offer except for the seller's changes; a counteroffer written on the back of the original, or on a separate sheet of paper, accepting your offer subject to certain stated changes; or revisions made by the seller's marking out unacceptable items on your offer and notes substitutions above or below, initialing each change. A time limit is noted, and the counteroffer is dated and signed by the seller.

This is delivered to you. If it's acceptable, you sign and date your acceptance. At that point the contract is considered ratified. If it's not acceptable, you could allow the counteroffer to expire or make a second offer—a counter to the seller's counteroffer. Have a new contract written out. Marking and initialing the document too extensively can only lead to confusion and mistakes.

Sometimes, negotiating goes on for days: offer, counteroffer, offer, counteroffer. More commonly, an agreement is reached on the second or third offer.

If the seller has other contract offers in addition to yours, he may try to play one against the other, often with oral messages. Sometimes a seller or seller's agent won't formally counter a contract but will tell the prospective buyer the offer is "too low," promising acceptance if it is raised. Don't respond; the seller has made no commitment to you, and you have no assurance you'll get the house if you do raise your bid. The seller could change his mind again and keep trying to jack up your bid.

Remind the seller that you have a formal offer on the table and would appreciate a written counterproposal stating the price and terms that would make your offer acceptable. A written response means you're still in the ball game. You can accept the counteroffer and nail down the deal, counter again, or let the response time lapse. Your strategy is to keep the seller involved with only you until your negotiation has run its course. The seller can give a counteroffer to only one buyer at a time; to do otherwise is to run the risk that both parties will accept.

Should you bend? That depends on how much you want the deal to go through. Say you like the house and it meets all major needs. You'd like to settle in time for your children to begin the year in their new schools. Why not give a little? On the other hand, if you're not pressed and you expect similar homes in the neighborhood to go on sale soon, focus on your priorities and hold firm. If this house gets away, you'll probably locate a similar one later. It's not uncommon to put in several bids on one property—or more than one property—before getting accepted. Who knows, you might get a second chance to buy the first house you bid on. You could even end up paying less than you originally offered.

If you're not pressed, focus on your priorities and hold firm. If this house gets away, you'll probably locate a similar—or even better—one later.

What an Accepted Offer Means

Once your offer is accepted by the seller, or you accept the seller's counteroffer, the agreement becomes a binding contract. If you change your mind after your contract offer has been accepted and signed by the seller, you stand the chance of losing your deposit and you could even be liable for damages for failing to live up to your contract.

Likewise, if the seller simply backs out, you can sue for damages or try to enforce the contract terms.

What if the owner dies before settlement? Your contract should bind the executors of his or her estate to proceed with the sale of the house to you. But you will need an attorney's help to assert your claim and keep the process on track.

Relocation Loans

Employers sometimes pick up the tab for employees they want to relocate. That can include help in selling the home you leave behind or even buying it from you, freeing you to buy a new home where you are being relocated. You may be offered the assistance of a relocation real estate specialist to help you sell your old home. In some cases, you could be offered a guaranteed price for your home if it doesn't sell within a specified period or for a preset price. Your employer might even carry the interest payments on the old home until it is sold.

Guaranteed Sale

In a twist on a once-popular option offered by real estate firms to help eager move-up buyers, some builders are promising to buy homes that owners leave behind when they move into one of the builder's new homes. Basically, it works like this: A builder enters into a "guaranteed purchase," or "buy-sell" agreement, with the buyer of one of its new or soon-to-be-built homes. In exchange for the buyer's noncontingent sales contract to buy one of the builder's homes, the builder agrees to buy the old home at a set price after a predetermined time, typically thee to six months. If the period elapses with no buyer signed on, the builder must purchase the property.

In the mid 1980s, guaranteed purchase plans were popular among real estate brokerage firms. Brokers, and sometimes even their agents, were quick to offer owners guarantees of 10% to 15% below market value. Then the market soured and brokers were forced to unload properties at big losses—or become landlords. Real estate firms offering such deals today usually bring in outside investors to act as guarantors.

A guaranteed purchase can work to your advantage. But it has a price tag. Builder purchase commitments are being set low, usually significantly less than the 85% to 90% of market value homeowners got in the mid '80s. You will be under pressure to sell, something that limits your negotiating hand. Do not sign a noncontingent sales contract before having it reviewed by your attorney.

Bidding on a Sale-by-Owner House

Theoretically, a house should cost less if bought directly from the owner rather than through an agent. And if the deal is structured right, the seller will do fine, too. What the seller wants is the maximum net proceeds from the sale, so a lower offer that is not reduced by a sales commission should net as much or more for the seller than a higher offer from which the commission is subtracted.

Many sellers will try for a few weeks to sell the house themselves before listing it with a broker at a slightly higher price. Even after a listing contract is signed by the seller, it may permit the seller to sell the house directly—with no sales commission to the agent—provided the seller finds the buyer himself, with no help from the agent. In either case, you may save by getting the house for a lower price than it would have sold for through an agent.

How much lower? Well, it could be a full 6% lower, which presumes all the savings of the commission end up in your pocket. More typically, the owner will want to share in the savings, perhaps by splitting the 6% evenly with you.

More typically, an owner who is selling his house himself will want to share in the savings, perhaps by splitting the 6% evenly with you.

CHAPTER

9

Have the Home Inspected

Serious structural defects may demand squashing the deal entirely. Common flaws may require negotiation.

You've made an offer, haggled over the contract and struck a deal. Now hire an home inspector to give you an objective evaluation of the condition of the home you'd like to buy.

Your purchase contingency should permit you to withdraw your offer if you aren't satisfied with the inspector's findings. If the report reveals serious structural defects, you may want to squash the deal entirely. More typically, the inspection will uncover common flaws and problems.

Your next move depends on your priorities and local sales activity. Don't do anything to void the contract until you've assessed your options. These include trying to bargain down the price or get the owner to pay for repairs. You always have the right to negotiate, and most sellers anticipate making some adjustments after an inspection. If you find yourself dealing with an owner who acknowledges that the house has problems but won't discuss lowering the price or making the repairs you deem necessary, he or she may be having second thoughts about the sale. One possibility: There's a better offer in the making and the owner is quite willing for you to withdraw your offer.

A seller may arrange for an inspection before putting a home up for sale. This helps market the property and shifts some disclosure responsibility from his shoulders to a third party's. Don't remove your inspection contingency until you've read the report and questioned the inspector yourself. Order your own if you have reservations about the report or the integrity or credibility of the inspector.

Finding a Good Inspector

Start by asking your attorney, friends, real estate agent and lenders for recommendations. You want someone with a good reputation and recognized professional credentials. Home inspection services may be listed in the Yellow Pages under "Building Inspection Services," "Engineers (Inspection or Foundation)" or "Real Estate Inspectors."

Look for these qualifications:

- **Experience.** A home inspector's experience in the building field usually comes from a background in contracting, architecture or engineering. By whatever route, the professional you want is one who knows homes inside and out, who makes a living poking into cellars and attics and crawl spaces looking for design, structural and equipment flaws, and who then gives you a detailed written report that takes some of the risk out of home buying.

- **Impartiality.** The inspector you hire should be independent, not beholden to the seller's real estate agent and not interested in promoting a repair or remodeling business.

- **Certification and/or professional affiliation.** Look for certification by the *National Institute of Building Inspectors*. The NIBI trains and certifies inspectors, requires annual continuing education, and sets acceptable levels of liability insurance coverage to be carried by members. Members must also abide by a code of ethics and standards of conduct. (A franchise business, HouseMaster of America Home

The inspector you hire should be independent, not beholden to the seller's real estate agent and not interested in promoting a repair or remodeling business.

Inspection Service, for example, requires its inspectors be certified by NIBI each year.)

Inspectors who are members of the American Society of Home Inspectors (ASHI) must pass a set of examinations, provide evidence of having done at least 250 fee-paid inspections, and take 40 hours of continuing education each year. Members are bound by a code of ethics and by prescribed standards of practice.

Many home inspectors belong to both organizations (see the accompanying box).

For More Information

• •

The National Institute of Building Inspectors (NIBI, 424 Vosseller Ave., Bound Brook, N.J. 08805) can tell you whether an inspector is currently certified.

The American Society of Home Inspectors (ASHI, 1735 N. Lynn St., Suite 950, Arlington, Va. 22209) can give you the names of its members doing business in your area.

The Cost

Fees for inspecting homes generally vary according to contract price and geographical area, and sometimes according to age, size and construction of the house. Assuming the home you are interested in is a fairly typical residential property, you might expect to pay anywhere from $150 to $350. Inspections in large metropolitan areas where homes are more expensive, for example New York City and San Francisco, may cost more.

An inspector may charge one fee for all homes under $150,000, for example, and bill for inspecting those over that amount on a sliding scale according to price. Inspectors may do specialized tests—such as those for radon or lead—for an additional fee. Inspecting very new or very old homes may take more time, which is reflected in the charge. Inspections on Sundays, holidays and after hours, and those that require any long-distance travel, also are likely to command premiums.

The Inspection

A thorough home inspection usually takes two or three hours. Most inspectors encourage buyers to accompany them. Arrange to do so and come prepared to ask questions and to get dirty. If the house has a crawl space, go down there with the inspector and see whether routine maintenance chores in that space will be within your capacity.

Let the inspector know whether you are handy with a pipe wrench or know something about carpentry so you can get an on-the-spot estimate of the repairs needed and how much they'll cost. Provide information about family size and habits. A water heater usually adequate for four people may be inadequate for your foursome if you all shower in the morning and then again after soccer or evening jogging.

The Report

An inspector may use checklist-type work sheets, adding brief remarks as necessary, or he may present a write-up of the overall condition of the property, along with suggested repairs and improvements.

The report should indicate potential as well as existing problems the inspector can readily observe. For example, the original wiring in a home built before World War II is probably not up to handling today's major electrical appliances. An inspector should note such a shortcoming and give you some idea of what would be involved in bringing the feature up to modern standards.

Special features such as a swimming pool, tennis court, well or septic system may require a specialist. If you are having a home inspected in winter, some testing may have to be postponed until warmer temperatures arrive; the wording of your contract should set out what obligations the seller must shoulder at that time.

A formula used by one inspector when calculating demands on a water heater counts a teenage girl with short hair as one person, a teenage girl with long hair as one and a half, and a teenage boy as two.

Before removing your inspection contingency, carefully review the written inspection report (see the accompanying box).

Back to the Seller?

When a seller finds that a qualified inspector has determined the roof needs repair or the water heater has outlived its expected life span, he may agree to make repairs or replacements or to knock down the price so that you can cover the cost of having the work done yourself.

Suppose something catastrophic is discovered? Perhaps the floors are heaving or the foundation is settling, causing cracks in the interior walls. At this point

What an Inspection Report Includes

The report should cover the house from basement to roof and include an assessment of the quality and condition of all the following:

- **Yard:** drainage, fences, garage, grading, landscaping, paved areas, recreational facilities, retaining walls

- **Exterior of House:** decks, doors, exterior walls (possibly including insulation), porches, steps, windows (including storm and screen)

- **Roof and Related Features:** chimneys, downspouts, gutters, hatches, roofing materials and construction, skylights, vents and fans

- **Crawl Space or Basement:** construction, settlement, structural stability, termite or rot damage, water penetration

- **Attic:** access, insulation, signs of leakage, ventilation

- **Electrical System:** capacity, fuses or circuit breakers, grounding, obvious hazards, outlets and switches, wires

- **Plumbing System:** drainage faucets, laundry appliances, pipes, sink traps, water heater, water pressure

- **Heating and Cooling Systems:** type, capacity and condition, controls, distribution of sources of heat and cooling, and humidifiers

- **Kitchen and Bathrooms:** fixtures and appliances, flooring, plumbing, tile, and ventilation

price is no longer the object; you want out. Assuming the deal was contingent upon an inspection "...which in the sole judgment of the purchaser, is deemed satisfactory," you're off the hook. Convey your decision to the seller in writing.

Special Situations: New Homes, Condos and Co-ops

If you're buying a not-yet-built home in a new development, determine whether covenants that dictate the size and style of housing in the development apply only to a particular phase or to all phases of the whole project. Developers sometimes give themselves escape clauses that, for example, permit them to change to a cheaper house if the market changes. Your contract should specify that the house is to be built to the quality standards of the model you saw. If covenants permit the builder to change the model from one phase to another or in response to market condition, and if that's not acceptable, your contract should stipulate what model and standards are to be used in building *your* home.

Insert a clause in your purchase offer giving you the right to have ongoing inspections done (at your expense) as construction proceeds, plus a final walk-through inspection. Inspection is particularly useful as the foundation is being built and before insulation and drywall go on. At that point, heating, cooling, plumbing and electrical systems in your house are in place.

Apartment-style condominiums and co-ops also require careful going over by inspectors knowledgeable about and experienced with the special problems and considerations inherent in these types of ownership. For example, an inspector should have the skills needed to assess the condition of large-scale heating plants and plumbing, common roofs, halls, stairs, elevators and swimming pools.

Insert a clause in your purchase offer giving you the right to have ongoing inspections done as construction proceeds, plus a final walk-through inspection.

A typical inspection of a single apartment unit would leave you with little or no information about the condition of the building as a whole. That's a potentially expensive shortcoming: Once you're a co-owner, you'll have to ante up your share of the cost of a new roof, electrical system or furnace.

Enter the Engineering Report

When an apartment building is converted to condo use, the developer-seller must provide tenants (as prospective owners of units) with an engineering report on the condition of the building. In addition, a tenants association or condo owners association may have, at some point, commissioned its own engineering report. Your contract to buy should be contingent on getting copies of all engineering reports *and* an inspection that in your judgment is satisfactory (see Chapter 8 for more on home-inspection contingencies).

When going through an engineering report, note recommended or suggested major work. Then find out whether it was done or still lies ahead. If work was done, how was it paid for—out of a reserve fund or by special assessment?

If you remain concerned about the building's condition, consider hiring the engineering or inspection firm that did the last study for a briefer inspection. (You could hook up with other would-be buyers to share the cost.) Commercial inspectors usually work by the hour, charging from $100 to $300 per hour. A two- to three-hour reinspection should give you the information you need. Weigh the expense against your ability

---

For More Information

• •

Inspection of a Single Family Dwelling, by Sol Sherman (American Association of Certified Appraisers Inc., 800 Compton Rd., Suite 10, Cincinnati, Ohio 45231; 800-543-2222; $22.95, including postage and handing).

The Homebuyer's Inspection Guide, by Warren Boroson and Ken Austin (John Wiley and Sons; $17.95).

The Home Reporter, by J. Barrett Irby (Home Reporter Systems, 10400 Chester Rd., Suite C, Chester, Va. 23831; call 800-328-6775 or 804-748-0182; $19.95, including postage).

to handle a large and unanticipated bill for major repairs soon after becoming a new homeowner.

New Home Warranties

Imagine that just two years after you buy a brand-new home the foundation begins to crack or the fireplace starts pulling away from its supporting wall. This kind of defect could threaten the soundness of your entire house; the remedy is sure to be costly. You don't believe you *should* have to pay—for the work or for legal bills, if it comes to that.

Implied Warranties vs. Extended Warranties

If your builder won't fix the problem, you have no alternative but to sue. Many states and local jurisdictions hold builders and developers to an "implied" warranty on the habitability of their homes. (Implied warranties are derived from common law as developed by case law.) In general that means a builder that is authorized to construct homes in a jurisdiction should for a specified time—at least a year or two—replace or repair anything that threatens a home's soundness and the safe functioning of its basic structures and components. While some states have statutes dealing with limitations on when certain actions can be taken in court, implied warranties *always* must be enforced through litigation.

The desire to avoid costly legal bills and draining court battles if something goes seriously awry helps sell thousands of homes constructed by builders who offer buyers long-term home protection plans backed by insurance. The idea behind long-term warranties is to provide consumers with recourse other than litigation. Warranty plans provide member builders—and buyers of their homes—with ten years of protection against catastrophic losses arising from major design and structural defects. If a member builder refuses or is unable

With a ten-year warranty, you are automatically covered when you buy a home from a builder affiliated with a plan issuer.

to fix a covered defect, insurance covers repairs that exceed the owner's deductible. (Not all plans charge deductibles—the New Jersey New Home Warranty Program, for example, doesn't.) A built-in dispute-settling process usually is available to mediate between buyer and builder.

What an Extended Warranty Costs, What It Covers

You don't buy a ten-year warranty policy as you do a homeowners insurance policy. Instead you are automatically covered when you buy a home from a builder currently affiliated with a plan issuer such as Home Owners Warranty Corp. Each member builder pays a one-time premium of about 0.25% to 0.5% of the home's selling price on each home it builds. (The following illustration is based heavily on HOW's plan; other extended-warranty plans will differ.)

During the first year, member builders warrant their new homes against defects in certain workmanship and materials, certain major structural defects, and certain flaws in the electrical, plumbing, heating, cooling, ventilating and mechanical systems. The warranty excludes appliances, fixtures and equipment.

During the second year, they warrant against major structural defects (defined in the warranty documents) and certain major electrical, plumbing, heating, cooling, ventilating and mechanical system breakdowns that render the home unsafe or unlivable during years two through ten. The warranty no longer covers defects in materials and workmanship.

During the first two years, you rely on the builder to correct covered problems. If, during that period, a builder defaults on the terms of the warranty or goes out of business, claims are paid through the plan issuer by an insurance company.

During the remaining eight years, each member builder remains insured against certain major structural defects.

You are reimbursed for authorized repairs, less the deductible (around $250), which applies to each claim. The builder's ten-year warranty stays with the home for ten years regardless of how often owners change.

The Limits of Coverage

But buyers who have new-home warranty plans are rarely aware of limits to their coverage. Foundation cracks and basement leaks generally are covered only during the first year. Certain wiring and plumbing defects are covered for two years. After that, coverage is generally limited to major structural defects that make the home unsafe, unsanitary or otherwise unlivable.

The sad reality for many owners in new homes that go bad is that they may not get much help from anyone. And they often have to fight to get anything. Builders go broke or refuse to make good. Serious problems appear only after statutory or warranty time limits have expired. Extended warranties that owners believe will protect them fail to do so. And so on.

A builder's ten-year homeowners warranty backed by insurance generally gives you an express warranty (as set out in terms of the contract) rather than an implied warranty. Assurances you get when your builder provides an extended-warranty plan may not be better or more comprehensive—particularly in the early years—than what you would have under an implied warranty. The plan's primary purpose is to offer the possibility of compensation—within terms of the plan's contract—without litigation. (In fact, most warranty claims are settled between builder and homeowner with no involvement by a plan administrator.)

Hashing Out Disputes

When homeowner and builder reach a stalemate over disputed warranted items within the first two years, either may request the plan administrator to arrange for an impartial third party to mediate, at no cost to the

The sad reality for many owners in new homes that go bad is that they may not get much help from anyone. And they often have to fight to get anything.

buyer. Referees for such disputes are not affiliated with the plan administrator or the builder.

If a mutually acceptable solution cannot be reached, the neutral party decides on the issue, *based on the warranty documents*. The builder is bound by the decision once it is accepted by a homeowner. He can appeal the decision but faces expulsion from membership if he ultimately refuses to comply. An unmollified owner is free to reject the arbitrated settlement and go to court. (The mandated New Jersey New Home Warranty Program provides that the decision of the neutral third party is final and binding on both parties.)

Most homeowners do accept the mediated decision. That may not mean they're satisfied, however. According to Peter Desch, chief of New Jersey's Bureau of Homeowner Protection, the biggest problems with extended warranties are that homeowners don't consult their warranty until a problem surfaces, that they fail to give the builder an opportunity to correct the defect, or that they wait too long before filing a claim. The National Academy of Conciliators, which provides mediators for many warranty disputes, agrees with Desch and adds that owners may feel dissatisfied with mediated decisions because they did not understand warranty limitations—either because they spent too little time reading their policies or didn't understand what they read.

Another problem is that plan issuers have no authority to get tough on delinquent builders, except by suing or expelling them from the program. An expelled builder can go on constructing homes unless

One State's Response

● ●

In 1979, New Jersey passed a New Home Warranty and Builders' Registration Act to protect new-home buyers. Under the law, all home builders in the state must register with the state's New Home Warranty Program. New homes are covered by a ten-year warranty issued through the state's warranty plan or a state-approved private plan.

For more information, contact the Department of Community Affairs, New Home Warranty Program, CN 805, Trenton, N.J. 08625-0805; or call, 609-530-8800).

local or state regulatory bodies decide to take action. (In New Jersey, if a builder fails to abide by the decision of a plan's dispute settler, its right to build homes in New Jersey can be revoked.)

Homeowners' Experience According to HUD

One assessment of how homeowners have fared with ten-year warranties comes from the U.S. Department of Housing and Urban Development (HUD). Prior to 1980, builders who wanted to sell new homes eligible for FHA-insured financing had to get the HUD's approval for all plans before starting construction. In addition, the builder needed HUD's okay on the foundation and framing work, and final inspection. In 1980, the department began allowing builders who offered ten-year warranty plans to start construction without submitting plans for approval—so long as they certified that construction plans and specifications met local building-code requirements. In addition, structures had to pass local building inspections and the builder must have had previous plans and construction approved by HUD.

HUD anticipated that these warranties would protect home buyers with three levels of protection. It expected warranty-plan administrators to exert pressure on builders when owners had problems; and it thought buyers would benefit by being able to rely on the insurance when a builder became insolvent and couldn't stand by his product; and HUD was assured that should a builder fail to correct covered defects or deficiencies, or to honor the terms of the plan, the insurance backer would act as a final fallback.

In 1991, HUD testified before a congressional subcommittee that while its overall experience with warranties on single-family homes had been positive, "consumers are too often denied full home protection when warranty companies unreasonably delay claim payments or claims adjusters use high-pressure tactics with homeowners." HUD was disturbed to find cases

"Consumers are too often denied full home protection when warranty companies unreasonably delay claim payments or claims adjusters use high-pressure tactics with homeowners."

where on-site claim adjusters used "hardball" tactics with homeowners when settling a claim. For instance, it found, the claims adjuster "may make a cash offer to repair damage but declare that the offer is only good until he reaches his car or office." (Warranty companies must now give homeowners with FHA mortgages ten working days' notice before they must respond to settlement offers.)

In response to its investigation, HUD revised some procedures to ensure that buyers using FHA mortgages to buy new homes are treated fairly and get more support when they go to arbitration over a claim.

In worst-case scenarios, homeowners have ended up in court anyway, suing the plan administrator and the insurance underwriter backing the warranty. Some of them would probably agree with Ernie F. Roberts, a Cornell University law professor, who believes ten-year warranties weren't intended to protect consumers but rather to protect builders from open-ended liability.

Homeowners who have taken warranty companies to court have also discovered there was little screening of builders and few controls on construction quality: Home Owners Warranty Corp. (a major plan issuer), for example, had only 12 people available nationwide to review more than one million homes in 1991.

Two Plan Issuers

• •

Home Buyers Warranty enrolls some 12,500 builders around the country. For a list of member builders, write to: Customer Service, HBW, 1400 Montreal Rd., Suite 240, Tucker, Ga. 30084, or call 800-488-8844.

Home Owners Warranty's 10,000 member builders operate in every state except Alaska. You can get a list of members by writing to HOW, P.O. Box 152087, Irving, Tex. 75015-2087; or call 214-402-7600.

What You Can Do

If you're faced with a new-home disaster and a recalcitrant builder, state law may permit you to sue *or* file a claim against the warranty company. Since an express warranty could stand *in the place of any implied builder warranty* in a court of law, it's helpful to find out what state law might make a builder do to fix a problem—and for how long—in order to judge the value of promises in a ten-year warranty plan. Your decision to buy from a builder whose homes are covered by an extended-warranty plan should take into account your assessment of the financial strength of the builder (the stronger the builder, the better you might fare in court with his stand-alone warranty instead of a ten-year warranty), how state courts have treated homeowners who sued builders, and your best guess as to what might

How to Make an Extended Warranty Work for You

Find out before you make a purchase offer or sign a contract how state warranty law could affect you.

Ask your attorney for an assessment and follow that with a purchase contract contingent on receipt of his or her opinion letter.

Read all the terms and conditions of any ten-year warranty policy your builder offers.

Have the terms of any warranties entered in the contract.

Hire your own inspector to monitor the job while the house is being built. Critical times: excavation, construction of the foundation, framing-in, and before the installation of drywall.

Check drainage and slope. Grading and drainage are extremely important—and a major source of problems. Make sure the foundation is high enough and the soil is sloped enough—at least 6 inches for every 10 feet—that water will drain away from the house and off the site.

Make contractors unambiguously responsible for everything and for everyone they choose to hire.

Keep records and act quickly. If you have a warranty and problems show up within two years, write directly to the builder. Send copies of all records to the warranty administrator. Hire an independent inspector to support your claims. Keep a diary and copies of correspondence.

Dig in your heels. Give the builder or the warranty administrator a reasonable time to review your claims and make repairs. Be prepared to fight—and put the responsible party on notice that if it doesn't take action, you will.

If you bought a new home with a VA or FHA mortgage, you may be covered under the agency's own four-year structural defect plan (see accompanying discussion). Complain to the nearest field office and provide copies of all correspondence and documents. If you think you could qualify at some point, keep the agency up-to-date.

go wrong in the house and when it might become apparent (get your inspector to help you with this).

Help from the FHA or VA

The Federal Home Administration and the Department of Veterans Affairs operate two little-known structural-defect correction programs for buyers who fail to get help from builders or warranty issuers and their insurers. To qualify, you must have bought your new home with either an FHA or VA mortgage, fulfill certain strict requirements, and apply for help within four years. (The FHA's so-called 518(a) program operates under Section 518(a) of the National Housing Act. The VA program comes under Title 38 CFR, Part 36.4364.)

Once your complaint has been reviewed and accepted, it becomes an official "application for financial assistance" and is subjected to further study and, probably, an on-site inspection. The FHA and VA may pay for correcting structural defects that meet their criteria. In certain situations, they may compensate an owner whose home becomes essentially unlivable due to structural defects. If a request is ultimately denied, you will be informed in writing.

To inquire about benefitting from these programs, your first contact point should be the FHA or VA field office that processed your loan. It can help you determine whether the house qualifies and the situation meets the agency's criteria, and can advise you on how to go about fulfilling all processing requirements.

How the FHA's Program Works

To qualify for the FHA program, a problem must meet HUD definitions and you must meet *all* the following criteria:

• The home must be covered by an individual FHA-insured mortgage.

- The property must have been approved for mortgage insurance *before* construction started and must have passed a final HUD inspection. (This clause eliminates many owners whose homes were inspected only during construction.)

- You must request assistance *no later* than four years after the date on the *first* HUD Mortgage Insurance Certificate issued on the property. (The Mortgage Insurance Certificate must have been properly endorsed and must be in force on the day your request is received.)

- You must have made reasonable, but unsuccessful, efforts to get the builder, seller or other responsible person to correct the structural defect.

How the VA's Program Works

To be eligible for the VA program:

- You must have bought a new home with a VA mortgage, and the Certificate of Reasonable Value (CRV) must have been "predicated upon completion of proposed construction" (see Item 13 on the original CRV). This means the builder sought VA approval before beginning construction and the home was checked by a VA compliance inspector during the construction phase. (If the house is enrolled in a ten-year warranty plan and a VA inspector made the final inspection, the home may be eligible.)

- In addition, you must have brought the problem to the attention of the VA no later than four years after the date on the initial Certificate of Reasonable Value. (In a few cases, veterans who brought problems to the attention of the VA within the first four years and kept them informed of efforts to get the builder and warranty plan administrator or insurance company to pay for correcting the defect have been eligible for assistance despite the fact that their official request for assistance was made *after* four years had elapsed.)

Unlike the FHA, the VA does not have special forms for you to complete. Instead, write a detailed letter to the loan guaranty officer of the appropriate regional VA office.

For information and details, contact the FHA or VA field office nearest you.

10

Pick the Right Mortgage

Time spent shopping for a mortgage is time well spent. A good deal can yield dramatic dividends in the short run and over time if monthly savings are invested elsewhere. Before you rule out one loan or another, read through this chapter and give some thought to your particular needs and aspirations.

Because you prequalified before house hunting, you're ahead of the game. Financial papers are at hand and up to date, and you know the general parameters (size and types) of mortgages you qualify for. But don't head back to the lender you prequalified with without shopping further.

The message is simple: Shop for a loan, not a lender. Mortgage lending is mechanical, impersonal and competitive. Hunt for the best loan—interest rate, points, processing costs and, on adjustable mortgages, the most favorable adjustment features. Don't pay much attention to who's originating the loan or where the lender is.

And don't place too much value on your current bank or thrift relationship, either. Odds are your loan will be sold once or twice over its term. (The firm servicing your new loan—collecting payments and holding taxes and homeowners insurance in escrow—may change as well.)

The next chapter explains how to shop for a mort-

The message is simple: Shop for a loan, not a lender. Mortgage lending is mechanical, impersonal and competitive.

Compare interest rates by asking for the annual percentage rate (APR) of the loans you're considering. The APR includes the cost of points and other fees.

gage—who originates them and how to use mortgage reporting or finding services. But before you go into the market, familiarize yourself with the choices and narrow your search to loans that best meet your needs.

Learn the pros and cons of fixed-rate and adjustable-rate borrowing. Get acquainted with the jargon of the mortgage business. Then you can ask lenders the right questions and compare confusing offers before putting yourself on the line.

The Basics

There are two basic ways mortgage lenders charge you for using their money: through the interest charges you pay each month over the life of the loan, and through "points," a one-time sum of money (one point equals 1% of the loan amount) that you pay up front.

Compare interest rates by asking for the annual percentage rate (APR) of the loans you're considering. While there are many ways to state interest rates, the APR includes the cost of points and other fees such as mortgage insurance, making it a useful tool with which to compare loans. Lenders are required by law to give you the APR on a loan if you request it.

A point is prepaid interest that raises the effective yield to the lender without raising the interest rate on a note. From your perspective, points discount the value of a loan. If you pay two points, or $1,800, to borrow $90,000, you've really borrowed only $88,200. But you will pay back the full $90,000 face value of the loan, plus interest.

Paying points to a lender is a standard part of the mortgage business. One point is roughly equivalent to an additional one-eighth of one percentage point on the interest rate of a 30-year fixed-rate mortgage; so the APR of a 10%, 30-year fixed-rate mortgage with no points is equivalent to the APR of a 9% loan with eight points.

In reality, you won't find lenders charging eight points because the cost of prepaying that amount would preclude all but the most affluent borrowers certain they'd be living in their homes for many years. Since most owners sell or refinance their homes long before their mortgages are repaid, they would be foolish to prepay so much interest. As a result, the differential between a 10% loan and a 9% one is apt to be around three points.

The cost of points on a buyer's loan is often shared between buyer and seller. (Like everything else in your purchase offer, who pays points should be set out in the contract.) In addition to points, lenders often charge an "origination" fee, usually calculated as 1% of the loan amount. Don't confuse the origination fee with the separate loan-application fees you'll pay to cover paperwork and loan approval. Application fees are not tax-deductible, but an origination fee is a charge for the use of borrowed money and, as such, is deductible.

Sometimes an origination fee is labeled a "prepaid point" because it's a prepayment of one of the discount points to be charged at settlement or closing. If, for example, a mortgage calls for a buyer to pay three points (3% of the loan amount) at settlement, a credit will be given for the 1% origination fee the buyer paid when he applied for the loan, and only the remaining 2% will be collected at settlement. For a discussion of tax implications, see Chapter 3.

Fixed or Adjustable Rate?

After all exotic mortgages are laid aside, the choice for most home buyers comes to this: Should you get a fixed- or adjustable-rate mortgage?

The standard fixed-rate, fully amortizing mortgage—with its preset, life-of-the-mortgage, monthly payments covering principal repayment and interest—came into being during the Great Depression and fueled the enormous expansion of homeownership in the decades following World War II. Its beauty was—and is—the peace of mind homeowners get from

With an ARM, you, the borrower, assume the risk of rising rates, and you stand to benefit should rates fall.

predictable monthly payments. Taxes, utilities and other costs of homeownership may rise, but principal and interest payments remain the same. An obvious drawback, of course, is that if rates fall, the holder of a fixed-rate mortgage cannot capture the benefit of a new, lower rate except by financing.

Lenders who made loans at fixed rates took a beating on the value of those loans when inflation and interest rates soared in the late 1970s. If they kept the loans, they had to settle for repayment in ever-devalued dollars. If they tried to sell them, they had to discount the value to reflect current and rising interest rates.

The increasing reluctance of lenders to make fixed-rate mortgage loans in a climate of rising interest rates led to creation of the adjustable-rate mortgage (ARM). With an ARM, the interest rate you pay rises and falls along with other rates charged throughout the economy. Put another way, you, the borrower, assume the risk of rising rates, and you stand to benefit should rates fall.

At one point in the early 1980s, when fixed-rate loans carried high interest rates, more than two-thirds of all new mortgages were adjustable-rate loans. As inflation and nominal interest rates declined in the mid 1980s, homeowners with high fixed-rate mortgages rushed to refinance. So did lots of homeowners with ARMs, because, although their payments were getting smaller, they wanted to lock in low fixed rates rather than take a chance on a resurgence of inflation.

As fixed-rate loans dropped into single-digit territory, the adjustable lost its appeal. By the spring of 1986, ARMs accounted for less than one-quarter of all new mortgages. (By then—unlike the 1970s—fixed-rate mortgage lenders were no longer shouldering the risk of rising interest rates, either. They were passing the risk on to investors by selling their mortgages in the secondary market.)

The 1990s brought more change. While the thrift industry—traditional loanmaker to the majority of home buyers—struggled to climb out of the hole dug during the days of deregulation, mortgage bankers quietly stole a huge chunk of its business. At the end of 1992, independent mortgage companies were originating more than half of all new mortgages—up from 35% just three years earlier.

In early 1993, 30-year fixed-rate loans hit a 20-year low of just over 7.5%. (New one-year adjustables were being offered for 4.25% or less.) Despite falling rates, 30-year fixed-rate mortgages continued losing market share, and by the fall of 1992, they made up just under half of originations—the lowest level since the ARM-dominated mortgage market of the early 1980s. This was due in part to low initial rates on adjustable-rate loans. In addition, 15-year and 20-year fixed-rate mortgages were gaining popularity, particularly among affluent families of the baby-boom generation coming to grips with the prospect of paying for their children's college educations.

A Personal Choice

• •

Your mortgage choice will depend on your answers to questions such as:

- Are you stretching to buy?
- Would you be able to handle a rising loan payment without major stress?
- Could you count on a higher income should inflation reappear?
- Could your spouse go to work? Could you swing another income?
- How long do you expect to live in the house you're buying?

What's Best for You?

Let's say that you *know* which direction interest rates will move. If so, you lock in low interest rates with a fixed-rate loan when it looks like they'll be heading up over the next few years. When it looks like rates will go down or stay about the same, an adjustable-rate mortgage should be considered.

But you don't know the direction interest rates will take, and neither do the experts. So leave interest-rate forecasting to those who dare, and concentrate instead on what *you* can manage. If you're stretching and a sooner-than-expected payment hike could strain your marriage, a fixed-rate mortgage is the safe bet. If not, a

Mortgages without prepayment penalties permit you to shorten the term of the loan at will and lower the ultimate interest cost.

one- or three-year adjustable-rate mortgage is worth considering. ARMs are attractive when the spread between fixed-rate mortgages and the starting rate on the ARM is two percentage points or more, or when you don't intend to stay put more than five years.

Don't accept an ARM without periodic and lifetime caps on interest rates; typical caps today are no more than a two-percentage-point hike in the interest rate from one year to the next, and no more than a five- or six-point increase over the starting rate during the term of the loan.

Fixed-Rate Loans

A fixed-rate loan locks in your interest rate. With an amortizing, fixed-rate loan, your total monthly payment of principal and interest remains constant, but the portion of each payment allocated to principal grows. By the end of the loan's life, or term, you will have repaid the original loan and all interest you owe.

Long-Term Mortgages

The most common long-term mortgages last twenty or thirty years.

Advantages

Predictability is the big plus. You know exactly how much interest you will pay over the term of the loan. Total monthly payment of principal and interest is fixed, and in early years it consists primarily of tax-deductible interest. Mortgages without prepayment penalties permit you to shorten the term of the loan at will—and lower ultimate interest cost—by making periodic payments against principal.

Disadvantages

Stability comes at a price. Interest rates on fixed-rate loans are usually higher than starting rates on adjustable-rate loans. Down-payment requirements on conventional, fixed-rate loans are steep—10% to 20%. If you opt for a low-down payment loan, you will have to pay for mortgage insurance—an added monthly expense that protects the lender from risk of loss. Interest rates on nonconforming or "jumbo" loans may be higher than on conforming loans, and you may pay more points. (The conforming loan limit is based on the change in average home prices from one October to the next. In 1992, the ceiling nationwide was $202,300. Anything above that was jumbo.)

While amortization costs remain level over the loan term, monthly payments will increase over the years as property taxes and insurance costs go up.

Attractive (that is, low-interest) fixed-rate mortgages usually can't be assumed by subsequent buyers, since lenders want to take every opportunity to replace a low-rate loan with a higher-interest one.

With 20-to-30-year terms, principal balance is reduced relatively slowly compared with shorter-term loans. Twenty-year loans usually don't carry a lower rate than 30-year loans. Though eased by tax deductions, total interest cost is high. A $100,000, 8%, 30-year fixed-rate mortgage costs $164,155 in interest over its term. An 8%, 15-year fixed-rate loan, on the other hand, has a total interest cost of $72,017—$92,138 less.

15-Year, Fixed-Rate, Fixed-Payment Mortgage

Advantages

Principal balance is reduced relatively rapidly compared to longer-term loans. The 15-year fixed-rate loan permits you to own your home debt-free in half the time, and for less than half the total interest cost, of a 30-year fixed-rate loan. It offers some individuals a useful financial planning tool. Interest rates may be lower than those offered on 30-year fixed-rate loans. FHA-insured, low-down-payment, 15-year fixed-rate loans are available; so are VA-guaranteed, no-down-payment, 15-year loans.

If you opt for a low-down payment loan, you will have to pay for mortgage insurance—an added monthly expense.

What Will Payments Be on a Fixed-Rate Loan?

This table allows you to calculate your monthly mortgage payment for each $1,000 that you borrow. Only principal and interest are included; insurance and property taxes would be additional expenses. To calculate your monthly payment for a new mortgage, locate the number in the

Interest Rate	15 Years	20 Years	25 Years	30 Years
4 %	$ 7.40	$ 6.06	$ 5.28	$ 4.77
5	7.91	6.60	5.85	5.37
6	8.44	7.17	6.45	6.00
6¼	8.58	7.31	6.60	6.16
6½	8.72	7.46	6.76	6.33
6¾	8.85	7.61	6.91	6.49
7	8.99	7.76	7.07	6.66
7¼	9.13	7.91	7.23	6.83
7½	9.28	8.06	7.39	7.00
7¾	9.42	8.21	7.56	7.17
8	9.56	8.37	7.72	7.34
8¼	9.71	8.53	7.89	7.52
8½	9.85	8.68	8.06	7.69
8¾	10.00	8.84	8.23	7.87
9	10.15	9.00	8.40	8.05
9¼	10.30	9.16	8.57	8.23
9½	10.45	9.33	8.74	8.41
9¾	10.60	9.49	8.92	8.60
10	10.75	9.66	9.09	8.78
10¼	10.90	9.82	9.27	8.97
10½	11.06	9.99	9.45	9.15
10¾	11.21	10.16	9.63	9.34

column and row corresponding to the length of the mortgage and the interest rate; multiply that figure by the number of thousands of dollars involved. Example: For a 30-year loan of $90,000 at 8%, multiply 90 by $7.34. The monthly payment of principal and interest would equal $660.60.

Interest Rate	15 Years	20 Years	25 Years	30 Years
11 %	$11.37	$10.33	$ 9.81	$ 9.53
11¼	11.53	10.50	9.99	9.72
11½	11.69	10.67	10.17	9.91
11¾	11.85	10.84	10.35	10.10
12	12.01	11.02	10.54	10.29
12¼	12.17	11.19	10.72	10.48
12½	12.33	11.37	10.91	10.68
12¾	12.49	11.54	11.10	10.87
13	12.66	11.72	11.28	11.07
13¼	12.82	11.90	11.47	11.26
13½	12.99	12.08	11.66	11.46
13¾	13.15	12.26	11.85	11.66
14	13.32	12.44	12.04	11.85
14¼	13.49	12.62	12.23	12.05
14½	13.66	12.80	12.43	12.25
14¾	13.83	12.99	12.62	12.45
15	14.00	13.17	12.81	12.65
15¼	14.17	13.36	13.01	12.85
15½	14.34	13.54	13.20	13.05
15¾	14.52	13.73	13.40	13.25
16	14.69	13.92	13.59	13.45

Disadvantages

Higher monthly payments make these loans more difficult to qualify for than longer-term mortgages. A 15-year mortgage reduces the number of homes you can afford to buy and locks you into making monthly payments roughly 15% to 25% higher than you'd make with a comparable 30-year loan. On a $100,000, 8% note, monthly payments would be $956 for 15 years and $734 for 30 years—a difference of $222.

Because the principal balance is paid down faster, total mortgage interest payments—a key tax-shelter benefit of homeownership—are reduced relative to a traditional 30-year mortgage (see the box below).

Convertible Fixed-Rate Mortgage

Often called a Reduction Option Loan (ROL) or Reducing Interest Loan (RIL), this mortgage can give borrowers the option of reducing their loan's interest rate following a specified drop in rates.

The Difference a 15-Year Loan Makes

This table shows the rapid decline in principal owed over the course of a 15-year mortgage compared with the slower pay-off of a 30-year loan. What a difference that makes in the *total interest* you would pay—$66,862 on the 15-year mortgage, which is less than half the $164,155 you would pay on the 30-year loan. (Note: The total interest you would pay on the 30-year loan by the end of year 15 is $108,859.)

Year	Payment Number	15-Year Fixed-Rate ($100,000 at 7½%)		30-Year Fixed-Rate ($100,000 at 8%)	
		Payment	Principal Balance	Payment	Principal Balance
1	12	$ 927	$ 96,249	$ 734	$ 99,165
3	36	927	87,850	734	97,280
5	60	927	78,096	734	95,070
7	84	927	66,769	734	92,477
10	120	927	46,263	734	87,725
15	180	927	0	734	76,782

Advantages

The option may enable you to reduce the long-term cost of the loan if interest rates decline. It gives you the option or right to obtain a lower rate on your fixed-rate mortgage. Typically, you can exercise your option between the 13th and 59th month of the loan should rates fall at least two percentage points below your initial rate during that period.

Disadvantages

You pay a fee of $100 to $200, plus a charge of one-fourth to one-half percent of the loan amount to exercise your option. If you want the right to adjust the rate on the mortgage without the cost of refinancing, you may have to pay a higher initial interest rate and a portion of a point. However, should rates fail to fall, an ROL could cost you more than a regular 30-year fixed-rate mortgage.

Biweekly Fixed-Rate Mortgage

Advantages

The biweekly payment schedule of this kind of loan speeds up amortization, reduces total interest costs and shortens the loan term—usually from 30 years to between 18 and 22 years. You make 26 biweekly payments—which amounts to 13 annual payments—instead of 12 monthly payments. Conversion to a 30-year fixed-rate loan is usually permitted. Payments are deducted automatically from your savings or checking accounts.

Disadvantages

Private companies and lenders usually charge for this service. Registration fees and biweekly debit charges can make this a costly way shorten the life of a loan and lower interest expense. The same objectives can be accomplished more flexibly with a 30-year mortgage by making an extra payment or two each year or by applying an additional sum to principal repayment

Registration fees and debit charges can make biweekly payments a costly way to shorten the life of a loan and lower interest expense.

when you make a monthly payment. As with other kinds of rapid-payoff mortgages, you trade total interest-cost reductions for reduced tax-shelter benefits.

Community Home Buyer's Program (CHBP)

This low-down-payment, fixed-rate mortgage was designed by the Federal National Mortgage Association (Fannie Mae) to help creditworthy buyers who can't qualify for standard conventional mortgages. You can choose between a 30-year and a 15-year loan. To qualify you must have income no more than 115% of your area's median household.

For More Information

• •

To inquire further about CHBP loans, contact lenders or Fannie Mae, 3900 Wisconsin Avenue, N.W., Washington, D.C. 20016. A Community Home Buyer's Program brochure is available free in Spanish and English.

Advantages

CHBP loans require less income and less cash. You may be able to pay as much as 33% of gross monthly income toward total housing payments (mortgage payments, taxes, insurance, and condo fees, if applicable) and still qualify. (Most mortgage lenders limit you to 28% or 29%.)

Your down payment can be as low as 5%. You may be permitted to use just 3% of your own funds if you obtain a 2% gift from a family member or a grant or loan from a nonprofit or public agency. Many community organizations and state and local agencies provide subsidized loans to low- and moderate-income families to help them buy a home.

You won't have to bring as much cash to closing. In most cases, buyers are required to put two months of mortgage payments in reserve at closing or settlement. This requirement is waived for CHBP borrowers.

Disadvantages

You will have to pay a monthly mortgage insurance premium.

Fixed-Rate, Adjustable-Payment Mortgages

Growing Equity Mortgages (GEMs)

Now rare, a fixed-rate GEM cuts the life span of the loan with payments that increase each year for a fixed number of years and then level off.

The interest rate is fixed. Once payments exceed what would be needed to amortize the 30-year loan, the excess is applied against principal outstanding.

Advantages

You save on total interest costs. Interest rates charged by lenders may be lower than for longer-term mortgages. Increases in monthly payments are applied to principal—most GEMs pay off in 12 to 17 years. The payment-hike schedule is determined when the loan contract is drawn up.

Disadvantages

GEMs are hard to find. Your income must be able to keep up with annual increases. Rapid principal repayment lowers total mortgage interest cost and reduces interest available as a tax deduction.

Graduated Payment Mortgages (GPMs)

A fixed-rate GPM starts out with low payments, which rise gradually (usually over five to ten years), then level off for the remaining years of the loan(see the following box).

Advantages

Lower initial payments enable buyers to qualify for a larger mortgage loan than they otherwise would.

Disadvantages

There are two big problems: high cost, and the

How Graduated-Payment Mortgages Work

Here's an example of a graduated-payment mortgage and how it compares with a level-payment, fixed-rate loan. Both mortgages are for amounts of $90,000 with a 9½% interest rate for the purposes of this example, though lenders typically charge half a percentage point more for a graduated-payment loan.

As you can see below, monthly payments on the graduated-payment mortgage increase 7.5% each year for five years and then level off for the remaining term of the mortgage. The early payments start lower than the $767.77 you would pay each month ($9,213.24 annually) for a comparable level-payment, fixed-rate mortgage.

In year five, the graduated payments catch up to and exceed the level payments, in order to amortize the loan. But, by this time, the total balance of the graduated-payment mortgage has actually increased, because the earlier payments weren't sufficient to cover the principal *and* all of the interest due (a process known as negative amortization). After the fifth year, you would owe $94,230.37, or $4,230.37 more than you did originally. At the end of the 30-year term, you would have paid $286,956 for the graduated-payment, fixed-rate mortgage—$10,559 more than you would have paid for the level-payment, fixed-rate loan.

The moral? The convenience of having smaller payments for the first four years does not come cheap.

Years	Graduated Payment	Difference From Level-Payment, Fixed-Rate Mortgage	Total Paid Annually
1	$ 573.47	$ 183.30 less	$ 6,881.64
2	616.48	140.29 less	7,397.76
3	662.71	94.06 less	7,952.52
4	712.42	44.35 less	8,549.04
5	765.85	9.08 more	9,190.20
6-30	823.29	66.52 more for 25 yrs.	9,879.40

risk of stable or falling home prices. Because low initial payments are not enough to cover monthly interest due on the loan, unpaid interest is added to the principal balance. Future interest payments are then calculated on the new higher loan balance. As a result, in order to pay off the debt, later GPM payments must be higher than they would have been with an ordinary loan. This process is called negative amortization, and that's another name for risky business.

With a GPM, you gamble that appreciation in the value of the home will offset your increased indebtedness. Should you sell after a few years, you would owe more on the home than you borrowed in the first place. If home prices fail to keep pace with your growing obligation, you could be stuck with a home you can't afford to sell. Assuming home prices escalate ahead of indebtedness, you'd still have less equity than you would have had with a standard fixed-rate loan.

Adjustable-Rate Mortgages

You may hear ARMs called variable-rate loans, adjustable-rate loans or adjustable mortgage loans. Whatever the name, they all carry an interest rate that can change periodically during the term of the loan.

Four Features All ARMs Carry

Initial interest rates

Starting rates are generally one to four percentage points below those on conventional 30-year fixed-rate mortgages.

Adjustment intervals

The adjustment schedule is set out in the mortgage contract. Changes in the rate to be charged on an ARM loan occur at the end of each adjustment period. These periods are equal in length and reoccur throughout the loan term. A loan with an adjustment period of one year is called a one-year ARM, and the interest rate can change yearly; a three-year ARM will have an adjustment three years after you get the loan and every three years thereafter.

Index

Each ARM is tied to an index that moves up and down in tandem with the general movement of interest rates. The index is used to figure the new loan rate for the next adjustment period. The calculation date—typically one to two months before the anniversary date of the loan—is set out in the contract.

Popular indexes include average rates on one-, three-, and five-year Treasury securities. Another is the Federal Housing Finance Board's National Average Contract Mortgage Rate (a monthly weighted average of loans closed). This is usually abbreviated to FHFB Series of Closed Loans.

Some indexes are more volatile than others. In certain circumstances the most volatile index will be the least expensive for borrowers over the long haul. While it will go up more quickly than most, it is less likely to "stick" at a high level when interest rates drop. For that reason, a mortgage tied to rates on one-year Treasury securities could give you the best deal when rates fall over a prolonged period.

Find out what index your ARM would be tied to and how often it would adjust. How has the index performed in the past? Where is it published?

Adjustment margin

The loan rate and the index rate move up and down together, but they aren't the same. "Margin" is the percentage amount the lender adds to the index rate to get the ARM's interest rate. Look for it in the mortgage contract. The margin amount, commonly one to three percentage points, usually remains constant over the life of a loan. Whatever the margin amount, add it to the index rate at the adjustment anniversary to get a new "adjusted" rate.

For promotional purposes, the starting rate of an

ARM may be less than the index rate plus margin. Don't be impressed with this kind of discount—it's usually temporary. Ask the lender what your interest rate (and monthly payment) would be at the first adjustment date, assuming the index rate didn't change between now and then. The payment will probably be higher (see later discussion of discount ARMs).

Two Features Many ARMs Carry

Caps on interest

There are two types of interest-rate caps.

Lifetime caps, required by law on all new ARMs and on assumptions, limit the interest-rate increase over the life of the loan. With a "5% lifetime cap," your rate can't increase more than five percentage points over the initial rate no matter how high the index rate climbs. Most adjustable-rate mortgage contracts limit lifetime caps to 5% or 6%. In some, lifetime caps apply to decreases as well as increases.

Periodic caps limit the interest-rate increase from one adjustment period to the next. For example, your mortgage contract could provide that should the index rate increase four points in one year, your rate could rise only two points. When rates rise rapidly, periodic caps cushion borrowers from overly steep payment hikes between one adjustment period and the next.

ARM contracts generally allow periodic decreases as well as increases. With ARMs that carry periodic caps, a drop in interest rates doesn't automatically lead to a drop in monthly payments. For example, take a one-year 5% ARM with a two-point annual cap. If the index to which it is tied rises three points during the first year, the second-year rate will be capped at 7%. At the end of the second adjustment period, *if the index stays the same*, the third-year rate will rise to 8%. This can happen because ARM contracts usually permit loan rates to rise—subject to annual caps—on any adjustment date when the index plus the margin is higher than the current rate you are paying.

With ARMs that carry periodic caps, a drop in interest rates doesn't automatically lead to a drop in monthly payments.

How ARM Payments Could Go Up or Down

Say you have a $100,000 one-year adjustable-rate mortgage (ARM) with an initial rate of 4%, an annual cap of two percentage points, and a lifetime cap of five percentage points. Here's what the monthly payment would be on a fully amortized loan if payments are adjusted up every year to the maximum and then remain at that level for the life of the loan.

Year	Rate	Years of Amortization	Monthly Payment	Principal Balance at End of Period
1	4%	30	$ 477.42	$ 98,238.96
2	6	29	596.32	96,942.24
3	8	28	723.92	95,975.59
4	9	27	790.00	95,097.78
5-30	9	26	790.00	.00

And this is what the monthly payments would be if interest rates on a $100,000, 7½% ARM dropped one-half percentage point every year for five years:

Year	Rate	Years of Amortization	Monthly Payment	Principal Balance at End of Period
1	7½%	30	$ 629.29	$ 89,170.35
2	7	29	599.34	88,189.10
3	6½	28	570.60	87,040.40
4	6	27	543.12	85,709.18
5	5½	26	516.95	84,181.67
6-30	5	25	492.12	.00

Checklist for Comparing ARMs

After you've prequalified for the amount of money you may borrow, use this work sheet to assess a lender's adjustable-rate mortgage (ARM) offering.

Lender's name _____

Telephone number_____

Down payment required   _____%

Beginning interest rate (APR)   _____%

Points   _____%

Beginning payment $_____

Lifetime cap on interest rate?   _____%

Periodic cap on the interest rate?   ____yes ____no

What is the cap?   _____%

How often can payment be adjusted?   _____

Is there a cap on payment?   ____yes ____no

What is the cap?   _____%

Does loan permit negative amortization?   ____yes ____no

How much negative amortization is allowed
    relative to the original loan amount?
    For example, can mortgage balance grow to
    105% of original loan, 110%, and so on?   _____

Loan is tied to which index?

    ____ 1-year Treasury securities ____ 3-year Treasury securities

    ____ 5-year Treasury securities ____ Other:_____

    ____ Federal Housing Board's National Average Contract Rate
        series for closed loans

Number of adjustments loan calls for_____

First adjustment occurs   _____ months/years

Second adjustment occurs _____ months/years

Third adjustment occurs   _____ months/years

Can loan be converted to a fixed-rate?   ____yes ____no

Under what circumstances?_____

Cost of conversion option $_____

Can loan be prepaid in whole or in part at
    anytime without penalty?   ____yes ____no

If yes, what are the conditions? _____

Is loan assumable by a qualified buyer?   ____yes ____no

Adjustable-rate mortgages sold to major investors in the secondary market—so-called *conforming ARMs*—*must* have periodic and lifetime limits on interest rate increases. Most ARMs today are sold by their originators; most limit interest-rate increases or decreases with periodic and lifetime caps.

Caps on payment

Payment caps limit payment increases to percentage of the previous payment.

Payment caps can result in "negative amortization" when rising interest rates call for payments higher than the cap would permit (see the earlier discussion of negative amortization under GPMs). At some point, you will be required to begin making monthly payments large enough to pay off all the principal and interest you now owe over what remains of the loan term. When the day arrives, you could find (assuming rates kept increasing during earlier adjustment periods) that the new monthly payment required to repay a bigger loan over a shortened term is very large indeed.

ARMs with caps on payments are rare today for two main reasons: They aren't a good deal for most buyers, and secondary-market purchasers of mortgages are reluctant to buy them after having been burned by higher-than-average foreclosure rates in the past.

Three Other Things to Ask About

There are three other things you should ask about when shopping for an ARM.

Assumability

Will you be able to transfer the mortgage to a prospective buyer under the same terms? By assuming the mortgage, the buyer takes on primary liability for the unpaid balance of your existing mortgage or deed of trust against the property. The lender usually must approve the buyer's assumption of liability in order for you to be released from obligation.

Convertibility

Can you convert the ARM to a fixed-rate mortgage? A convertible ARM may enable you to lock in a lower rate at some future point. Expect to pay extra for an ARM with a conversion clause—via a higher-rate, an upfront fee, a conversion charge imposed on the date you make the change or some combination of these charges. Some ARM contracts permit you to do this at a predetermined time, commonly after the end of the first adjustment period. When you convert, the new rate generally is the current market rate for fixed-rate mortgages.

ARMs purchased by Fannie Mae may permit you to convert to a 15- or 30-year fixed-rate mortgage by paying 1% of the original loan plus an additional $250. The new loan would carry the going market rate. Alternatively, you may be able to pay a smaller fee in return for a fixed-rate loan about one-half percentage point higher than the going rate.

The Whole Truth

Lenders must provide you with a "Truth in Lending Disclosure Statement" within three days after they receive your application for financing. Use it to double-check important information about your proposed loan. The statement shows you the annual percentage rate (APR), total finance charges, amount financed, total number of payments, amount of scheduled monthly payment, late payment charges, prepayment penalty (if one applies), and applicable assumption restrictions.

Prepayment

Will you have to pay a fee or penalty if you refinance or pay off the ARM early? Prepayment penalties sometimes are negotiable before you sign the loan documents. In many cases, however, you will be permitted to pay off the ARM loan at any time, in full or in part, without penalty.

Two-Step Mortgages

A two-step mortgage allows you to borrow at a lower initial rate for the first five years. At the end of

Two-step loans can be attractive to first-time buyers, foreign service and military buyers, and those who are regularly relocated by their employers.

the fifth year, the interest rate is reset for the remaining 23 years of the loan. The new rate is based on a formula tied to ten-year Treasury securities. Another two-step mortgage makes an adjustment after seven years but is otherwise identical to the 5/23 loan. Two-step loans can be attractive to first-time buyers, foreign service and military buyers, and those who are regularly relocated by their employers.

Advantages

Monthly payments are lower in the early years relative to a 30-year fixed-rate mortgage. Two-step mortgages are available for as little as 10% down. Borrowers are assured fixed-rate financing at the end of the fifth or seventh year—at no additional charge—and do not have to requalify. Any interest rate increase at the end of five or seven years is subject to a six-percentage-point cap above the initial rate.

Disadvantages

You pay for the convenience and flexibility with a higher interest rate. If you don't sell after five or seven years, the two-step mortgage could end up being more costly than a traditional 30-year loan.

Seven-Year Balloon Mortgage With Refinancing Option

When periodic payments aren't enough to pay off principal and interest over the life of a loan, a remaining balance, or balloon payment, will be due. Balloons can be fixed-rate or adjustable-rate loans. Fannie Mae's seven-year balloon is treated as an ARM because it carries a refinance option. In most cases, the balloon lender has no obligation to help a borrower obtain a loan to pay off the expiring balloon mortgage.

Advantages

Interest rates on seven-year balloons are lower than going rates on 30-year fixed-rate mortgages. Monthly payments are based on 30-year amortization—that is, monthly principal and interest payments would pay off the debt in 30 years. The balloon can be refinanced with a 23-year fixed-rate mortgage in most cases.

Buyers who stay in their homes less than seven years will pay less than they would have with a 30-year fixed-rate loan. If their plans change, they should be able to refinance without requalifying, providing the rate for the new loan is calculated to be no more than five points higher than the balloon-note rate.

Monthly payments can be lowered with a temporary buy-down. Lenders may permit borrowers or builders to buy down initial loan interest rates. A typical charge is 1% of the mortgage loan amount for each one-quarter-point reduction in the interest rate. (The less time you stay in the home, the less you benefit from buying down the rate.)

Disadvantages

You could lose the right to refinance by falling behind on monthly payments or by putting a lien on the property. In addition, if interest rates rise significantly by refinancing time, you could be turned down. If the new rate is more than 5% above the balloon-note rate, you could be required to requalify for the new higher rate and have your home reappraised.

You will be charged fees and costs to refinance.

Discount ARMs Require Caution

As the name implies, "discount" ARMs are offered at initial rates below the sum of index rate plus margin. The discounted rate lasts until the end of the first

The cost of a permanent buy-down of the interest rate is usually passed along to the buyer by way of a higher price tag on the property.

adjustment period set out in the mortgage contract. Discount ARMs may carry large initial loan fees and possibly extra points, both of which serve to increase overall loan costs.

Discount ARMs are called buy-downs when the lender is paid a lump sum at settlement in exchange for a lower rate to the buyer. (The payment may be designated as so many "points".) Buy-downs can be permanent or temporary and may be paid for by sellers, builders or buyers. The cost of a permanent builder or seller buy-down is usually passed along to the buyer by way of a higher price tag on the property. (Fixed-rate loans can be bought down, too. In such cases, the borrower gets a discounted rate that gradually increases to the agreed-on fixed rate, often over a three-year period.)

Discount ARMs can give unwary borrowers payment shock. If the ARM has a periodic rate cap, you may find it applies only to adjustments made after the discounted rate expires. As a result, there is actually no cap on the first adjustment. Let's see what could happen to your monthly payment with a discount ARM:

- **loan amount:** $100,000

- **index rate:** 3%

- **adjustment margin:** 2%

- **regular ARM rate:** 5% with two-point annual cap; $537 monthly payment during first year

- **discount ARM rate:** 3% with no cap on first annual adjustment, 2% annual cap thereafter; $422 monthly payment during first year.

If the index rate sticks at 3%, your monthly payment will increase $115 to $537 in the second year when the discount ends. If the index rate increases 2% during the first year, when the first annual adjustment is made 2% will be added to the 5% undiscounted index-plus-margin rate, making your new rate 7%. Your second-year payment jumps to $658—an increase of $236 a month.

You could end up paying more on a discount ARM than you would on a regular adjustable-rate loan if the full index-plus-margin rate is higher than going ARM rates to begin with. In most cases the discount period is too short to offset the higher base rate you would have to carry during the remaining term of the loan.

Discount ARMs can give unwary borrowers payment shock. A periodic rate cap may apply only to adjustments made after the discounted rate expires.

Government Backed-Loans

FmHA Guaranteed Home Loans

In addition to making various types of loans to farmers and rural businesses, the Farmers Home Administration (FmHA) guarantees fixed-rate home loans by private lenders to qualified low- to moderate-income individuals and families. (FmHA also makes direct loans and insures, rather than guarantees, others.)

To qualify, you must live in the home you buy, build or repair, it must be situated in an area defined by the FmHA as rural, and you must have been unable to obtain a mortgage loan with a reasonable interest rate from a private lender.

You will be expected to pay for title insurance, credit reports and other loan-closing costs, but most of these expenses can be rolled into the loan.

Apply to the FmHA county office in the area where the home is or will be located. FmHA offices are listed under "Department of Agriculture" in the "U.S. Government" section of telephone directories. Office addresses can be obtained by writing to the Farmers Home Administration, U.S. Department of Agriculture, Washington, D.C. 20250.

FHA lenders will qualify you using a set of debt-to-income ratios a bit more generous than those applied by mortgage lenders making conventional loans.

FHA-Insured Home Loans

The Federal Housing Authority insures a wide variety of mortgages, including fixed-rates, ARMs, GEMs and GPMs. Down payments are low—5% or less. You can be charged an origination fee for services of up to 1% of the loan amount, and you are not restricted from paying points. The FHA doesn't set the interest rate on loans it insures, so you'll need to shop around for the best rate.

The FHA limits the amount it will insure to whichever is less: 95% of the local median home price or 75% of the loan limit set by the Federal Home Loan Mortgage Corporation (Freddie Mac), a large buyer and reseller of mortgages. In 1993, the cap could be as high as $151,725 in some high-cost areas such as Los Angeles, San Francisco and Washington, D.C. An FHA-approved lender can determine the cap in your area.

FHA-mortgage insurance premiums usually will be collected in one lump sum at settlement. For single-family homes (what the agency calls Section 203(b) property) the premium is 3% of the loan amount. You may be allowed to increase the size of your mortgage to cover the cost. (Loans repaid at an early date may entitle you to a refund.)

FHA lenders will qualify you using a set of debt-to-income ratios a bit more generous than those applied by mortgage lenders making conventional loans. Family housing expenses may not exceed 29% of gross income and total indebtedness may not go over 41% of income. Rules permit lenders to make exceptions where there are "significant compensating factors." Just what those factors may be isn't set out in black and white, so don't rule out a low-down-payment FHA loan without checking with more than one major lender in your area.

Other FHA-loan features are:

- **You are allowed to include all closing costs in the mortgage amount.** This is a change from 1991 and

1992 requirements, when FHA borrowers were required to pay 43% of those costs in cash (see Chapter 3 for information on how points and other loan-origination fees are handled for tax purposes).

- **FHA loans are assumable.** In most cases the FHA will require a credit check on the assuming home buyer.

- **Loans carry no prepayment penalty.** You can make additional payments at any time.

- **FHA loans are available from FHA-approved lenders,** including savings institutions, mortgage bankers and commercial banks. Mortgage bankers, however, do the bulk of the business.

    So-called direct-endorsement lenders can process your loan, which should reduce the time to loan approval. (You'll have to ask whether a lender is direct-endorsement—lenders won't tell you.) And, because appraisals are the bottleneck in loan approvals, you'll want to find out whether a direct-endorsement lender has an appraiser on staff.

VA-Guaranteed Loans

The Veterans Administration protects lenders against losses on mortgage loans made to eligible veterans by guaranteeing the timely payment of principal and interest on mortgage securities backed by VA loans. VA-guaranteed loans are, for the most part, fixed-rate loans with repayment periods of as long as 30 years and one month. (The VA is currently testing an adjustable-rate mortgage.)

Until recently, interest rates were set by the VA at a level somewhat lower than those on conventional mortgages. Rates are now set by lenders, not by the government. In conjunction with this change, the VA will permit veterans to pay points but not to finance them in their loans. In the past, veterans were not permitted to pay more than one point; this kept them from paying an effective rate higher than the VA's maximum. VA retains the right to go back to setting the rate if it appears that "negotiated" interest rates (agreed on by veterans and lenders) haven't benefitted veteran home buyers.

In most cases, no down payment is required by the VA. You'll have to fork over cash if you can't qualify for the monthly payments, if you want a graduated-payment loan, or if the cost of the property is more than the VA establishes as its "reasonable value."

The VA sets no limit on the size of mortgage it will guarantee, but Freddie Mac, Fannie Mae and other investors in the secondary market do. As a rule, your entitlement (the guarantee amount) must be at least 25% of the loan amount. If you are also making a cash down payment, that amount plus the entitlement must equal 25%. The VA does have a maximum guarantee, however. It will guarantee no more than $46,000 on loans over $144,000. Using your full VA entitlement for a no-down-payment loan, the maximum you could borrow would be $184,000.

You will be responsible for the following closing costs: discount points, appraisal, credit report, survey, title search, recording fees and VA funding fee. You should not be charged brokerage fees for your loan. On no-down-payment loans, the VA collects a one-time funding fee equal to 1.25% of the loan at settlement. (This is reduced to 0.75% of the loan amount with a 5% down payment, to 0.5% when the down payment is 10%.) You will pay a higher funding fee if you are a reservist, if you borrow to refinance (interest rate reduction refinancing loans, or IRRRLs) or if you buy a manufactured home. Certain disabled veterans may be exempt from paying.

Loan Opportunities

For the first time, members of the National Guard and military reservists with six or more years of service will be eligible for VA-guaranteed loans. They will pay a higher funding fee. In addition, a direct loan program for American Indian veterans buying on trust lands (reservations) should be available by the end of 1993.

You will have to negotiate paying loan points with the seller (see Chapter 3 for a discussion of points). Until 1993, veterans weren't allowed to pay more than one point (an origination fee) in connection with their VA loan. This restriction eliminated bargaining and left sellers to pick up the tab. (Conventional and FHA-insured loans impose no restrictions on how points are to be divided between buyers and sellers.) The VA's limitation may have saved a veteran money, but it probably also narrowed his or her choice of homes during periods when lenders were charging several points to make VA mortgages. At such times, sellers may have refused to consider VA contracts because they realized that points beyond the 1% cap would come from their own pockets.

VA loans can be paid off in full at any time without penalty. You can prepay principal when you make regular monthly payments so long as additional payments are $100 or more. (If you have an old mortgage and your monthly installment is less than $100, the prepayment must be at least as much as the payment.)

If you buy a new home that was appraised by the VA prior to construction and inspected along the way to ensure compliance, the property may be covered by the VA's structural-defect program. Builders of such homes must warrant that they were built according to the approved plans and specifications. A similar builder warranty may be provided on new manufactured (mobile or modular) homes (see Chapter 9 for information on builders' extended warranties and the VA/FHA structural-defect program).

Regional VA offices can provide you with information on eligibility requirements and other details. Look

More From the VA

• •

In addition to guaranteeing traditional fixed-rate loans, the VA also guarantees graduated payment mortgages (GPMs), buy-downs, growing-equity mortgages (GEMs), energy-efficient mortgages (EEMs), and interest rate reduction refinancing loans (IRRRLs). VA also guarantees its new adjustable-rate mortgage with a five-percentage-point lifetime cap and one-point annual cap.

If you are self-employed, involved in a divorce or otherwise unable to qualify for a mortgage originated by a bank, thrift or mortgage company, one alternative is seller financing.

in the phone book under "U.S. Government" for the VA office nearest you.

Other Types of Financing

Those who don't fit the mold designed by secondary-market mortgage buyers such as Fannie Mae, Freddie Mac and Ginnie Mae can have a hard time buying a home. If you are self-employed, involved in a divorce or otherwise unable to qualify for a mortgage originated by a bank, thrift or mortgage company that will turn around and sell your loan to the secondary market, one alternative is to look for property being sold with seller financing. Another is to seek out a mortgage broker who will try to locate an investor to buy your note.

Obviously, the more a buyer has to pay in interest each month, the less house he can afford to buy. So when interest rates are high, many would-be purchasers can't qualify for long-term mortgages big enough to buy many homes listed for sale. As a result, sellers must step in to fill the gap between down payment and first mortgage. In the 1970s and early '80s, this type of lending was called "creative financing" and was, for the most part, a euphemism for below-market-rate financing subsidized by sellers. Sellers who took back below-market-rate notes in effect discounted the prices of their homes.

With rates now hovering at 20-year lows, sellers who own homes free and clear of debt have become more willing (and in some instances, even eager) to finance purchases. In such cases, a seller is doing essentially the same thing as a commercial lender—carrying the entire note and securing it with a first mortgage or deed of trust. What's in it for sellers? When yields on certificates of deposits, money-market funds and short-term bonds are so low, a seller may earn much more on a note secured by property—in this case a former home. He may be able to get an *above-market* rate (more than the going long-term mortgage rates), enough to compensate for the added risk and complications of having documents drawn and executed. Where homes aren't selling promptly, one being offered with seller financing may pull more prospects—particularly those who can afford to buy but who are nevertheless outside institutional lending parameters for one reason or another.

First Mortgage Financing

As a buyer, the appeal of this kind of financing lies in its flexibility. Assuming documents are properly and carefully drawn, you'll be in the same basic situation you would have been had you obtained a mortgage or deed of trust from an institutional lender.

Since you are likely to be trading a higher price for favorable terms, be prepared for more lengthy negotiations. What rate you pay, how often and how much, prepayment and late-payment penalties, and whether the note carries a due-on-sale clause are all subject to bargaining. To protect your interests, you will need your own representatives—a buyer's broker and an attorney—to assist you in negotiating and reviewing documents.

In their book, *Sell Your Property Fast,* Bill Broadbent and George Rosenberg point to four areas, in addition to the interest rate and payment frequency, likely to require negotiation and compromise between buyer and seller:

Due-on-sale provision

This clause enables a lender to demand full payment of the remaining loan balance should you sell or transfer all or part of the property without her consent. You want a loan without a due-on-sale clause, because your loan would be assumable. The seller (soon-to-be lender) will want to include this clause to protect her stake in the property.

Possible compromise: A due-on-sale provision that gives the seller/lender the right to approve a new buyer

Postpone the balloon payment as long as possible. The more time you have, the better your chances of refinancing at favorable terms and before the deadline.

after checking character references, credit and loan-paying ability.

Balloon payment

Though payments on seller carry-back loans are commonly structured to amortize principal and interest over 30 years, most are due in full—hence the name balloon—three to seven years after the sale. Because the seller/lender doesn't want her sale proceeds tied up too long, you should expect a balloon payment as part of the deal. Your concern should focus on your ability to refinance the loan when it comes due. Suppose rates are much higher then or your spouse is unemployed. Then what?

Possible compromise: Postpone the balloon payment as long as possible. The more time you have, the better your chances of refinancing at favorable terms and before the deadline. The loan balance will be lower, too. Try for ten years and negotiate a protective clause into the note giving you the right to extend the term for a specified period of time. You could suggest a two-year extension, for example, coupled with a higher rate, a bigger monthly payment, a one-time partial payment on the balloon, or even a combination of those.

Late-payment charge

The seller will want a penalty big enough and soon enough, say 6% of the payment amount if payment is not received within five to ten days, to discourage delinquency. You don't consider yourself a deadbeat and you don't want the clause.

Possible compromise: Keep the seller's penalty at 6% but extend the time to a more reasonable 15 days.

Closing costs

You want the seller to pay all closing costs. The seller wants you to pay them.

Possible compromise: Split them equally. Even if that's not acceptable, suggest the 50/50 split as a starting point for further negotiations.

Seller financing isn't restricted to situations in which the owner has no mortgage debt. Seller carry-back second mortgages and wraparound loans are options when there is an assumable mortgage on the property.

Carry-Back Second Mortgage

Here a note, secured by a second mortgage or trust deed, closes the gap between the price of the property and the combined amounts of the down payment and the balance due on an assumable first mortgage. The interest rate is negotiated between seller and buyer and may be more or less than the going rate on commercially originated second mortgages.

As Broadbent and Rosenberg make clear in their book, carry-back financing can be a "win-win transaction for both buyer and seller." That's because a seller/lender may be able to earn a higher rate on a carry-back note than he could earn elsewhere, and the buyer/borrower's overall cost of funds may be no more than if he got a loan from an institutional lender.

You will want to be sure the first mortgage you intend to assume is, indeed, assumable and what, if any, conditions or fees the first-mortgage lender or servicer may impose on you or the seller. You could be required to get approval by passing certain income and credit tests, for example. Failure to fulfill the requirements could cause the lender or servicer to call in the loan using a due-on-sale provision in the mortgage.

Payments on seller carry-backs typically are figured as though the loan would be paid back over 25 or 30 years, but loans are due in full, in the form of a balloon payment, three to ten years after the sale. This means you will have to refinance by that time.

Should a buyer default and foreclosure result, the seller/lender gets reimbursed after the first-mortgage holder's claim is satisfied. If a property ultimately sells for less than (or close to) the sales price it commanded when the carry-back second note was placed on it, the seller/lender could lose money.

Wrap-Around Mortgage

When there is an existing, legally assumable first mortgage on a property you want to buy using a down payment plus seller carry-back second (see above for discussion of carry-back notes secured by second mortgages or trust deeds), you can expect a savvy seller or agent to start throwing around terms like "wrap" or "wraparound." The reason: Such financing may provide a better return to the seller. Wraps—like other forms of creative financing—typically carry balloon payments.

Instead of financing the second-trust or second-mortgage note, the seller may suggest carrying back what is called an "All-Inclusive Trust Deed" note for an amount equal to the assumable first plus equity. The rate you will be offered on the wrap will be less than what you would have paid for a carry-back second and more than the rate on the assumable first. You'll be making one payment to the seller/lender covering the

More on Mortgages

- *A Consumer's Guide to Home Buying & Mortgage Financing,* by Peter J. Anderson (Anderson Publishing, P.O. Box 5675, Saginaw, Mich. 48603; or call 800-468-7331; $19.95, including shipping and handling).

- *A Guide to Homeownership* (Fannie Mae, Consumer Education Group, 3900 Wisconsin Ave., N.W., Washington, D.C. 20016-2899; free). Fannie Mae also makes available a useful brochure, "Unraveling The Mortgage Loan Mystery" (free).

- *Consumer Handbook on Adjustable Rate Mortgages* (Publications Services, Board of Governors of the Federal Reserve Systems, MS-138, Washington, D.C. 20551; free; also available from lenders).

- *How to Shop for a Mortgage* (a brochure, Mortgage Bankers Association of America, 1125 15th St., N.W., Washington, D.C. 20005; free).

- *The Common-Sense Mortgage, How to Cut the Cost of Home Ownership by $100,000 or More,* by Peter G. Miller (Harper Collins Publishers).

assumable first and the amount you'd otherwise be paying for the carry-back second—at a blended rate. This puts more money in the seller's pocket and also earns her the benefit of principal reduction that is occurring as payments are made on the first. The blended rate plus the value of principal reduction on the assumable first boosts the seller's overall yield or return on the all-inclusive trust deed.

Wraps remove the seller/lender's concern that the buyer won't make payments on the assumable first loan because the buyer will now make just one payment—to the seller. The seller then makes the payment on the first loan. Broadbent and Rosenberg suggest that you, as buyer/borrower, protect your interests by requiring the seller to select a neutral collection agency where you can send your wrap payment. The agent then becomes responsible for making payments on the assumable first loan and disbursing remaining funds to the seller.

> ## *More on Seller Financing*
> •
>
> *Sell Your Property Fast: How to Take Back a Mortgage Without Being Taken,* by Bill Broadbent and George Rosenberg (Who's Who in Creative Real Estate, P.O. Box 23275, Ventura, Cal. 93002; 800-729-5147; $25, plus $3 for handling and shipping; $23 total for readers who mention *Kiplinger's Buying & Selling a Home*). This book addresses take-back mortgages in detail from a seller's viewpoint. But it should reward anyone who intends to buy a home with seller financing and is willing to study and act on what the authors propose.

Land Contract

Also known as a conditional sales contract, contract for sale, or contract for deed, this type of financing is actually an installment sale whereby the buyer gets only the *right* to obtain absolute ownership to the property. The buyer doesn't get title to the property but must wait until some point agreed on in the contract—usually after a certain amount has been paid towards principal or when the contract is fully paid. Often that's years down the road. In the interim, the seller retains what is known as "bare legal title."

Much can go wrong with land contracts. As part of

the deal, the buyer may agree to take over payments on the seller's existing mortgage—an arrangement that a mortgage lender may contend violates the "due on sale" provision of its mortgage contract. Lenders may be able to foreclose on such mortgages, leaving the buyer/borrower with nothing to show for his payments except a worthless contract. Never sign a land contract before obtaining expert legal advice.

Equity Sharing

In a shared-equity arrangement, the home buyer and an investor—frequently a parent, relative or friend—buy a house or condo apartment together. It is one way for first-time buyers who otherwise couldn't afford to buy, or who wouldn't qualify for a mortgage, to do so. For example, rather than making a loan or gift to help a child into homeownership, parents become part owners and rent their share of the place to the child. As investors, the parents share in the appreciation of the house. As landlords, they also get rental income and the tax deductions that go along with rental real estate (for a discussion of the investment aspects of equity sharing, see Chapter 23).

Both parties enter into a contract that specifies who pays what portion of the down payment, mortgage interest, property taxes and monthly costs, how much rent the child will pay, and how equity will be split when the house is sold. Parents could make the down payment and pay most of the mortgage interest and taxes. Or equity could be split 50/50, with each party putting up half the down payment and agreeing to pay half of ongoing expenses. The possibilities are limited only by the needs and desires of the contracting parties.

Making a Mortgage Choice

Deciding which mortgage is best requires a close look at your present circumstances, future earnings and financial goals. Clear forecasting of economic conditions a few years down the road would help, too—but don't hold your decision hostage to your predictions about interest rates and economic cycles. That's something even experts fail to do with precision. Instead keep your needs in the forefront. Do you intend to stay put for many years? Then getting the best interest rate is important. Paying 7.5% rather than 8% on a $100,000, 30-year fixed-rate mortgage will save you $34.50 each month. Tuck that amount each month in a mutual fund and you've saved $414 a year, not counting long-term appreciation and compounding (see the accompanying table).

On the other hand, say you plan to put the home up for sale three to five years hence. Then points and closing costs (and the ability to pay off the mortgage without penalty) are more important than getting the absolute lowest available rate.

For most home buyers, the choices are these:

- Will your down payment be small or large?

- Do you want a long-term or shorter-term loan?

- A fixed-rate or adjustable-rate mortgage?

- Will you pay points for the lowest-rate mortgage or will you shop for a loan with few or no points and therefore a higher rate?

Go for Equity?

Another way to look at the problem is to ask yourself what you want from your home in addition to its shelter value. Choose a mortgage that helps move you closer to those objectives.

Suppose ten years from now you will need a home-equity loan to finance college educations for your children. From your perspective, tax benefits from mortgage interest payments are less of a priority than equity buildup. You could accomplish this by making a large down payment, of course, and borrowing it back

Don't hold your decision hostage to your predictions about interest rates and economic cycles. Even experts fail to do that with precision. Instead keep your needs in the forefront.

An ARM and Fixed-Rate Example

Let's say that you are expecting a job-related move within three to five years. You could consider a 30-year, three-year adjustable-rate mortgage (ARM) with a 2% periodic-adjustment cap and a 5% lifetime cap. Assume that you could get this ARM with an initial interest rate that is three percentage points lower than what you could get with a 30-year fixed-rate loan (points paid at settlement are equal). The following figures show how you would fare with an upward adjustment of two percentage points at the end of year three.

Over a five-year period, monthly payments on the three-year ARM would cost you nearly $9,000 less than those on the fixed-rate loan, and you would have reduced your mortgage balance by $2,285 more than you would have with the fixed-rate loan. If rates on the ARM increased less than two percentage points in the third year—or fell—savings would be greater.

5%, 30-Year, Three-Year ARM $100,000 Mortgage

Year	Interest rate	Payment	Balance
1	5%	$ 537	$ 98,525
2	5	537	96,974
3	5	537	95,344
4	7	656	94,109
5	7	656	92,785
6	7	656	91,366

8%, 30-Year, Fixed-Rate $100,000 Mortgage

Year	Interest rate	Payment	Balance
1	8%	$ 734	$ 99,165
2	8	734	98,260
3	8	734	97,280
4	8	734	96,219
5	8	734	95,070
6	8	734	93,825

as necessary. If that's not possible, you could choose a 15- or 20-year loan—using the mortgage as a form of forced savings, as it were. Or you could opt for a fixed-rate 30-year mortgage and make additional voluntary payments against the principal. (Before you choose the latter, determine whether your loan contract would permit the lender to charge you a prepayment penalty. If so, and you can't get that provision removed, chances are you'd do better not prepaying but investing that extra sum elsewhere.)

Before embarking on a major campaign of prepaying principal, however, give thought to alternative uses of the money. What kind of return on your money could you anticipate from stocks, bonds, mutual funds and other types of investments? How does that compare with the amount of equity you could "accrue" in your home over the same time period? Keep in mind that once you put money into repaying your mortgage, you will earn no current income, and you can get it out only by borrowing it back via a home-equity loan or some sort of refinancing.

The Vanishing Point

From time to time, the points (prepaid interest charges on mortgages) you will be asked to pay to get a mortgage loan shrink or even vanish. This can be a boon because you can borrow for less and drive a harder bargain on price.

In late 1992, for instance, lenders were sometimes waiving points on conventional loans. (Points on FHA-insured and deeply discounted adjustable-rate mortgages remained customary.) Lenders could afford to forgo points because the yield curve was skewed in their favor: Lenders were paying 3% or 4% for money they could lend out to would-be homeowners at 8% or better. That was profit enough without points. Lenders were also finding that borrowers were shopping hard to minimize closing costs. Should you take a zero-point loan? The irony is that if you plan to stay in the house,

Should you take a zero-point loan? If you plan to stay in the house, it may be wiser to pay a point or two to get the lower interest rate.

it may be wiser to pay a point or two to get the lower interest rate. Pay one point ($1,000) on a $100,000 mortgage with a rate of 8.25% instead of 8.5% and you break even in four years, assuming a 28% tax bracket.

If the spread between short-term and 30-year rates close to around three percentage points, mortgage points will return.

Whatever your decision, keep in mind that as circumstances change and interest rates rise and fall, your initial loan choice in most cases isn't set in stone. You can refinance or take out a home-equity loan, even sell and move on. You don't have to bet right on the cheapest loan to come out ahead in the long run. Buy the home you like in a good neighborhood, and odds are it will appreciate modestly in line with inflation over the coming years.

Finding a Lender, Getting a Loan

After you've picked the type of mortgage best suited to your needs, you're ready to find a lender.

As noted in the previous chapter, lender name recognition and location are less important than the quality of the deal. A decade or two ago, finding a mortgage didn't require much comparison shopping. Loans were fixed-rate and rates didn't vary much, so most people dealt with a local institution they already had a relationship with. Today things are more complex.

Despite a plethora of loans and lenders, comparison shopping has been eased by the emergence of computer-loan origination systems and mortgage-reporting services—firms that survey major lenders in metropolitan areas every week or so and publish information sheets on who is offering what loans on what terms. Both can help you narrow the field. One caveat if you rely on a real estate agent, broker or firm for help in finding a lender: Because of recent changes, the Real Estate Settlement Procedures Act (RESPA) does not require agents using computer loan origination (CLO) systems to maintain a minimum number of lenders on the system, nor does the revised law limit the amount you can be charged for using such a service.

True, you will be given a written disclosure state-

Despite a plethora of loans and lenders, comparison shopping has been eased by the emergence of computer-loan origination systems and mortgage-reporting services.

You'll save time dealing with the same company that prequalified you, but you aren't obliged to do so.

ment along these lines: "You are advised that you may avoid this fee entirely if you approach a lender or mortgage broker directly. Additionally, lower mortgage rates or other lower fees may be available from other mortgage lenders who are not listed on this computer system." This is technology tuned to benefit real estate agents, not consumers. So our advice remains:

Shop for lenders offering the best deals. Check with several mortgage companies and use one or more reporting services. Rely on your own efforts, lots of telephone calls and possibly some old-fashioned legwork.

If there isn't a reporting service covering your area, begin the search at your own bank or savings and loan. Real estate agents have extensive contacts in the local lending community but may be less than enthusiastic about giving you free advice when they can charge you for tapping their CLO system. The local board of Realtors may have surveyed lenders in the community. Ask the board for names of s&l's, banks, mortgage companies and mortgage brokers, but don't be surprised if the board refers you back to your agent.

If you were prequalified by a lender or mortgage company, by all means determine whether the firm can offer you a competitive deal. You'll save time dealing with the same company, but you aren't obliged to do so.

The Role of the Secondary Market

Most home mortgages are sold once they have been closed. The buyers—organizations with such names as Fannie Mae, Ginnie Mae and Freddie Mac, as well as a number of private firms—make up what is known as the secondary market. It acts as a conduit, linking the world of the home buyer to Wall Street by purchasing mortgages from lenders and reselling them, or securities backed by them, to investors. Because it is so big, the secondary market affects what loans are available and what buyers have to do to get them.

By selling the loans they originate, savings institutions, mortgage companies and commercial banks get their cash back to reinvest, and they also earn fees for continuing to service the loans. Those who buy the loans, usually government or government-backed agencies or large mortgage bankers, get the right to receive the principal and interest paid by borrowers. They, in turn, package their mortgages and sell securities backed by the pooled loans. Pension funds and other institutional investors are the biggest market for mortgage-backed securities.

The secondary market helps redistribute available mortgage funds by buying mortgages in regions where the demand from homeowners outstrips lenders' deposits and selling them in other markets where available credit exceeds loan demand.

Sources of Mortgage Money

The lender you choose will take your loan application, follow through on credit checks, property appraisal, and other details leading to settlement and transfer of title. (These days, a "lender" is likely to be a loan originator who immediately sells your loan and others to secondary-market mortgage buyers and repackagers such as Freddie Mac or Fannie Mae, as described above, rather than an institution that lends you money and holds your loan in its own portfolio of investments.) An originator will have the promissory note prepared—establishing the amount of debt, terms of repayment and interest rate you have contracted to pay—and have the mortgage or deed of trust drawn to secure the property for the lender should you default on the note.

Independent Mortgage Companies

Independent mortgage companies—such as Countrywide Credit Industries, to name one of the largest—make just over half of all home mortgages, including most VA-guaranteed and FHA-insured loans. Mortgage bankers work closely with the secondary market by selling their loans to agencies buying standardized, or conforming home mortgages. You will be expected to meet secondary-market standards covering creditworthiness, down-payment size and appraisals. Once your application is approved, you will get a loan commitment binding the lender for a specified length of time to the rate and terms set out in the contract. Originating mortgage bankers are considered lenders of record even after their loans have been sold, so initially you will send monthly payments (of interest, principal and escrow) to the originating mortgage company.

Locate a Mortgage Broker
• •

State and local boards of Realtors may be willing to give you names of mortgage brokers active in a particular area. Or, contact the National Association of Mortgage Brokers, 706 E. Bell Rd., Suite 101, Phoenix, Ariz. 85022 (602-992-6181).

Savings Institutions

Savings and loan associations and savings banks originate close to a quarter of home mortgages. Most are conventional loans—those not guaranteed by the VA or FmHA, or insured by the FHA—and most conform to standards set by secondary-market agencies because these institutions, like mortgage bankers, sell the mortgages they originate.

Commercial Banks

Commercial banks are active in residential lending. Many have affiliations with mortgage bankers or operate their own mortgage banking subsidiaries. Banks also are a major supplier of loans for mobile-home buyers.

Mortgage Brokers

Mortgage brokers act as intermediaries. A broker keeps tabs on the mortgage market through ties to local, regional and national lenders, and can refer a prospective borrower to a mortgage banker, savings institution, commercial bank, or even an individual investor interested in buying mortgage paper. Brokers don't lend and can't approve loans or make loan commitments to borrowers.

If you are having trouble getting a loan, consider using a mortgage broker. You may pay a flat fee, or you may pay an additional point or so to the lender, who then pays the broker at settlement.

Credit Unions

Close to one-third of all credit unions make first-mortgage loans. You must be a member, however, and membership is often based on some criterion of affinity, such as residency in a given city or state, employment or membership in an association or club. Loans are generally available from the largest credit unions. If you are a credit union member or are eligible to become one, you may find the mortgage rates and terms it offers quite competitive.

Public Agencies

State and local housing finance agencies make below-market-rate financing available to eligible low-

Sources of Help

• **If you aren't able to locate the correct agency providing help to low- and moderate-income first-time buyers in your state,** contact the National Council of State Housing Agencies, Suite 438, 444 North Capitol St., N.W., Washington, D.C. 20001 (202-624-7710).

• **If you can't get credit from private providers of mortgage funds but you meet certain income and rural residency requirements,** you may be able to buy a home through the Farmers Home Administration's rural housing program. Contact the FmHA office in the county where you'd like to buy or build. Addresses of offices can be obtained by writing to the Administrator, FmHA, U.S. Department of Agriculture, Washington, D.C. 20250.

and moderate-income first-time buyers, through the sale of tax-exempt bonds.

Employers and Unions

Don't overlook your employer as a source of assistance. An employer may pay points, subsidize the interest rate or even act as lender. Such programs are most commonly available to employees who have been asked to relocate from areas where home prices are modest to areas where they are sky-high.

Unions are another possibility. The AFL-CIO offers what it calls "Union Privilege" to affiliated unions. Unions that sign on can make first-time home loans available to eligible members for as little as 3% down. (The other 2% is an unsecured loan from union-owned Amalgamated Bank of New York.) Interest rates are at or below national averages. What's more, buyers who sign up for the program, use a Century 21 agent and register the mortgage they select with Union Privilege may be eligible for a credit against origination fees.

Certain parts of the program are open to parents and children of union members.

Help for Union Members

• •

For information about the AFL-CIO's first-time home loan program for affiliated unions, contact your union or write to Union Privilege, AFL-CIO, 1444 Eye Street, N.W., Washington, D.C. 20005.

Using a Reporting Service

Reporting services provide details on a variety of mortgages, including conventional, FHA and VA loans. Some may include rates on second mortgages and other types of loans as well. You should be able to get a handle on the types of loans being offered (adjustable-rate and fixed-rate, for example), loan life spans, interest rates, points, and length of time the lender will guarantee the rate you're offered at application time. For adjustable-rate mortgages, look for information on the index base, adjustment margin, and periodic and lifetime caps.

Reports are updated on a regular basis, often weekly, and you should be able to buy just one or two. Many metropolitan newspapers publish abbreviated lists in weekly business or real estate sections (see the

Mortgage-Reporting Services

Listed below are firms that provide information about lenders in more than one state:

- **Gary Myers and Associates** (308 W. Erie St., Suite 300, Chicago, Ill. 60610; 800-472-6463 or 312-642-9000). Myers reports mortgage rates weekly for Boston; Chicago; Cincinnati; Detroit; Kansas City; New York City; Norwich, Conn.; Washington, D.C.; and all of California. Each report costs $22. Myers also provides rate information to some 200 newspapers in more than 44 states.

- **HSH Associates** (1200 Route 23, Butler, N.J. 07405; 800-873-2837 or 201-838-3330). HSH surveys more than 2,000 lenders weekly in more than 30 states and many metropolitan areas.

  Its *Homebuyer's Mortgage Kit* provides a list of lenders and information on at least three loans from each, including discount points, down payments, interest rates, annual percentage rate, terms and maximum mortgage amounts. The $20 kit contains a 44-page booklet, *How to Shop for Your Mortgage*. The booklet discusses the basics of mortgage financing, the loan process from application to closing, how to choose a mortgage, and various types of mortgages and features

that could save or cost you money. Work sheets are included.

PC Mortgage Update, an electronic version of the kit, is available for IBM or IBM-compatible PCs at the same price.

- *National Mortgage Weekly* (P.O. Box 360991, Cleveland, Ohio 44136; 216-273-6605; residents of Ohio and Michigan may call toll-free, 800-669-0133). NMW covers the greater Cleveland, Columbus and Detroit areas. The company surveys more than 80 lenders in each area. Subscribers pay $4 per week for one to 12 weeks, or $32 for 13 weeks.

- **Peeke LoanFax Inc.** (101 Chestnut St., Suite 200, Gaithersburg, Md. 20877; 301-840-5752). Peeke provides mortgage reports for metropolitan Washington, D.C., including northern Virginia and suburban Maryland. The report, issued daily by facsimile to subscribers, lists rates offered by 43 lenders. The cost is $15 per report; $50 for reports on five consecutive days.

  Residents of the Washington, D.C., metropolitan area can use a free, 24-hour, seven-day-a-week mortgage hotline (301-258-1000).

Rate quotes are usually guaranteed for a particular period; some are not guaranteed at all, giving the lender the right to charge you the current market rate on settlement day.

accompanying box for information about other mortgage-reporting services).

Fine-Tuning Your Choice

Try these tips for getting the best possible mortgage for you:

- **Use reports and other loan sources to identify the best loan prospects.** Discuss details with promising lenders over the phone or in person before making a final selection. Make sure advertised loans and rates are available.

- **Use the annual percentage rate (APR) to compare loans.** The APR is the cost of your mortgage loan expressed as a yearly rate. It reflects the effect of origination fees, points and (if applicable) mortgage insurance by adding them to the loan rate as though they were spread out over the term of the loan. Lenders often promote a particular mortgage loan by advertising the interest rate or the monthly payment. By law, they also must divulge the APR.

- **Find out how long an advertised or stated loan rate will stick.** In other words, if you applied for a loan today at an advertised rate, could the lender raise it tomorrow? At the end of 30 days? Would it be available at settlement 45 days or 60 days hence?

  Rate quotes are usually guaranteed for a particular period; some are not guaranteed at all, giving the lender the right to charge you the current market rate on settlement day. If the rate at closing is much higher, you conceivably could be shocked with "disqualification" at the eleventh hour.

- **When rates could be upwardly mobile, lock in the rate you want by paying a loan-commitment fee.** This charge ranges from 0.25% of the loan amount to as high as 1%. A lock-in guarantees you the rate quoted at the time of application for the lock-in period, commonly 45 to 60 days. Look for a lock-in that gives you the right to close at a lower rate if mortgage loan rates fall during that period.

The Loan Application Process

You've found the mortgage you want and you're ready for the next step: loan application. The process costs money, anywhere from $100 to $350 or so, usually nonrefundable. Lenders levy the fee to cover the costs of running credit reports, filling out mortgage-insurance applications, and the like. For budgetary reasons alone, you'll want to avoid multiple applications. But if you feel shaky about the prospects of approval, or want to play one lender against the other for the best rate, you may be tempted to apply to more than one. Don't do it. A lender will almost certainly discover that you've applied elsewhere. After all, you just gave the company the right to examine your credit history—including the names and dates of all recent credit-check inquiries. If you applied elsewhere or have been turned down, it will show up on the computer screen. You may be able to rescind a contract you signed, but using that right to obtain the lowest rate isn't kosher, and you won't get back nonrefundable fees. Worse, you could get turned down everywhere else as a result.

What to Expect

- **You will need raw material, and lots of it, for the application:** income and balance-sheet figures and evidence, copies of past income-tax returns, and the title to your car (to prove it either free of liens or encumbered by an auto loan). Take with you the paperwork you pulled together during the prequalifying process. Much of the information should be directly applicable.

More About "Lock-Ins"

A useful brochure, *A Consumer's Guide to Mortgage Lock-Ins,* is available free from the Federal Reserve Board. Write to Publication Services, Board of Governors of the Federal Reserve System, MS-138, Washington, D.C. 20551.

- **Be prepared to give the name and phone number of someone who can verify financial information about you**—most likely, your employer's personnel office. If you have substantial nonsalary income from investments, you'll be asked to substantiate this through an accountant, stockbroker, trust officer or similar source. If you are self-employed (a definition that could be triggered by as little as a 5% to 10% ownership stake in a closely held company you work for), you may be asked to submit financial information about the company.

- **Application forms are usually filled out during the interview,** with the help of a loan officer, but you could also fill them in at home and return them.

- **For conventional loans carrying private mortgage insurance (PMI),** check with your lender regarding the necessary documentation.

- **In addition to the application fee, you may be asked to pay a "loan origination fee" or "prepaid point"** —typically 1% of the loan amount—when you apply, before approval is made. This is just another way of charging you prepaid interest—the points you may have to pay at settlement.

- **Find out what will happen to your origination fee if the lender decides not to approve your loan.** Will the 1% origination fee be refunded? Get the answer in writing before you pay.

- **Check whether the quoted interest rate is guaranteed, and for how long.** If you think that interest rates may rise while your application is being processed, consider paying for a "lock-in," (above).

- **The federal Real Estate Settlement Procedures Act (RESPA) requires a lender to provide you with** a "good faith" estimate of closing costs once you complete a loan application or within three business days. The RESPA statement reflects the lender's experience in the area where your property is located. The estimate must include costs for such items as points, an appraisal, title search, title insurance, survey, recording of deeds and mortgages, and attorney's fees. You can ask for a hypothetical calculation of such items as property taxes and hazard insurance, based on your anticipated closing date (see discussion of settlement costs in Chapter 13).

Private Mortgage Insurance

Lenders usually require buyers getting conventional loans with down payments of less than 20% to carry insurance provided by a separate private mortgage-insurance company. The insurance is designed to protect lenders from losses in the event borrowers stop paying on their loans; premiums typically are paid by home buyers.

Insured, low-down-payment mortgages are more attractive—and less risky—investments than uninsured ones, and lenders who wish to sell low-down-payment loans must have them insured. FHA-insured and VA-guaranteed loans also protect lenders against borrower default.

Private mortgage insurance generally covers 20% to 25% of a first-mortgage loan. This permits lenders to make loans up to 90% or 95% of the appraised value of a home while taking about as much risk as they would assume making a loan of 71% to 72% of value. A loan-to-value ratio (LTV or LV) expresses the relationship between the amount of a loan and the value of property being pledged as security. For example, on a $100,000, 90% LTV-ratio loan, the borrower making a 10% down payment assumes the first $10,000 risk of any loss in property value. The insurer takes 20% on the remaining $90,000, or $18,000. The lender then is left holding the bag only for losses beyond $28,000. In other words, the down payment plus insurance togeth-

Lenders usually require buyers getting conventional loans with down payments of less than 20% to carry insurance provided by a separate private mortgage-insurance company.

er serve to reduce the lender's loan-to-value ratio on the property from 90% to 72%.

Insurance premiums vary from company to company and according to the type of loan being insured. Coverage is available for conventional fixed-rate and adjustable-rate mortgages with down payments of at least 5%. First-year premiums may range from 0.35% to 1.65% of the mortgage amount depending on, among other things, the loan amount, the size of the down payment, and the type of loan. Thereafter, premiums range from 0.25% to 0.75%.

You will be expected to pay one or more monthly premiums, or the entire premium, in advance on the day of settlement. A newcomer to the business, Chicago- based Amerin Guaranty Corp., intends to streamline the process. The company has eliminated commissioned salespeople, and it will set standards in advance, thus allowing lenders to issue new policies without having to send documents to the insurance company for approval. Lenders will include premium costs in the fees and interest they charge rather than collecting at settlement and monthly through escrow accounts.

Can you ever stop paying? Loan documents are the final word on terms and conditions for canceling mortgage insurance. Conventional, conforming loans sold to Freddie Mac or Fannie Mae are covered by special rules. A lender is usually required to cancel insurance when you meet certain conditions and make the request in writing to your loan service company. You should be able to cancel once equity in your home reaches 20%, provided that monthly payments have been on time. Freddie Mac makes you wait two to five years before becoming eligible; both Freddie Mac and Fannie Mae permit lenders to demand an appraisal.

More on Mortgage Insurance

• •

For more information on FHA mortgage insurance, you can obtain a free brochure, *Guide to Single Family Home Mortgage Insurance,* by writing to the U.S. Department of Housing and Urban Development, 7th & D Sts., S.W., Washington, D.C. 20410-3000.

With a loan insured by the FHA, cancellation depends on the lender's approval—something you're not likely to get.

Credit Life Insurance

Your lender may try to talk you into buying credit life insurance that would pay off the mortgage in the event of your death. Even if your lender doesn't offer it, you may be deluged with mortgage life insurance solicitations after you buy your home.

Mortgage life insurance is usually decreasing-term insurance, in which the premium stays the same but the amount of coverage declines each year, in step with the declining balance owed on your mortgage. It is often promoted as valuable protection for your family, to keep them from losing the house if you die.

Mortgage life insurance does this, but there are better and cheaper ways to provide the same protection. One problem with mortgage life insurance is that the beneficiary is the mortgage lender, not someone you designate. Perhaps your spouse, for example, needn't and *shouldn't* pay off the balance on the mortgage, because the interest rate on it is much lower than the then-prevailing rate and there is sufficient income to keep making the payments. Since mortgage life insurance automatically pays off the lender, your spouse won't have a choice about how to use the insurance money. He or she would own the house free and clear but may have to refinance, possibly at a higher interest rate, to tap the equity for some worthwhile purpose, like college expenses.

Undeniably, any new homeowner with a family to protect should boost his or her life insurance coverage, so that the insurance proceeds—if invested conservatively—would yield enough income to continue paying the mortgage and other basic expenses of living. For a young person, annually renewable term life insurance offers the most coverage for the lowest current cost,

Insure a Second

Private mortgage-insurance coverage of second mortgages may be hard to find, but at least one company, United Guaranty Corp., in Greensboro, N.C., was writing such policies in 1992.

Make sure you haven't been forgotten. Remind the loan officer of your settlement date and check on how everything is going.

even though the premiums will rise each year. Before buying mortgage life insurance, shop for the best deal in term coverage.

The Wait and the Tension

From the time you submit your completed loan application—and appraisal and credit reports are received—the lender has up to 30 days to approve or reject your request and inform you of its decision. If you are turned down, you must be told why.

When homes are selling briskly, the time between a loan application and loan approval will gradually increase. Appraisers and credit bureaus get swamped. Harried mortgage-loan officers slip less-than-perfect applications back into the pile and move on to the most routine and trouble-free applicants. Before long, the whole process slows to a crawl.

Make sure you haven't been forgotten or put on a back burner. During the process, remind the loan officer of your settlement date and check on how everything is going.

Buyers with impeccable credit records who are able to make hefty down payments may be able to locate a "no-doc" loan through a mortgage broker. Because you do not have to provide the extensive income verification and credit documentation usually required to obtain a mortgage loan, the time to closing may be shorter. However, you can expect to pay extra points and fees and possibly a higher interest rate for the convenience.

You should have assessed how long the application process would take and proposed a suitably distant date back when you submitted your purchase contract. If it now appears you miscalculated, ask the seller for a new, later settlement date and explain that processing delays beyond your control have made it necessary. Most sellers will agree to a good-faith postponement of settlement, and this kind of delay is generally not grounds for voiding a contract.

During the wait between application and approval, the settlement clock is ticking and you are at the lender's mercy. When interest rates are falling, though, you may have some leverage. If rates have come down since you applied, remind the loan officer that he or she could lose your business by delaying settlement. If delays force you to reschedule the settlement, you might be inclined to reshop the mortgage and shift to another lender who can offer a new, lower rate or assure you of faster approval. If this is a real possibility (or a persuasive bluff), make sure your loan officer knows you're considering it; it could speed things up.

Getting a Good Title

When you take title to your home, you want assurance of secure ownership and marketable title now and in the future.

If you build a new house and it burns to the ground, you'll still own the land, even if you failed to cover the house with insurance. But if you buy a home with a faulty title—perhaps due to fraud, forgery, conflict between long-ago heirs, unpaid liens from contractors, or just a title-search error—you could lose everything.

When your lender requires title insurance on the home you intend to buy, it is not for your benefit. Lender coverage assures the institution that it has a valid first lien and that it will be protected against title defects that aren't listed as exceptions in the policy. Lender's title insurance is issued in the amount of the mortgage and decreases as the mortgage is paid off. It leaves your equity unprotected.

When you take title to your home, you want assurance of secure ownership and marketable title now and in the future, if you wish to sell or pass the property along to someone else. Unfortunately, the title being conveyed to you—essentially the seller's right to own, possess, use, control and dispose of the property—may not be all it seems. Rights conveyed to you in a properly executed and recorded deed may be seriously compromised. That's why you'll want the protection of owner's title insurance, regardless of the customary closing practices in the state where you're buying. If providing you with a policy isn't customary and automatic, make your purchase offer contingent on being able to obtain such insurance.

How the Process Works

You should also request a title insurance interim binder to be issued before closing. An interim binder is a preliminary commitment to insure and is based on a search and examination of the public records. It gives a description of the property and shows the owner, title defects, liens or encumbrances of record.

Following examination of the title evidence, the company will normally insure the title. If problems are discovered, the company may still agree to insure the title if certain conditions have been met by the closing date. Alternatively, it could make the insurance coverage subject to specified exceptions.

Basically, an interim binder gives you the chance to decide whether you want the seller to take remedial action or whether the problems merit canceling the purchase. If problems show up after the binder is issued, the title company may be liable, depending on the provisions in the policy.

Title examination takes place before your purchase is completed, usually while your mortgage loan application is being processed. Attorneys or other title specialists—often selected by you—handle the work.

If title problems turn up, they should be cleared up before settlement, or otherwise they could force a delay. Clearing a title can require the release of a debt lien or use of a quitclaim deed. If the snag is the result of record-keeping neglect, such as the failure to show a paid-up second mortgage as satisfied in the record, the task may be simple. But problems such as contested wills can be nightmares. You could even be faced with trying to void your contract. If it comes to that, don't try canceling without skilled legal advice.

Insist on being kept informed and on understanding each step in the title-checking process.

Title problems are numerous and varied, and they are on the increase.

If a title problem threatens to delay settlement, let your lender know how much time may be necessary to clear the title. Loan commitments often expire after 30 or 45 days, sometimes earlier. If you don't get a commitment extension in writing, you could lose your loan, or at least the interest rate you were promised.

Hazards of a Cloudy Title

There are circumstances, such as assuming an old loan or using seller financing, that may tempt you to save money by foregoing a title search and new owner's title insurance. The savings aren't worth the risk. Regardless of how great a deal you've found or the customs of the region, you should obtain an owner's title insurance policy.

The wisdom of buying title insurance boils down to this: You need the protection. Title problems are numerous and varied, and they're on the increase. Some possibilities:

• You are buying a house from a supposedly single man or woman. The title search reveals two names on the ownership record and describes them as married: "John and Jane Clark, husband and wife."

• You are buying from a middle-aged brother and sister from out of town. They are selling you a home their parents bought for their retirement. The father died several years ago and the widowed mother passed away just recently. A title search reveals that the property is in her name, but there is no will on file to direct what she wanted done with it.

• You are buying from a couple who borrowed $20,000 seven years ago to add a room to their house. They have long since paid back the loan but have forgotten that her parents recorded it as a second mortgage when they made the loan. A title search shows the second mortgage but no evidence of its having been paid.

- You are buying a house to which the owner added central air-conditioning two years ago. He had a fight with the air-conditioning contractor over some damage to a ceiling that occurred during installation. When the contractor refused to correct the damage, the seller refused to pay the final installment on his contract. The contractor filed a mechanic's lien on the property, and it has never been removed.

- Or, you are buying a property that is beautifully landscaped. A title search shows that the landscaper has a lien on the property. The seller explains that several of the trees died and when the landscaper refused to replace them, he refused to make final payment.

Avoiding Surprises

Never take title to a property—not even as a gift—without full knowledge of its legal and financial condition. Common problem areas include:

Unpaid taxes. Make sure there are no unpaid property taxes from prior years. The title policy or interim binder should note the pro rata portion of taxes unpaid in the current year.

Restrictions. Restrictive covenants or easements tell you where and what you can and can't build. The title company may be responsible for damages caused by restrictions it failed to list. If a listed easement, such as a utility right-of-way, concerns you, get a legal opinion before closing.

Community standards. Within the private restrictive covenants section, the title policy should certify that structures comply with existing community standards. Then you'll be protected if, for instance, the previous owner built the deck two feet too close to the road and your neighborhood association demands you dismantle it. The title company will have to pay to bring the deck into compliance.

Encroachments. Be sure the policy affirms that nothing on your property encroaches on your neighbor's property, and vice versa.

Inadequate land description and the resulting defective deed occurs in the city, too, when neighbors get together and swap bits of land.

- You are buying a house at a great bargain from a man who is in trouble with the Internal Revenue Service, which has placed a lien on the property.

- You are buying a house from an aged widow. She and her husband bought the property many years ago, and when he died last year, she thought she was the sole owner. Now a title search reveals that the deed by which she and her husband acquired title was defective. The deed says only "Horace and Henrietta Jenkins." It should have shown their relationship and the manner in which they intended to take title.

- You are buying a house that has a newly paved driveway. Your seller is proud of having improved the value of his property by converting his joint driveway into a private driveway. He bought his neighbor's half in a friendly deal last year when the neighbor built a new driveway on the opposite side of his house. There is just one problem: The expanded driveway doesn't appear in the public records.

- The paving, sidewalks and gutters in front of the house you have under contract are all new. A title search shows that your seller has not paid the city's special assessment for the improvements.

- You plan to build a garage on the west end of your lot as soon as you move in. A title search reveals an easement of eight feet over the length of your future yard, extending across the garage site. The gas company owns the easement, which was granted by the development company that built your house.

- You are planning to get away from it all by building a house on a piece of land 50 miles from town. A title search reveals that your property was carved out of a large farm that was never legally subdivided. The land description was one of those down-home "from the apple tree to the stone marker" jobs.

That sort of inadequate land description and the resulting defective deed occurs in the city, too, when neighbors get together and swap bits of land. Sometimes an owner with an oversize yard sells a rear 20 feet to a neighbor with a short yard. Or neighbors buy a vacant lot between them and split it. They erect a fence along the newly created lot line and consider the job finished, never thinking to get a survey and a proper deed for their new half lot and have it recorded.

Sometimes it is the owner's financial manipulations in a business that cloud the title. In the case of a bankruptcy or an unincorporated business or partnership, the owner's personal residence may be attached to satisfy part of his business debt. Another business owner may not be in trouble, just expanding, and has pledged his personal residence—the one you're about to buy—as part of the security required to obtain a business loan. Until that lien is paid or he arranges with his creditor to substitute other property as security, he can't deliver a clear title to you.

Less Than Best

By the time you close you should feel sure that the title you're getting is what you expected and what it's represented to be.

You could encounter the following methods, other than title insurance, for assuring that a title is good. Neither, however, carries the legal or financial protection of title insurance.

- **Abstract plus an attorney's opinion:** Title is usually in the form of an abstract, which is a historical summary of everything found in a search of public records that affects ownership of the property. It includes not only the chain of ownership but also recorded easements, mortgages, wills, tax liens, judgments, pending lawsuits, marriages and anything else that affects the title. When a property is sold, the abstract is examined by an attorney, who gives a written opin-

In most states, title insurance rates vary enough to make shopping around worthwhile.

ion as to the title—including who the owner of record is and her judgment on whether anyone else has any right to or interest in the property. The opinion is often known as the certificate of title.

- **Attorney's record search and opinion:** The attorney searches through the public records and issues her certificate of title.

Buying Title Insurance

Regardless of customary title assurance practices in your state, you can buy title insurance for a one-time fee. (Iowa has a state title guaranty fund, but private title insurance is available to residents through insurance companies located outside the state.)

You pay for title insurance at settlement. Title insurance companies are regulated by state law, but in most states, rates vary enough to make shopping around worthwhile. An owner's policy could cost about $3.50 per $1,000 of home value; lender protection about $2.50 per $1,000 of the loan amount.

When you're checking the fees charged by different firms, find out exactly what is covered in each case. In some areas of the country, companies routinely quote a single fee that includes the costs of handling the closing as well as the search, title report and insurance risk premium. In others, the quote may include only the report and risk premium, and in a few states, only the premium.

The easiest way to get coverage is to piggyback on your lender's coverage. As mentioned, the lender will generally require mortgage (lender's) title insurance to protect its interest in the property and improve the mortgage's marketability.

The face amount on the lender's policy is the amount of the loan and will decline gradually as the debt is paid off. The lender's policy does not protect you. To protect yourself, you must request and pay for an owner's policy. (In some localities, the seller custom-

arily provides owner's title insurance for the buyer.)
While you may be able to buy owner coverage at some
later time, it's easier and cheaper to buy both the
lender's and the owner's title insurance policies at once.

Your owner's policy is for the purchase price and
will continue to protect you and your heirs after you
sell. Your policy is the title insurance company's contract with you to make good
any covered loss caused by a
defect in the title or by any
lien or encumbrance that was
recorded in the public
records and was not revealed
to you when the policy was
issued. It doesn't cover title
defects you cause while you
own the property. The title
company also will identify
title problems and pay for a
legal defense against an
attack on the title, in whatev-
er manner is provided for in its policy. The company
has a number of options for handling valid claims: It
can pay, negotiate an acceptable settlement or appeal
the claim in court.

Ordinarily, you can expect an owner's policy to
cover you against such things as loss or damage from
forgery, failure to comply with the law, impersonation,
acts of minors, and marital status and competency questions. Policies are sometimes amended by adding
special endorsements or by removing exclusions. For
example, the insurer may include a rider that will
increase the face amount on the contract as your home
appreciates.

Nearly all title policies follow the same standard
format, regardless of the issuing company. Take time to
read yours, and if possible have someone knowledgeable go over the details with you before closing. Pay
close attention to what it covers and to the exceptions
and exclusions.

One Way to Save

• •

One way to save money and still get full title
protection is to get a reissue rate. If the seller has
owner's title insurance, find out whether the
company offers a reissue rate. You may get a
break even when a company reissues insurance
on a title policy made as long as ten years ago. In
a few cases a reissue rate may be obtained from a
company other than the original issuer.

Be sure you understand what kind of deed you will receive from the seller and what rights will be conveyed to you.

Title Documents You'll See at Closing

You'll be wading through a dizzying number of legal papers at closing, and you'll find yourself signing your name over and over again, sometimes on several copies of the same document. Obviously, that's not the most auspicious time to be asking dozens of questions about deeds, titles and insurance protection—or for getting good answers. The time for that is before making a purchase offer. Get information and answers as you proceed. Here's a brief rundown on some of the common documents relating to title transfer.

Warranty deed

This document officially transfers title to the buyer. The seller, not the buyer, signs it and thereby agrees to protect the buyer against losing the property because of claims against it. Generally, the closing agent will then have the deed recorded at the local courthouse and send you a copy.

In some states a different type of deed, such as a bargain and sale deed, security deed, grant deed or special warranty deed, is used in lieu of a general warranty deed to transfer title. Be sure you understand what kind of deed you will receive from the seller and what rights will be conveyed to you.

Quitclaim deed

This is a device often used to deal with title problems. Anyone with a potential claim against the property can sign it, thereby releasing rights he or she might have.

Mortgage or deed of trust

The basic purpose of either document is to secure the loan. When a debt is secured by a mortgage, the borrower signs a document that gives the lender a lien on the property.

When a debt is secured by a deed of trust, the buyer conveys title to a third party, who holds it until the note is paid in full. The lender does not receive title but only the right to request that the property be sold should the borrower default. Both documents should be recorded.

Owner's affidavit

The seller swears in this document that there are no unpaid liens, assessments or other encumbrances against the property. The affidavit protects the purchaser, lender and title company. If the seller is lying, he or she can be sued for damages.

Purchaser's affidavit

Sometimes the buyer is required by the lender to swear that there are no existing or pending suits, judgments or liens against him or her. If the buyer is lying, that is sufficient grounds for foreclosure.

Get Ready for Settlement

Expect minor problems and delays, but remember, at this point, neither party is likely to be looking for a way out of the deal.

There is no way to guarantee a smooth path from ratified contract to settlement table, but doing your part is at least half the job. Major steps at this stage are finding the right loan and getting the application under way.

Expect minor problems and delays along the way. On the seller's side, title problems are a common cause of postponed settlements. On your side, bureaucratic snags such as extensive credit checks and slow appraisals can bog things down. In many cases, there isn't much you or the seller can do but wait.

Should you run into problems—say, a delay in mortgage approval that would prevent you from being ready to close—contact the seller immediately and work out an extension. You shouldn't be penalized if the problem is one you couldn't have anticipated. At this point, neither party is likely to be looking for a way out of the deal.

While you're waiting for completion of all the processes now in motion, you should:

- **Decide how you want to take title to the house.**

- **Apply for homeowners insurance on your new home.**

- **Get an exact accounting of settlement costs, and**

make sure the money and necessary documents will be there at closing.

- **Select a date for the walk-through of the house.** You may wish to have a walk-through two weeks or so before you intend to close if you expect work will need to be done by the owner. Then a final inspection can be made just prior to settlement.

- **Contact the utility companies about starting service in your name.** Arrange for electricity, gas, oil and water to be turned on in your name the day of settlement so there will be no interruption in service. Make arrangements a few weeks in advance, since utility companies may require deposits, credit checks and advance notice.

- **Review the adequacy of your disability and life insurance policies.**

How to Take Title

Before you can take title to your new home, you'll have to decide what form of ownership you want.

If you're single, you'll probably buy the house in your name alone.

Husband and wife generally own their property through joint ownership, in the form of either joint tenancy with the right of survivorship or tenancy by the entirety.

Under either form of joint tenancy, when one spouse dies, the other becomes sole owner of the property. This happens automatically, bypassing probate, avoiding delays and usually trimming the costs of settling the estate. For federal-tax purposes, half the value of all property owned by a married couple as joint tenants is included in the estate of the first spouse to die.

The two kinds of joint ownership differ in some respects, and many states don't recognize tenancies by the entirety. Get your lawyer's advice. If you live in a

It's wise for two single owners to have a written agreement setting out each individual's rights to deal with his or her legal interest in the property.

community-property state (Arizona, California, Idaho, Louisiana, Nevada, New Mexico, Texas, Washington and Wisconsin), state law may affect the availability and treatment of certain joint ownership arrangements.

The advice of a good trusts-and-estates attorney is particularly important if you are a member of a step-family or are wealthy. For example, a couple whose total wealth exceeds $1.2 million and who die more or less simultaneously would spare their heirs federal estate taxes if their property was divided equally between them so that each spouse's estate gets the benefit of the $600,000 starting point for taxation.

To save on estate taxes someday, you may want to put the new home in the name of one or the other spouse alone. But your lender may not want the house owned by one spouse exclusively if all or most of the earnings to pay the mortgage will be derived from the other spouse.

And consider this: Titling the house in only one spouse's name could affect the division of property in case of a divorce.

If you are buying with a partner who is not your legal spouse, you can choose among the forms of ownership discussed below. Consult your attorney on which is most suited to your needs.

Tenancy in Common

Each owner has separate legal title to an undivided interest in the whole property, and each is allowed to independently sell, mortgage or give away his or her interest.

It's wise for two single owners to have a written agreement setting out each individual's rights to deal with his or her legal interest in the property. The agreement also should specify the percentage of ownership interest each person has in the property, particularly if they have not contributed equal amounts. When one of the owners dies, the other does not automatically get the deceased's share unless that person specifically made such an arrangement in his or her will. If the will doesn't cover this, or if an owner dies without a will, state law determines who gets the deceased owner's share.

Joint Tenancy

Under this arrangement, each person has an equal interest in the property regardless of the amount contributed at purchase. If one owner dies, that person's share passes automatically to the other without going through probate.

Partnership

If title is in the name of a partnership, it is the partnership that owns the property, not the individual partners. This arrangement calls for an agreement that sets forth how each partner will share in the management of the partnership. The death of a partner does not affect the partnership; that person's heirs would acquire the interest. This form of ownership is useful if one or more of the partners are investors who don't plan to live on the property. Another plus for a partnership arrangement is that you may avoid some problems that can arise with the other two forms discussed above if one person goes into bankruptcy or has other legal problems that could cloud the title.

Partnership is a useful form of ownership if one or more of the partners are investors who don't plan to live on the property.

Insurance on Your New Home

Your lender will require you to take out a homeowners insurance policy, something you would want to do anyway. The lender wants to cover the amount of its mortgage loan so it could recover the money in the event of a total loss; you want full-value coverage, perhaps enhanced by an inflation-adjustment mechanism that keeps the coverage rising with home values. You may want other special protections as well.

Standard policies cover much of what you own, give you personal liability protection, and protect you from credit card losses and medical bills.

HO What?

The term *homeowners insurance* is to some extent a misnomer: Standard policies cover much of what you own, give you personal liability protection, and protect you from credit card losses and even medical bills.

There are five types of homeowners policies, called HO-1, HO-2, HO-3, HO-6 and HO-8. (A sixth type, HO-4, covers renters.) The first three differ in the number of perils they cover and the degree of protection they offer:

- **HO-1** affords basic protection, with many restrictions, and is available in only a few states.

- **HO-2,** which costs 5% to 10% more, can protect you from costs arising from misfortunes such as burst pipes and exploding furnaces.

- **An HO-3,** or "all risk," policy, which can cost up to 30% more than an HO-1, covers everything not specifically excluded, including features that are part of the structure, such as wall-to-wall carpeting and built-in dishwashers.

If you are buying a condominium, you will use an HO-6 form; and unique older houses may be insured with a special HO-8 policy, available in some states.

All of these policies exclude floods, earthquakes, war and nuclear contamination. Policies may differ by company and according to state requirements.

Property and Liability

A typical homeowners HO-3 policy combines two basic types of insurance with some additional coverage:

Property protection
This part of the policy reimburses you for losses or damages to the house and its contents. The amount of

insurance coverage is based on the anticipated cost of replacing the entire structure, with coverage on personal property usually figured as the cash value at the time of loss. There are set monetary limits for specific classes of objects. They range from $200 for currency, to $1,000 for jewelry, furs and manuscripts, to $2,500 for silverware.

Liability insurance

This protects you against personal liability, medical payments for injuries to others and damage to other people's property. It typically applies to you and other family members living in the house.

Liability coverage usually pays up to $100,000 to others for injury or damage that you or a family member might have caused, or for an accident that occurs around your home. You will be covered, for example, if the mailman trips on the front-porch steps. If someone is injured at your home, medical-payments coverage typically will pay at least $500 of the injured person's bills. Injuries to someone by a family member who is away from the home may also be covered. And the injury need not have been your fault for the coverage to apply. You would also be covered for legal defense if you needed it.

Extended personal liability or umbrella insurance may be worth considering. It dramatically increases your personal liability coverage at comparatively little cost and extends your coverage beyond damages assessed for physical injury to such things as libel, slander, character defamation, shock, mental anguish, sickness or disease, false arrest, wrongful entry or eviction, and malicious prosecution.

Additional coverage

You can select a policy that will help cover costs, including provisions for housing and restaurant bills, should your home become uninhabitable. Many policies routinely pay up to $500 if a credit card is stolen or forged in your name.

Extended personal liability or umbrella insurance extends your coverage to such things as libel, slander, mental anguish, false arrest, and malicious prosecution.

How Home Insurance Policies Compare

When shopping for homeowner's insurance, you can choose between the standard, one-size-fits-all "HO-3" (or "Form 3") policy, to which you may need to add extra coverage, or a package plan that already includes the extras you want—and some you might not care about.

The listing of coverages at right gives you an item-by-item comparison of two homeowners insurance policies—their features and costs—as offered by a national insurer. Both the basic plan and the package plan cover a $100,000 house and feature a $250 deductible.

The summary at left shows that the base price of the package plan is only $9 more than the basic policy's ($381 versus $372) even though the package plan provides greatly enhanced coverage, including guaranteed replacement of the dwelling, replacement cost coverage on contents, and better coverage on jewelry and furs. When you add the most important missing coverage to the basic plan, however, the net premium for the package policy is lower.

How the Premiums Compare

• •

	Basic Plan	Package Plan	Your Plan
Premium With			
$250 deductible	$ 372	$ 381	$_____
500 deductible	- 63	- 65	_____
Smoke alarms, other credits	- 15	included	_____
Option (1)	+ 1	included	_____
Option (2)	+ 31	included	_____
Option (3)	+ 15	+ 15	_____
Option (4)	+ 13	+ 13	_____
Total Net Premium	**$ 354**	**$ 344**	**$_____**

See table at right for description of options 1-4.

So, in sizing up competing plans, do consider which extras you really want, and don't assume you will save money by choosing less coverage. Some package plans impose tougher standards than the basic policy—say, a higher minimum deductible—but if you really want most of the extras, a package deal is often your best buy.

*ACV is actual cash value: the policy reimburses you for the estimated depreciated value of the item being claimed.

**RC is replacement cost: the policy reimburses you for the estimated cost to buy the item new. When you add replacement cost coverage, it applies to all contents, including valuables.

	Limits of Coverage	
	Basic plan	**Package plan**
Coverage of Structure	100%	100%
Risks covered	all risks	all risks
Guaranteed replacement (1)	optional: no cap	no cap
Loss of use coverage	100%	100%
Other Structures		
Limit as % of policy limit	10%	10%
Coverage of Contents		
Limit on coverage	$55,000/ACV*	$75,000/RC**
Replacement cost coverage (2)	optional: $75,000	included
Per item coverage cap	no limit	no limit
All risk on contents	—	some items
Coverage of Valuables		
Jewelry and furs	$1,000	$2,500
Added coverage	$10 per $1,000	$10 per $1,000
Silverware	$2,500	$2,500
Added coverage	$5 per $1,000	$5 per $1,000
Additional Coverage		
Business property	$500	$500
Computer/data	$3,000	$3,000
Lock replacement	$100	$100
Cash	$200	$200
Securities	$1,000	$1,000
Boats/trailers	$1,000	$1,000
Debris removal	—	—
Sewer/sump pump backup	$5,000	$5,000
Liability Coverage		
Personal liability	$100,000	$100,000
Personal liability at vacation property (3)	optional: $100,000	optional: $100,000
Libel/slander protection (4)	optional: $100,000	optional: $100,000
Medical payments	$1,000	$1,000

How to Get Your Money's Worth in Home and Auto Insurance, by author Barbara Taylor (McGraw-Hill). This book, written under the sponsorship of the Insurance Information Institute, offers clear explanations and helpful information to consumers who need to buy insurance protection for their homes.

How Much Coverage Do You Need?

Once you've pinned down the type of policy that suits your needs, the next step is to figure out how much coverage you want on the house and its contents. The basic building block of any policy is the amount of coverage on the house. This should be based on the replacement value—that is, what it would cost to rebuild the structure.

Because you are unlikely to experience a total loss on your home, you may be tempted not to insure for the full value. But insuring for less than full value is false economy. You won't be fully protected for a partial loss unless your coverage at the time of the loss is at least 80% of replacement cost. That provision could become a problem as construction costs rise or as you improve the house. You can protect yourself by getting an inflation guard, which automatically raises your coverage in step with rising prices. But check on the value of the house and contents at least every two years to see that you are adequately covered.

A better solution is to shift the responsibility for keeping replacement-cost coverage up to 80% from your shoulders to the insurance company, through what is called a replacement-cost endorsement. This option can cost as little as 10% of a year's base premium or as much as three times the standard coverage. You can also buy replacement-cost coverage for personal property.

Most policies can be customized to meet your needs. You should be able to buy add-on coverage to insure silverware or art, for example, not covered in standard policies (see also the discussion of package plans in the preceding box).

Cutting Costs

Prices for equivalent homeowners policies can vary by hundreds of dollars from company to company.

As you shop, take the following steps to ensure that you are getting the most for your money:

- **Get price quotations from at least three companies.**

- **Ask about package plan prices.**

- **Find out whether you'd get a price break** if the insurer provided both your home and automobile coverage.

For each policy, compare these items:

- **The amount you wish to insure the house for and the cost of a replacement-cost endorsement on your policy.**

- **The cost of content coverage.** Half the amount of coverage on the structure (minus depreciation) is standard; decide if more coverage seems necessary.

- **The cost of replacement coverage versus actual cash coverage on the contents.** If possible, opt for replacement coverage.

- **The deductible.** As a general rule, don't ask for a deductible lower than $250; it's too expensive.

- **The cost of floaters** you may need for antiques, jewelry, computer software and the like.

- **The liability limits.** The standard amount is $100,000, but $300,000 is desirable and not that much more expensive.

Fair Access

• •

If you discover that the home you want can't be insured privately, you may be able to buy basic coverage under the Fair Access to Insurance Requirements (FAIR) plan. FAIR is in effect in 29 states and the District of Columbia. For information, contact your state insurance department, the Insurance Information Institute (110 William St., New York, N.Y. 10038; 212-669-9200) or the National Insurance Consumer Helpline (800-942-4242).

Flood Insurance

The most important risk excluded from most homeowners policies is damage caused by flooding from rivers, dams and other natural sources. If you buy a home in an area designated by the government as flood-prone, you may be able to purchase flood coverage through the National Flood Insurance Program (NFIP). You buy it from a licensed property/casualty insurance agent or broker, or from a private insurance company (see the accompanying box).

Earthquake Insurance

Although standard homeowners policies don't include coverage for earthquake damage, you should be able to buy a special earthquake endorsement with your homeowners policy or get coverage with a separate policy.

Unfortunately, cost deters most owners from even taking out earthquake insurance. And that in turn makes coverage more expensive because the risk is being carried by a smaller pool of individuals. In California, for example, an earthquake endorsement usually runs from $2 to $4 per $1,000 of coverage on houses built with wood frames—as much as or more than the underlying policy. The deductible

Federal Flood Help

• •

Some 18,000 communities participate in the federal government's NFIP, administered by the Federal Insurance Administration, part of the Federal Emergency Management Agency (FEMA). Most owners living in such a community will be eligible for some coverage once required flood-management programs have been initiated. Protection isn't cheap; the average homeowner's annual premium is $300. Minimum deductibles are applied separately to the building structure and to its contents, although both may be damaged in the same flood. You may be able to buy replacement-cost coverage on a single-family home under certain conditions.

For more information, call the NFIP at 800-638-6620. In Maryland, call 800-492-6605. In Alaska, Guam and Hawaii, call 800-638-6831.

FEMA puts out a free booklet, *Answer to Questions About the National Flood Insurance Program.* Request it by name and number (#FIA-2) from the Federal Emergency Management Agency (P.O. Box 70274, Washington, D.C. 20024, Attn: Publications).

is typically 10% or so of the policy amount ($10,000 on a $100,000 home).

This is much higher than the typical $250 to $500 deductible on a homeowners policy. Earthquake insurance pays off only on devastating claims and it will not shield you from having to absorb a major financial loss. In addition, the deductible usually applies separately to the structure and its contents.

Despite the cost, it's important to consider buying earthquake insurance if:

- Your home was construct-ed before World War II, when codes covering a structure's ability to with-stand shifts in the earth were weaker; this is partic-ularly important for homes not framed with wood.

And You Thought You Were Safe?

• •

California isn't the only part of the country where homeowners are at risk for earthquakes. Homes situated in parts of Arkansas, Colorado, Idaho, Illinois, Indiana, Kentucky, Massachusetts, Mississippi, Missouri, Nevada, New York, South Carolina, Tennessee, Utah, Washington and Wyoming are also at higher-than-average risk.

- Your home is located within ten miles of a fault.

- Your home is on unstable soil, such as a hillside, landfill or flood-control plain.

Insurance on Your Life

If your new home represents a higher financial burden than you've ever carried before, and you have a spouse or children to protect in the event of your death or disability, this is a good time to review your insurance needs. Have an accountant, trusts-and-estates attorney, financial planner or trusted insurance professional review your situation on disabil-ity and life insurance.

Depending on your age, your best bet may be con-ventional term life insurance whose proceeds, if invested wisely, would produce enough annual income

The more planning and monitoring you have done, the more likely you are to have a peaceful closing.

to pay the new mortgage and other basic living expenses (see the discussion of credit life insurance and its drawbacks in Chapter 11).

On to Settlement

You are only days away from becoming an owner. The search has been expensive in terms of both time and money. Now it's time for you to pay for the property and for the seller to deliver the deed.

There is no standard name for this next step. Depending on where you live, it is known as title closing, settlement or closing of escrow. The closing officer in your area may be a title company, an abstract attorney or a regular real estate attorney. Occasionally, it is a broker or lender.

When closing involves an actual meeting, the process commonly is called settlement. If no meeting occurs, it's often known as escrow and is handled by an escrow agent. In escrow cases, the buyer and seller typically sign an agreement requiring each party to deposit certain funds and documents with the agent. When all the papers and money are in, the escrow is "closed." The agent records the documents and makes the appropriate disbursements.

Settling on a home can be as serene as a treaty signing or as stressful as divorce proceedings. All in all, the more planning and monitoring you have done, the more likely you are to have a peaceful closing.

As the buyer, you probably selected the person or firm to perform the settlement, so you can rely on their competence and integrity. If for some reason the seller specified the settlement agent, you should take along your own attorney or have an attorney of your choice review the documents before you sign them.

The Costs You Face

The key to reducing money shock at settlement is to know ahead of time what you'll have to pay. You got

GET READY FOR SETTLEMENT

ballpark figures to work with when you started looking, and once your purchase offer was accepted, you received detailed estimates from the lender with whom you made an application.

Settlement costs are influenced by such things as the state in which you live, your closing date, how you financed your purchase and what the lender required as an inducement to lend you money.

It's difficult to say how much these costs run on a national basis, simply because there is no uniformity in how costs are tallied and calculated. But within local markets you generally can get a good estimate. For example, in Atlanta closing costs on conventional loans commonly come to about 3.5% of the loan amount. In California, 2% is closer to the mark. Neither estimate includes discount points (one point is equal to 1% of the loan amount) or brokerage commissions (usually paid by the seller)—and these, as you know by now, will be the big-ticket items on your settlement sheet. With points included, totals approach 6% in some high-cost metropolitan areas.

The federal government's Real Estate Settlement Procedures Act (RESPA) applies to most home loans, including VA, FHA, FmHA and other government-backed or government-assisted loans; loans eligible to be purchased by FNMA, GNMA, or in other federally related secondary-mortgage markets; and loans made by lenders who invest or make more than $1 million in residential loans each year. Assumptions and seller financing are excluded.

When you apply for a new loan from a lender covered by RESPA, you must be given a "good faith" estimate of fees or be sent one within three business days. You must also be given a Department of Housing and Urban Development pamphlet entitled *Settlement Costs and You*, which describes how the closing process works and explains terms you will encounter.

The day before settlement, you are entitled to see the Uniform Settlement Statement. This is a duplicate of what you will get at settlement. Where there is no

It's difficult to say how much these costs run on a national basis, but within local markets you generally can get a good estimate.

meeting, the escrow agent is required to give you a copy when escrow is closed.

Use the following work sheet to check the lender's and agent's estimates against actual amounts as you get them. This may give you some warning if there are substantial changes before settlement. The work sheet, like HUD's Uniform Settlement Statement, breaks total settlement charges into broad categories including:

Costs associated with getting a loan

These include the lender's charge for processing the loan, loan discount points and/or origination fees, appraisal fee, borrower's credit report, mortgage insurance, and, if relevant, loan-assumption fee.

Items to be paid in advance at closing

Among them are mortgage interest, property taxes, and mortgage and hazard insurance premiums.

Once you become an owner, you pay interest on your monthly mortgage loan in arrears; that is, you pay for the use of the loan at the end of each month. Payments made on the first of each month cover interest owed from the previous month. To make this work, the lender collects interest in advance at settlement for the period between closing and the end of the month. For example, if settlement is August 15 and you make your first mortgage payment October 1, the lender will collect interest through the end of August.

In addition, lenders often require payment of as much as the first year's premiums for mortgage and hazard insurance at closing. In some cases a buyer can arrange for the seller to transfer the remaining hazard insurance, paying the seller on a prorated basis for the remainder of the policy term.

Reserves for insurance, taxes and assessments

The borrower may be required to pay an initial amount at closing to set up a reserve fund, or escrow account. Each month a portion of the regular payment will be added to the reserve to assure sufficient sums to pay future taxes and insurance premiums.

Title costs

These pay for various transactions, notably the title search required by the lender. An examination is made of the public records to determine whether the title you receive has any ownership or financial claims against it or restrictions on the use of the property. Other related charges include title insurance, document preparation, notary fees and the lender's attorney fees.

Recording and transfer charges

Such charges cover recording of the loan and property documents at the county courthouse, as well as related transfer taxes.

Additional fees

These might cover attorney and buyer broker services, property survey and pest inspection.

In general, items paid for in advance by the seller, such as property taxes, would be prorated in favor of the seller at closing. Items paid in arrears, interest on an assumed loan, for example, would be prorated in favor of the purchaser.

Run through the work sheet and note which items are to be paid in full or in part by you. Local custom influences whether buyer or seller pays a particular charge. You can do things differently, but only if your purchase contract stated clearly how each item was to be handled. Otherwise, it's not unreasonable for the seller to expect you to abide by the prevailing custom.

In some areas, for example, buyers pay for a title insurance policy because their lenders demand it. In others, the seller absorbs the charge as a selling cost. Likewise, you may discover that buyers always pay the local tax for recording the deed, or that sellers always pay it. (To find out what closing costs might be involved in the purchase of a $150,000 home, see the example following the Settlement Costs Work Sheet.)

The borrower may be required to pay an initial amount at closing to set up a reserve fund, or escrow account, for insurance, taxes and assessments.

Settlement Costs Work Sheet

You'll receive a copy of this form—or one with similar language, sequence and numbering of the line items—from your real estate agent, prospective lenders, and whoever conducts your settlement. Required by the Department of Housing and Urban Development, this format makes it easier for you to compare estimated settlement charges and to identify and question any unexplained items. (Unless otherwise stated, the word "to" refers to who will receive the payments.)

			Agent's Estimate	Lender's Estimate	Actual Cost
800. Items Payable in Connection With Loan					
801. Loan origination fee	% (of loan)				
802. Loan discount (points)	% (of loan)				
803. Appraisal fee	to				
804. Credit report	to				
805. Lender's inspection fee					
806. Mortgage insurance application fee	to				
807. Assumption fee					
808.					
809.					
810.					
811.					
900. Items Required by Lender to Be Paid in Advance					
901. Interest from (date) to	(date)@$	/day			
902. Mortgage insurance premium for	months to	(end date)			
903. Hazard insurance premium for	years to	(end date)			
904.	years to				
905.					
1000. Reserves Deposited With Lender					
1001. Hazard insurance(number of)	months @$	per month			
1002. Mortgage insurance	months @$	per month			
1003. City property taxes	months @$	per month			
1004. County property taxes	months @$	per month			
1005. Annual assessments	months @$	per month			
1006.	months @$	per month			
1007.	months @$	per month			
1008.	months @$	per month			

	Agent's Estimate	Lender's Estimate	Actual Cost
1100. Title Charges			
1101. Settlement or closing fee to			
1102. Abstract or title search to			
1103. Title examination to			
1104. Title insurance binder to			
1105. Document preparation to			
1106. Notary fees to			
1107. Attorney's fees to			
includes above item numbers:			
1108. Title insurance to			
includes above item numbers:			
1109. Lender's coverage $			
1110. Owner's coverage $			
1111.			
1112.			
1113.			
1200. Government Recording and Transfer Taxes			
1201. Recording fees: Deed $; Mortgage $; Release $			
1202. City/county tax/stamps: Deed $; Mortgage $			
1203. State tax/stamps: Deed $; Mortgage $			
1204.			
1205.			
1300. Additional Settlement Charges			
1301. Survey to			
1302. Pest inspection to			
1303.			
1304.			
1305.			
1400. Total Settlement Charges			

What to Bring to Closing

In order for things to go smoothly, each person is responsible for bringing certain documents and for being prepared to write the necessary checks. Many closing costs can be paid by personal check, but ask the closing attorney. A certified or cashier's check may be required; find out to whom checks should be made payable—the seller or settlement attorney, for example.

The seller and his attorney, or the settlement attorney you've both agreed on, are responsible for preparing and bringing the deed and the most recent property-tax bill. They also will bring other documents required by the contract. This can include the property insurance policy, termite inspection, documents showing the removal of liens, a bill of sale for personal property, loan documents and so on.

Your responsibilities include having adequate funds in your checking account for the down payment and other settlement costs, arranging for your attorney to represent your interests at the meeting, bringing the loan commitment and informing the lender of the meeting's time and place.

If your lender requires payment of the first year's premiums for mortgage and hazard insurance at closing, be prepared to pay or to bring proof that they've already been paid. Finally, it's a good idea to bring a copy of the purchase contract. You may need to refresh your memory.

The Final Inspection

The house you're buying must be handed over to you in the condition specified in the contract (see the discussion of condition in Chapters 8 and 9).

To verify this, schedule a walk-through of the house shortly before settlement; several days in advance is best, to allow time for the seller to correct any last-minute problems.

Hypothetical Settlement Costs

In this example:

(1) The buyer is paying a 1% loan origination fee, and the seller has agreed to pay one point on the buyer's $120,000 home mortgage.

(2) Because interest is paid in arrears—for the previous month—and because the buyer's first regular monthly payment won't be due until March 1, the lender collects interest for the period from January 2 through February 1 at closing.

(3) Each month lenders frequently collect one-twelfth of the annual property taxes—along with the principal and interest payment—and hold them in escrow until payment is due. How much is paid at settlement depends on the closing date and when taxes are collected in a given locale.

(4) The lender is collecting and will be paying a full year's premium on hazard insurance covering at least the value of the mortgage; the lender is also starting a reserve fund for future premiums.

In other locales and in other circumstances, the buyer's closing costs may include an assumption fee (if the buyer is taking over the seller's mortgage), mortgage insurance, and various other charges.

Total settlement charges are generally less if the buyer is assuming an existing loan or paying all cash, rather than getting a new mortgage.

(These settlement calculations were provided by Bank One Mortgage Corp., Chevy Chase, Maryland.)

The Purchase

Location	Montgomery County, Maryland
Date of Closing	February 1
Sale Price	$ 150,000
Down Payment	$ 30,000

Buyer's Costs

Credit report	$ 48.00
Loan origination fee (1%) (1)	1,200.00
Interest to February 1 (2)	936.90
Six months' property tax (3)	640.50
Hazard insurance premium (4)	211.00
Two months' insurance reserve (4)	35.16
Attorney's fees (includes title exam fee and binder)	350.00
Recording fee	50.00
Survey	125.00
State recordation tax	660.00
State transfer tax	750.00
County transfer tax	1,500.00
Title insurance (lender's coverage)	260.00
Title insurance (borrower's coverage)	250.00
Total	**$ 7,016.56**

Seller's Costs

Sales commission (6%)	$ 9,000.00
Loan discount point (1%) (1)	1,200.00
Appraisal fee	250.00
Closing fees	125.00
Termite inspection	45.00
Total	**$10,620.00**

You shouldn't test the air-conditioning when outside temperatures are cold—arrange for a test once warm weather returns, and have an expert verify that it's in working condition.

If the house is vacant, it should be empty of debris and in the "broom-clean" condition you specified in the contract. Take along a simple device for testing all the electrical outlets—a plug-in nightlight, for example. Turn on the furnace and air-conditioning. Flush toilets and turn on faucets. Put the washing machine and dryer through a cycle. In short, put the house through its paces.

If anything needs fixing or further cleaning (aside from things that were conveyed only in "as is" condition), tell the seller immediately. Neither you nor the seller wants to postpone the settlement, but make it clear you won't go to closing until a second walk-through is satisfactory.

Save All the Documents for Your Taxes

Congratulations! You're now a homeowner. Tax benefits weren't your primary motivation for buying, but now they take on more importance.

If you haven't read Chapter 3 carefully, do so after closing. Now is the time to begin keeping meticulous records of every cost you incur on your new home—from settlement expenses to improvements that add to the home's value. Some expenses can be deducted from taxable income in the year you buy the home; others will merely increase the tax basis, lowering the taxable gain when you someday sell the house, whether next year or 40 years hence. The better your records, the easier those calculations will be later on.

Mortgage, Mortgage, Who's Got the Mortgage?

It may not be long after you assume ownership of your home—possibly after only one or two mortgage payments—that your mortgage lender will sell your mortgage. Servicing mortgage loans—collecting monthly payments, and reserving taxes and insurance premiums in escrow—is big business and quite separate from mortgage lending. Some lenders sell the servicing immediately after originating the loan; others sell blocks of loans as a way to raise cash. At least half of all mortgage debt in America is being serviced by companies other than loan originators or lenders. Problems with loan service are common, particularly once a loan is transferred from lender to service company.

Here's how to respond to four of the most common servicing problems:

Notification

It seems little enough to ask that somebody promptly let you know if your mortgage is transferred. Several states have laws requiring timely notification. On loans in which they have an interest, Fannie Mae and Freddie Mac require both the old and the new servicers to advise you of the transfer. The Mortgage Bankers Association recommends its members to notify you as well.

If your loan is transferred, you should get a "good-bye" letter from your old servicer before receiving a "hello" letter from the new one. Don't redirect payments unless you've been told to do so by your current servicer. If your first notice comes from the new servicer, contact your current lender to make sure the transfer is on the up-and-up.

Homeowners Insurance

If your mortgage servicer fails to pay an insurance premium, you should get a warning from your insurer before the policy is canceled. Some companies send just one notice to the homeowner and mortgage servicer. Should you get such a notice, don't ignore it.

Problems with loan service are common, particularly once a loan is transferred from lender to service company.

Lenders must pay interest on funds held in escrow accounts in California, Connecticut, Iowa, Maine, Maryland, Massachusetts, Minnesota, New Hampshire, New York, Oregon, Rhode Island, Utah, Vermont, and Wisconsin.

Contact both your servicer and the insurer to see that coverage is maintained. In theory, if a mortgage servicer is responsible for paying an insurance premium and fails to do so, resulting in a loss of coverage, the servicer would be liable for losses suffered by the homeowner. But such a situation would compound an already upsetting and stressful event and could force you to sue in order to recoup.

Property Taxes

Many borrowers have complained that their servicer failed to pay property taxes on time. Some found that when the company got around to paying the bill, the late payment was deducted from their escrow account. If you get tangled in that kind of mess, write to both the lender and the taxing authority. You may have to wrestle with the lender to get him to pay what he's already taken your money for, and persuade the taxing authorities to stop harassing you over a problem you didn't create.

Escrow Problems

Mortgage transfers are often accompanied by an increase in your monthly payments. And although terms of the loan don't change, there's a good chance that the amount required for deposit into your escrow account will.

It's difficult to know whether you're being asked to pay too much into your escrow account. Because insurance and tax bills come due at different times of the year, lenders are allowed to keep a cushion in the account. That means the amount you pay into escrow each month will be more than the total of your tax and insurance bills divided by 12. Many contracts permit lenders to keep a cushion covering up to two months, the maximum allowed under the Real Estate Settlement Procedures Act (RESPA). Lenders may use a combined total to calculate the cushion or view taxes and insurance as separate accounts.

Keep track of what is in your account. You should get periodic statements of exactly how much is in there and when payments are made from it. If it appears that the amount is too much, ask for an escrow reanalysis.

If you have a problem that you can't get fixed, find out from the original lender the name of the secondary-market firm—like Fannie Mae or Freddie Mac—that bought your loan. These giants have a strong interest in the proper servicing of the loans they buy and resell; they want to know about problems with servicing firms that do business with them (for contact information, see the accompanying box).

Your servicer must respond within 20 business days and must abide by certain other procedures. When the National Affordable Housing Act was passed in 1990, certain provisions were added to RESPA dealing with complaint resolution. Among them: a stipulation that under certain conditions an aggrieved consumer may recover actual damages up to $1,000.

Calling in the Cavalry

If you have an intractable problem with your mortgage servicer, it's time to contact the owner of your loan. In any correspondence, be sure to include the mortgage company's name, your loan number, name, address, and home and work phone numbers.

If Fannie Mae bought the loan, send a letter (a note jotted on your mortgage payment coupon won't do) to your mortgage company outlining the problem, and send a copy to: Public Information Officer, Fannie Mae, 3900 Wisconsin Ave., N.W., Washington, D.C. 20016-2899. The letter will be forwarded to the appropriate regional office.

For Freddie Mac loans, call or write to the Regional Director of Loan Servicing at the regional office closest to your mortgage company (ask your original lender for the address).

Regional offices are in:
- New York City (212-418-8900)
- McLean, Va. (703-902-7200)
- Atlanta (404-438-3800)
- Dallas (214-702-2000)
- Chicago (312-407-7400)
- Sherman Oaks, Cal. (818-905-0070)

14

Buying a Vacation Home

There's more than one way to own a vacation home, each with financial, legal and tax consequences to consider before the fun begins.

A simple log cabin in the Ozark mountains. A weathered cottage on Cape Cod. A ski condo in Aspen. A secluded home tucked into a cove on the Caribbean island of St. Lucia. A resort timeshare in Pennsylvania's Pocono Mountains.

The words *vacation property* may be used by the owners of each, although the financial, legal and tax consequences of ownership can be as different as the environments.

There are many reasons to buy a second home—some personal, some financial. You could enjoy a vacation spot so much you believe you'll want to keep returning over and over. Rather than renting a different house or hotel room each time, you want to *feel* at home and be recognized as part of a community—and that means having your own place where you can put down roots, entertain friends and family, and stash vacation gear.

If your goal is merely to lock in predictable vacation costs where you like to go each year, a fractional interest or timeshare might make sense. Some kinds of timeshares are not real estate per se but are in effect a prepaid right to use a given unit for a certain length of time each year. If so, keep expectations for financial gain low or nonexistent; it's usually difficult to sell a timeshare for what you paid for it.

You may dream of buying a vacation home where you believe you'll retire one day and convert that second home to your primary residence.

Or you may have financial motivations uppermost in your mind. If this describes you, make sure you check out all the angles before succumbing to the fast talk of a resort salesperson. Buying a vacation home to avoid rising rents might make sense in some communities, but not in others; it often costs the vacationer less to rent the nicest house in a given community for a month than it costs the owner to pay the mortgage, taxes and maintenance on that same house for a month, particularly in the early years of the ownership period.

Price appreciation is another matter. Some people buy in a given vacation community because they've witnessed firsthand a rapid rise in home prices (and probably rents, too) over the previous several years; they want to get in on the action. Carefully selected homes in the most sought-after communities can, in fact, appreciate nicely, making them good investments as well as nice places to spend a vacation. But appreciation is highly variable from region to region and resort to resort. Some who hastily bought timeshares or resort houses from persuasive salesmen have found they can't even recover their original investment in the slender resale market.

Why a Vacation Home?

Define your needs carefully.

- How large a residence do you need?

- What style is practical and desirable?

- How far from your home is acceptable—a few hours drive? a long plane trip?

- How frequently will you want to visit your vacation home? Weekends? Just two weeks annually?

- Will the home be exclusively for your own use, or will you want to rent it out for part or all of the year?

- If the latter, are you willing to curb your taste for the unusual and buy what renters want and like?

Study Before You Buy

It takes study, cool analysis and good luck to make a smart decision. In many ways, though, buying a vacation property is like buying a principal residence, so the preceding chapters of this book should be useful to you. There are also special considerations, such as those addressed in the accompanying box.

Then, as you head out with your dreams, your maps and the classified ads, keep these points in mind:

A depressed price isn't the same thing as a bargain.

The property may have been grossly overpriced to begin with or severely inflated by a speculative orgy. If there's an abundance of listings, try to find out why from independent sources, such as the local tax assessor or a real estate agent. If a lot of people were burned, it could happen again. Or maybe the area has become less socially desirable.

Location, location, location.

That trilogy is just as important for a vacation home as it is for your principal residence. Overbuilding tends to run in cycles, and it generally happens in bigger, better-known, heavily promoted areas with large numbers of builders and hard-charging chambers of commerce. You may find better prospects in older, quieter and less-exotic communities with fewer absentee owners. The more time you can spend looking and comparing, the better you're likely to do.

Check the financial viability of resort operators.

When you buy a home near ski slopes or golf greens, your property's value is directly tied to the quality of the resort's management. Investigate its financial health before you risk your own. You should be able to obtain quarterly statements and annual reports on a publicly held development. A privately held resort is not required to disclose financial information, but some sleuthing can uncover clues about its well-being.

Try to find out whether the company pays creditors and employees on time. Ask homeowners about the company's reputation. Search libraries and electronic data bases for articles about the resort and its owners, and then follow up.

At some resorts—such as Wintergreen, in Virginia's Blue Ridge Mountains—ski, golf, and racquet amenities are owned by a partnership of homeowners. That means you can probably get copies of federally mandated property reports and other financial documents.

Don't speculate.

Don't assume today's prices make appreciation a sure bet. Remember that many investors' hopes were dashed even when all the tax benefits were in place and prices were steadily moving up. Most of today's buyers are families who plan to use the property for vacations and weekend getaways. If a rental market does start to hum, overbuilding could soon spoil things.

Check your access rights.

Find out whether homeowners are guaranteed preferred access to golf courses or ski slopes. Does the guarantee transfer with the property? Get it in writing.

Understand tax benefits.

Albeit to a lesser extent than in the past, Uncle Sam still subsidizes your home away from home. You can probably fully deduct mortgage interest and property taxes you pay on a second home.

Buy for enjoyment.

Buying a place where you can escape for fun, relaxation, tranquility and companionship could do wonders for your health and spirits, and could be one of the best investments you'll ever make. In terms of real value, a well-established, desirable, family-oriented community with good recreation facilities could be a far better choice than a neon-splashed strip of high-rise condominiums and cocktail lounges.

Uncle Sam still subsidizes your home away from home. You can probably fully deduct mortgage interest and property taxes you pay on a second home.

Never buy a home on a first visit to a new resort community or a timeshare resort that uses intensive sales pressure to convince people to commit themselves on the spot.

Don't buy where you haven't visited many times as a vacationer. Most of all, never buy a home on a first visit to a new resort community or timeshare resort that uses intensive sales pressure to convince people to commit themselves on the spot.

While on a vacation in the community you're considering, devote a few days to a thorough investigation of the market. Look at the houses or timeshares for sale. Find out how much homes have sold for in that area, and ignore advertised asking prices. Talk to leading real estate brokers in the community. If you're planning to rent the house out, contact several management firms who specialize in finding tenants, collecting rent, maintaining and making repairs when you're not around. Talk to all the year-round residents you can find, and drop by the local newspaper, chamber of commerce or local library to learn what you can about zoning, future developments, and commercial growth in the area.

Vacation-Home Strategies

Most would-be buyers soon have their choices limited by the lofty price tags attached to the most attractive vacation properties. The scenarios below show the kinds of properties that make the most sense depending on your plans for its use.

Personal Use Only

Affluent buyers are often looking for a unique or unusual property. They want it to reflect their status in life and aren't interested in rental income. They intend to use the property for their own and their family's enjoyment, but long-term appreciation and estate building are primary *investment* objectives. The home may qualify as a second residence; if so, mortgage interest will be fully deductible as long as the combined debt secured by the vacation home and principal residence doesn't exceed $1.1 million.

Good bets include the most sought-after (and expensive) categories of vacation property: rural acreage near growing metropolitan areas; waterfront property; and apartments or townhouses in cities that are hubs of international travel and cultural and recreational attractions.

Some Rental and Business Use

Other affluent buyers look at vacation property with a sharper focus on its potential medium-term investment return. Appreciation and some tax shelter are important financial objectives. They may own more than one property—because it is financially rewarding and because it gives them more than one getaway place. They actively seek rental income and use professional management. Such owners may restrict personal use of a property to maintain deductions and tax shelter (a strategy that demands careful analysis). And they may use it for business purposes, such as entertaining clients or customers.

Choices of vacation property purchased for financial reasons could include condos or townhouses in popular resort areas, or perhaps a condo hotel suite in a sought-after area where the climate permits either one long vacation season or two peak seasons.

Limited Personal Use, Heavy Renting

Less-affluent vacation-home buyers need rental income to help carry their investment. They also need appreciation and tax shelter to make ownership sustainable. They may manage the property on their own or seek renters to supplement those lined up by their manager. They may not use the property themselves in the early years of ownership, or may do so only out of season (see the discussion below on the trade-offs between personal and rental use). Owning in an area that becomes overbuilt—driving down rental rates and slowing appreciation—is a serious financial risk.

*"You can't spend
all your time on
vacation, so why
own a vacation place
all the time?" If you
belong in this
category, consider
fractional interests
and timeshares
in quality
developments.*

Best purchase prospects include resort property in areas with perennial popularity and with, as in the above category, either one long rental season or two rental seasons (for example, a part of New England with winter skiing and summer camping).

Less-Than-Full-Time Ownership

Finally, there are those who dream of owning a beach cottage or a mountain hideaway but cannot afford the down payment or the cash outlay that an unrented property would drain from their budget. "You can't spend all your time on vacation, so why own a vacation place all the time?" they reason.

And, because so many people are in this group, developers and salespeople have spent hours upon hours figuring out how to help them "own"—ways that people wouldn't consider for a primary residence but that may make sense for a vacation home.

If you belong in this category, consider fractional interests and timeshares in quality developments. Resort developers in states including California, the Carolinas, Florida, Hawaii and Texas offer fractional interests in their properties.

Fractional Interest

Fractional interests may be sold as quarter-shares (13 weeks), fifth-shares (ten weeks) or tenth-shares (five weeks). Essentially, you buy title to a number of weeks spread throughout the year. If you buy a quarter-share, for example, you get to use the property every fourth week. Each year, the sequence shifts forward a week, giving you the opportunity to use all the weeks of the year within a four-year period. Some fractional-interest contracts use a mix of floating and fixed time periods.

Fractional interests offer better prospects for appreciation than timeshares (see below). Pay attention to marketing costs, which range from zero to 25%.

Buyers paying a 25% premium in sales expenses such as commissions will have to wait a long time before counting paper profits.

The resort developer is the most likely source of funds to finance a fractional interest, and terms vary widely. Prices for "fractionals" range from $25,000 to $100,000 or more. Check with a knowledgeable accountant regarding tax consequences and interest deductions.

Timeshares

This is a popular means of dividing vacation-property ownership, and it's often the cheapest way to buy into a resort. You become one of the owners of a property, typically a condo apartment. Usually, ownership is divided into 52 parts—one for each week of the year—and the parts are sold one or more at a time. A one-week timeshare rarely sells for more than $10,000.

Timeshare ownership can be in the form of tenancy-in-common (sometimes called time-span ownership) or interval ownership. Tenancy-in-common gives you an undivided interest in a property, prorated according to the amount of time you purchase. Interval ownership lasts only for a specified number of years. When those years are up, you and the other interval owners become tenants in common. Under either type of ownership, you don't always get a specified unit for a fixed time period. Instead, you may choose from interchangeable units and floating weeks.

One form of timesharing—known as a vacation license, vacation lease or club membership—carries no ownership rights at all, only the right to use the property each year for a number of years. Ownership stays in the hands of the developer.

Whatever the form of purchase, you normally cannot get a mortgage to buy a timeshare. Financing typically is covered by a personal loan over a five- to ten-year period with a 10% down payment, and the lender usually is the developer. Check with your

A timeshare doesn't make sense if you'd like to sell at a profit eventually. This caveat is particularly pertinent if the unit is new and the developer still is selling others.

accountant and attorney about the tax implications. Don't rely on assurances from a salesperson.

If guaranteeing yourself a slot at your favorite resort once a year is your goal, a timeshare may suit the bill. It locks in the cost of staying at a particular place, yet provides the flexibility to vacation elsewhere, too. For an annual fee, usually about $50 or $60, you can use a timeshare exchange that works out vacation-place swaps with other timeshare owners around the world.

But a timeshare doesn't make sense if you'd like to sell at a profit eventually. This caveat is particularly pertinent if the unit is new and the developer still is selling others. Heavy marketing costs, which may include free airfare and lodging to lure potential buyers to the resort, push up cost of units. Developers don't devote time to reselling units until a resort is completed and sold out. According to the International Resale Brokers Association, most timeshares are resold for *half—or less*—of what their owners originally paid and take months to sell, if they can be sold at all.

Buying With Partners

Friends often get together to buy a vacation home, either as tenants in common or in a legally constituted partnership.

Owning as tenants in common, friendly as it sounds, can cause headaches. Head off problems by anticipating and addressing them in a written partnership agreement. Use your real estate lawyer to draw up the agreement, but ask an attorney in the vacation locale to check relevant regulations.

Make sure the contract addresses the following:

- **How ownership will be divided,** which in turn determines who pays how much of the down payment, monthly payment, maintenance and repairs. The contract should also describe how any profits or losses from rent or sale of the place will be divided and how tax benefits will be distributed.

- **Who gets to use the property when.**

- **What constitutes a deciding vote** and under what circumstances a vote is considered necessary.

- **Which owner will act as managing partner** and thus be responsible for signing checks and paying the routine expenses.

- **How much advance notice** a withdrawing partner must give and how the buyout price will be set.

A partnership may also protect the existing mortgage when a new owner enters the picture if the documents make clear that it is an interest in the partnership—not an interest in the property—that is being transferred.

Ideally, a general partnership should try to find a lender who is willing to limit each partner's liability on the loan to his or her percentage of ownership, even though such agreements are unusual. Otherwise, each partner is responsible for 100% of the loan, so a lender could single out any partner to sue for the money if there's a default, instead of going through complicated foreclosure proceedings.

Taxes Take No Holiday

One thing you can't get away from at your get-away-from-it-all vacation home is taxes and some exasperatingly convoluted tax rules.

When It's Just for You and Yours

First, look at the bright side. If your home away from home is only that—a second residence that's never rented out—the tax benefits come with few complications. You can deduct the mortgage interest on a second home just as you can on your principal place of residence.

Rent for more than 14 days, and you become a landlord in the eyes of the IRS. You must report rental income, and you qualify to deduct rental expenses.

Only two homes to a customer, though. Congress apparently figures that anyone who can afford more than two homes can handle the mortgage interest without the help of a tax deduction. Interest on any additional homes—and on any debt on the first and second homes that exceeds the $1.1 million cap—falls in the category of nondeductible personal interest.

A motor home or boat can qualify as a second residence for purposes of this deduction. To meet the IRS definition of a home, the boat or recreational vehicle must have basic living accommodations, including cooking facilities, a place to sleep and a toilet. (However, if you are subject to the alternative minimum tax, interest on a loan for a boat you use as a second home can't be deducted as mortgage interest.)

Property taxes are deductible, regardless of how many homes you own. However, points paid to get a mortgage on a vacation home are not deductible in the year paid. Instead, they're deducted proportionally over the life of the loan.

When You Also Rent

It's when you start renting out the vacation home—as many owners do to help pay the freight—that things get tricky. The IRS does not care about rental income you receive if you rent the place for 14 or fewer days a year. You can charge as much as you want, and as long as your tenants stay no longer than two weeks the rent you receive is tax-free. Rent for more than 14 days, though, and you become a landlord in the eyes of the IRS. You must report rental income, and you qualify to deduct rental expenses.

How much time tenants use the property compared with how much time you enjoy it yourself determines whether the house is treated as a personal residence or a business property. This distinction is the key to the tax ramifications.

If your personal use accounts for more than 14 days during the year or more than 10% of the number of days the place is rented (26 or more personal days compared with 250 rental days, for example), the house is considered a personal residence. Hold personal use below the 14-day/10% threshold, however, and the house is considered a rental property.

Because the tax consequences turn on personal use, it's important to know that the IRS takes a broad view of what counts. Personal use includes:

- **Any day the property is used by you or any part-owner** (unless it is rented as a principal residence to a part-owner under a shared-equity arrangement).

- **Any day it is used by a member of your family,** whether or not rent is paid. For this test, a member of your family includes your spouse, brothers and sisters, parents and grandparents, and children and grandchildren.

- **Any day it is rented for less than fair market rent.**

- **Any day the property is used by someone in connection with an arrangement that gives you the right to use another dwelling,** such as if you trade a week at your beach home for a week at a mountain resort.

- **Any day it is used as a result of your donating its use.** If you donate use of your vacation home to a charitable organization—to be auctioned off at a fund-raising event, for example—the period the property is used under the arrangement counts as personal use.

Note that time you spend at the place doing repairs or general maintenance does not count as personal use. As long as that is the primary purpose of staying at the vacation home, the day isn't counted. You must keep detailed records showing the dates of personal use, rental use, and repair and maintenance days.

Tax losses—available only if the property qualifies as a rental — can often be used to trim your tax bill by sheltering other income.

The breakdown between personal and rental days is crucial because it determines whether the property can produce tax losses. Such losses—available only if personal use is limited so that the property qualifies as a rental rather than a residence—can often be used to trim your tax bill by sheltering other income, such as your salary.

But limiting personal use no longer automatically opens the door to big tax losses. The law limits the deduction of "passive" losses, a category that includes all losses on rental property. There is an important exception, though, that protects many vacation home-owners. If your adjusted gross income (AGI) is less than $100,000, you can deduct up to $25,000 of rental losses each year. The $25,000 allowance is gradually phased out as AGI rises to $150,000. To sidestep the passive-loss rules, you must "actively" manage the property, a requirement you can probably meet as long as you're involved in such decisions as approving tenants, rental terms and repairs.

Expenses you can't deduct because of the passive-loss rules aren't lost forever. Unused losses are held over to future years when they can be used to off-set income from the vacation home or other passive investments. Also, any passive losses unused when you sell the property can be deducted against the profit on the sale or any other income.

Even if the $25,000 exception will protect your rental write-offs, you have to watch out for another potential trap. Limiting personal use of your vacation home may mean giving up the right to some mortgage-interest deductions.

Remember, the law only permits mortgage-interest deductions for loans secured by your first and second *residence*. If your vacation place is a business property, then the mortgage isn't covered. Part of the interest could still be deductible—the portion attributable to the business use of the property—but the rest would be considered personal interest, and therefore is not deductible.

That rule has led some tax advisers to recommend that taxpayers intentionally flunk the 14-day/10% test by increasing personal use of vacation property. That way, you preserve the full interest write-off. Part of the interest would be deducted as a rental expense and the rest as personal mortgage interest. What you give up, of course, is the opportunity to claim a tax loss.

Allocation of Expenses

To figure your vacation-home deductions, you have to allocate expenses to personal or rental use. There are two ways to do this—the IRS method and another approach that has been approved in court cases—and the one that's best for you depends on your circumstances.

According to the IRS, you begin by adding up the total number of days the house was used for personal and rental purposes. Then figure the percentage of time it was used for rental. That's the percentage of total expenses you can deduct against rental income.

For example, assume you have a cabin in the mountains that you use for 30 days during the year and rent out for 100 days. The 100 days of rental use equals 77% of the total 130 days the cabin was used during the year. Using the IRS formula, 77% of your expenses—including interest, taxes, insurance, utilities, repairs and depreciation—would be rental expenses.

The IRS is also particular about the order in which you deduct those expenses against your rental income. You deduct interest and taxes first, then expenses other than depreciation, and then depreciation. The sequence is important, and detrimental, because of the rule that limits rental deductions to the amount of rental income when personal use exceeds 14 days or 10% of total use. Remember that mortgage interest and property taxes not assigned to rental use could be claimed as regular itemized deductions instead. But by requiring you to deduct those expenses against rental income—that might otherwise be offset by depreciation you won't get to claim—the law squelches the write-off for taxes and interest as an itemized deduction.

By using a different allocation formula, though, you can limit the interest and tax expenses used to off-set rental income and thereby boost the write-off of other rental costs. Courts have allowed taxpayers to allocate taxes and interest over the entire year rather than over just the total number of days a property is used. In the example above assuming 100 days of rental use, that method would allocate just 27% (100 divided by 365) of the taxes and interest to rental income. That would leave more rental income against which other expenses can be deducted. The extra taxes and interest can be deducted as regular itemized deductions.

Although the court-approved formula can pay off when the 14-day/10% test makes the property a personal residence, the IRS version can be more appealing if

For More Information

Periodicals and Newsletters

- *Hideaways International* (15 Goldsmith St., P.O. Box 1270, Littleton, Mass. 01460; 800-843-4433). Directory of vacation homes for rent and for sale worldwide; published twice a year; subscription includes a quarterly newsletter. Trial subscription available.

- *Island Properties Report* (4061 Bonita Beach Rd., Suite 201, Bonita Springs, Fla. 33923; 813-495-1604). Monthly newsletter on the Caribbean; eight islands are covered in depth each year, along with four quarterly reports covering the region generally. Each issue features 30 to 40 properties, along with a list of real estate brokers.

- *John T. Reed's Real Estate Investor's Monthly* (Reed Publishing, 342 Bryan Drive, Danville, Cal., 94526; 800-635-5425). Plain talk and cautionary counsel from an expert in the field.

Advisers, Brokers and Clearinghouses

- **American Society of Real Estate Counselors,** 430 N. Michigan Ave., Chicago, Ill. 60611; 312-329-8427.

- **Condolink,** 723 N. 120th St., Omaha, Neb. 68154; 800-877-9600.

- **Timeshare Resales International,** 745 E. Market St., Harrisonburg, Va. 22801; 800-368-3541 (East Coast), 800-423-6377 (West Coast).

the place qualifies as a business property. You need to look at the specifics of your situation to determine the best method for you.

Retirement Plans?

What if you were to buy a second home before retirement, rent it out for four or five years, then retire to it? It would be classified as a rental property and you could deduct your expenses—including mortgage interest, property taxes, operating costs and depreciation—up to the amount of your rental income. Any excess expenses would be subject to the passive-loss rules.

Unfortunately, when you finally sold your home and retired to the rental, you wouldn't be able to roll over the profit from your old home into the rental. To qualify for the rollover, a new principal residence must cost at least as much as you got from the sale of the old one, and you must buy or build and occupy the new home within two years—before or after the sale of the old one. If you want to buy a retirement home and rent it until you move in—and still keep the rollover right—you must buy the new home, sell the old, and move into the new within two years.

If you are age 55 or older when you sell your old home, and have owned and lived in it for at least three of the five years leading up to the sale, you may qualify for the special provision that permits taxpayers to exclude from income up to $125,000 of profit on the sale of a home (see the discussion in Chapter 16).

P A R T

T W O

For Sellers

CHAPTER

15

Alternatives to Selling

There are as many reasons for selling a home as there are for buying. Some people sell because they're relocating and believe they must sell their current house to get the cash they need for a new home. Others sell because they need more space for a growing family—or less space because the children are grown. Still others, due to retirement, ill health or a reduction in income, sell because they need the money that's tied up in their home for living expenses.

Whatever the reason, give some thought to whether you might meet your objectives without selling. Don't expect to hear about these alternatives from real estate agents. In a business fueled by sales commissions, it's a rare agent who will advise you not to sell. Nor should an agent advise you on something that is really a financial-planning decision. If you're unsure about selling, check with your lawyer or accountant—or seek advice from a financial planner.

If your present home is too small, what about remodeling or adding on? Moving to another home is usually the most expensive solution to the tight-space problem. Sales commissions, closing costs, moving and decorating costs—not to mention picking up and moving—take a big toll financially and emotionally.

Would remodeling make sense? Do you like the neighborhood well enough to justify the cost and hassle

Before you spend the money to pack up and move, consider financial strategies that will help you make the most of what you have.

of a building project? Is your lot big enough for an addition? Would your improved house be too big or fancy for the neighborhood, making it hard to recover the cost of your improvements if you had to move?

Moving to a new job? Study housing markets in your current and future hometowns. If houses are appreciating in value rapidly where you live now, but less so where you're headed, consider converting your home to a rental property (see Chapter 23 for a discussion of the implications of turning your home into a rental property).

But where will the money for remodeling or for a down payment on a place in the new hometown come from? It could be right under your nose. You could tap the equity in your current home via a full refinancing, traditional second mortgage, or home-equity line of credit. These possibilities are discussed below. Beginning on page 279, is a discussion of special options for older homeowners who want to stay put but need the money they could get from selling the house.

Tapping Your Home Equity

Your home equity is the difference between what the place is worth and what you owe on loans secured by the property. If you could sell for $100,000 and the balance on your mortgage is $60,000, for example, your equity is $40,000.

Your equity should increase each year as your home appreciates in value and monthly payments reduce what's owed on the mortgage. Home equity could be the major building block of your net worth.

In recent years more and more homeowners have been dipping into that equity by borrowing against it. The appeal of this kind of debt is that interest paid on the loan is generally fully deductible on your tax return, while interest paid on other consumer loans is not. If the money will be used to improve your home substantially, the sky's the limit. You can deduct up to $1 million of mortgage debt used to buy a home or make major improvements. For other home-equity debt, the cap is $100,000 (beyond the loan you took to buy the house). It's deductible for any use except buying tax-exempt bonds or single-premium life insurance.

In other words, the government subsidizes the cost of borrowing *if* the loan is secured by your home. Consider what that means on a $10,000, ten-year loan at 10.5%. In the first 12 monthly payments, interest totals $1,022. If the loan is secured by your home and the $1,022 is deducted in the 28% bracket, the federal government effectively pays $286 of the interest. (Your state government might help, too, assuming you also get the benefit of the deduction on your state return.)

Home-Equity Line of Credit

This has become the preferred method of tapping money needed for home improvements, college expenses or a new car. Unlike a traditional second mortgage (discussed on page 271), a home-equity line is a form of revolving credit, somewhat like a credit card. Your home serves as collateral for the home-equity line. The lender sets a credit limit and you may borrow up to that amount by writing checks. Convenience and tax-deductible interest give these loans great allure. But casual use will drain your home equity (and lower your net worth); worse, it could cause you to lose your home.

How It Works

Your maximum credit limit is based on the loan-to-value (LTV) ratio of your home. If a lender uses a 75% LTV ratio, for example, you could borrow up to 75% of the appraised value of your home. If you own a $100,000 home free and clear, for example, you could be eligible for a credit limit of up to $75,000. If you owe $60,000 on the mortgage, though, the limit would be $15,000—$75,000 minus the $60,000 already borrowed against the house.

Loans usually carry a variable interest rate figured

Convenience and tax-deductible interest give these loans great allure. But casual use will drain your home equity; worse, it could cause you to lose your home.

by adding one to three points to a floating rate, commonly the prime rate. The rate can vary as often as monthly. And, although home-equity loans must have a cap on how high the interest rate can go, there is no limit on how high a lender can set that cap.

You pay interest on what you borrow, not on the amount of credit available to you. You'll be required to make at least a minimum monthly payment on any outstanding loan amount.

Home-equity lines are usually structured to expire far sooner than 30-year mortgages, although a few come due only when you sell. Generally, the loan period is divided into two segments—a "draw" period and a "payback" period. During the draw period, typically five years or so, you can borrow at will simply by writing a check. As you pay back the loan, your credit limit is restored accordingly. The length of the draw period is set out in your contract, along with minimum withdrawal amounts and any restrictions on how often you can tap the credit line.

The contract also spells out what happens when your draw period ends. You may be able to renew the credit line, for example, or be required to pay the outstanding balance at once. Alternatively, you could be required to repay the outstanding balance over a fixed period—say, ten years.

See Your Own Banker First

• •

Some lenders are more comfortable putting a second mortgage behind their own first, and that could be reflected in their rates or terms. Great Western Bank, which lends in California and Florida, lets borrowers tap 80% of their equity if it holds the first mortgage but only 75% if another lender made the loan.

What to Look for When You Shop

When lenders are competing hard for home-equity loan business, you may find temporary low teaser rates dangled before you. Lenders may reduce application and closing charges to "cost." A few may even offer to set up equity lines free of all closing costs.

But more often, appraisals, title searches, credit reports and the like are added to the cost of the loan. Few banks or thrifts dare dump all these costs on you, but many levy whatever the competition or market will bear. Beware: Even when an ad touts "no points" or "low fees," that may mean no *bank* fees. Outlays for paperwork, taxes and assorted services can still total hundreds of dollars.

Lenders generally calculate closing costs as a percentage of the credit limit or charge a flat fee plus actual costs. As a rule, the larger the line of credit, the more you pay. That's because the amount charged is based on the maximum loan available, not on what you actually borrow. Generally, you pay these costs when you open the credit line, although in certain cases you may be able to roll them into the first loan advance.

The shorter the borrowing term, the more critical it is to hold up-front costs down. On the other hand, if you're using the loan to pay for major home improvements, you'll probably be repaying over a period of five years or more. In that case reasonable up-front fees and transaction costs are less important than the interest rate and the index to which the rate is pegged.

Recently, the stiffest competition for your money has been in credit lines with adjustable rates. The battle has lowered rates and generated new options. But most home-equity borrowing is still local, so going to a national lender is no guarantee of getting the lowest rates.

A minimum credit line is typically $10,000. Interest rates are adjustable—usually the prime interest rate plus one to three percentage points. Loan terms are all over the lot. Lines of credit typically provide for a period of five to 20 years during which you can tap the account by writing checks, using a special credit card or making a telephone transaction. The payback periods typically range from ten to 20 years. Once you reach the end of the advance period, you must stop borrowing and make regular payments of principal and interest for the rest of the loan term or you'll face a balloon payment.

Even when an ad touts "no points" or "low fees," that may mean no bank fees. Outlays for paperwork, taxes and assorted services can still total hundreds.

Nearly 80% of home-equity loans are now pegged to the prime rate. Lenders add one to three points, or more, to get their index rate. Should you turn up an equity line pegged to some other index—for example, the 90-day Treasury bill—ask the lender to provide you with an historical example showing how changes in the index rate in the past would have affected minimum payments due on the home-equity line compared with what you would have experienced tied to the prime. (An index that responds quickly to rising rates will also reflect a drop in rates much more

Home-Equity Loan Work Sheet

	Lender 1	Lender 2	Lender 3
Name	_____	_____	_____
Rates			
Rate	_____	_____	_____
Points	_____	_____	_____
Annual percentage rate (APR)	_____	_____	_____
Index	_____	_____	_____
Margin	_____	_____	_____
Introductory rate	_____	_____	_____
Maximum rate	_____	_____	_____
Terms			
Minimum line	_____	_____	_____
Maximum line	_____	_____	_____
Minimum advance	_____	_____	_____
Advance period	_____	_____	_____
Payback period	_____	_____	_____
Balloon?	_____	_____	_____
Fees			
Application fee	_____	_____	_____
Annual fee	_____	_____	_____
Prepayment fee	_____	_____	_____
Closing costs	_____	_____	_____
(taxes, appraisal, credit report, title insurance, etc.)			

quickly than a sluggish one such as the index of 52-week Treasury bills.)

Compare each loan you consider according to these points:

Payment terms

These should be spelled out clearly. For example, you might be told that your line of credit is good for ten years, with a minimum monthly payment of $100 or 1/360 of the loan balance plus finance charges, whichever is greater. At the end of this ten-year draw period, you would have another five years to pay any remaining balance. Minimum terms during the repayment period would be 1/60 of the outstanding balance plus finance charges.

Watch out for negative amortization, which means that interest payments are too low to let you pay back the loan during its term. The balloon payment at the end could catch you off guard. If you can't pay or refinance, you may have to sell or face foreclosure.

Payment example

You must be given an example of what the minimum monthly payments would be if you borrowed a certain amount—say, $10,000—and the interest rate reached its maximum level.

Lenders' fees

These include loan-application fees (typically around $150), one or more "points" (each at 1% of your credit limit) and a maintenance fee (often $75 or so).

Third-party fees

Fees usually include amounts for home appraisals, credit reports and legal fees, and might total between $500 and $900.

Variable-rate features

As noted earlier, you must be told what interest index is used, along with any annual or lifetime rate caps that apply. The index must be one that is out of the lender's control. Banks aren't allowed to use their own cost of funds as an index or change the index at their discretion.

As a rule, lenders can't accelerate payments or change the contract terms once the line has been opened. But a rainy-day fund could dry up just when you need it. Most home-equity lenders check borrowers' credit every year or so. If something on your credit report turns sour, your borrowing rights could be frozen or reduced. A sudden drawdown when you haven't used any credit for an extended period or a request to switch to easier payback terms could also trigger a check. Lenders have the right to reappraise your home periodically to make sure there's still enough equity cushion for their safety.

Once you've found a good home-equity loan, compare the deal with a traditional second mortgage (see the following page) before you commit. You can't simply compare the APRs on the two loans, however. The APR on second mortgages—just as with first mortgages—takes into account the interest rate charged, plus points and other finance charges, while the APR on a home-equity loan is based only on the periodic interest rate and excludes points and any other charges.

After you commit yourself, you have three business days to back out of the loan if your principal residence serves as collateral.

Paying off the loan when you sell

You may be required to advise the lender when you put your house on the market. In any case, at settlement you must repay the home-equity loan along with your original mortgage. You'll face minor additional fees because clearing title involves an extra step. Your settlement attorney must prepare a release, which can cost from $10 to $50, and file it, usually at a cost of another $10 to $25.

Second Mortgages

Lenders typically offer second mortgages—also called second trusts—of up to 15 years. Unlike an open-ended equity line, second mortgages involve borrowing a fixed amount of money up front and then making payments of principal and interest over a fixed period to amortize the loan. You generally can borrow up to 75% or 80% of your home's appraised value; if you can find a lender willing to count the value remodeling will add to the property, you may be able to borrow more. (Check out Fannie Mae's HomeStyle remodeling loans.)

Interest rates are higher than those on conventional ARMs and fixed-rate first mortgages and adjustable-rate home-equity loans. Adjustable-rate second mortgages may be more competitive, but their spread over the index rate is commonly two to four and one-half percentage points. Rates are most often adjusted monthly.

The application process for a second mortgage is similar to that for a first. You won't get approval until your home is appraised, your credit checked and title insurance written. Turnaround time for approval can be fairly short; you could close within two or three weeks of applying.

You'll also have to pay closing costs, which typically amount to 2% or 3% of the loan amount. For second mortgages of less than $15,000, lenders are often satisfied with a drive-by appraisal, verification of existing title insurance and a credit report. As with home-equity loans, lenders may allow you to finance the closing costs as part of the loan.

Even with a higher interest rate, adding a second trust on top of a first mortgage usually costs far less, over the whole term of your homeownership, than refinancing with a new first.

You generally can borrow up to 75% or 80% of your home's appraised value— more if you can find a lender willing to count the value remodeling will add.

FHA Loans

You can borrow $25,000 or less for specific improvements to your home (sorry, no swimming pool) with an FHA Title I loan. FHA-insured Title I loans are fixed-rate and can be obtained through contractors or from banks or other lenders. (Lenders inspect finished projects when you borrow more than $7,500. On lesser loans, you'll be asked to certify that the work qualifies as a home improvement.) Loan terms run from six months to as long as 15 years.

If you borrow less than $5,000, the loan won't be secured by a lien on your home. But interest payments on such unsecured personal loans are not deductible as mortgage interest for federal tax purposes. Larger loans are secured by your home and interest is deductible. Unlike with home-equity lines and second mortgages, the combined total of mortgage debt and Title I loan can go as high as 100% of equity.

For More Information

● ●

To learn more about FHA Title I loans for home improvement, call HUD at 800-733-4663 and leave your name and address on the recording. HUD staff will send you a brochure describing the program and a list of lenders operating in your area.

Full Refinancing

First, the good news. An owner who trades a $100,000 fixed-rate, 30-year mortgage at 10% for the same loan at 8% is happily saving $144 a month before taxes. Refinancing means paying off your old loan and getting a new first mortgage. Now the bad news. It generally means paying fees for origination, appraisal and credit check, and points, too.

What if your rate is 9.5%, or you paid to refinance a couple of years ago, or you have an adjustable-rate mortgage (ARM) with an adjustment due soon? Is refinancing worth it?

A home-equity loan or second mortgage may be the fastest way to tap your equity, but refinancing could be the better route in any of the following situations:

- interest rates are 2% or more less than what you are now paying;

- rates aren't quite 2% less, but you plan to stay put; or

- you figure you could pay off a new loan in less time with roughly the same payment you are making on your current mortgage.

Do you have remodeling in mind? Say your home is worth $200,000 and the mortgage balance is $75,000. You could refinance for $125,000 at a new lower rate, use $75,000 to pay off the old loan and free $50,000 of home equity for remodeling. Lower interest rates mean you could get a bigger loan without a big increase in monthly payments. For example, the principal and interest payment on a $100,000, 10%, 30-year, fixed-rate mortgage is $878. With rates at 7.5%, if you refinanced for $130,000 and used the money left after paying off the old loan for home improvements, monthly principal and interest payments on the new loan would be $910—just $32 more than on the old loan.

Refinancing can make sense even if you don't need to tap the equity in your home. In fact, *consider refinancing anytime there's a difference of two percentage points or more between your fixed-loan rate and current rates.* The two-point rule works in your favor when you stay in the house long enough for lower monthly payments to offset the costs of refinancing— usually four to seven years. Refinancing with less than a two-point differential can be advantageous if you plan to live in your home for a long time. Even a 1.5-point spread can do the trick when you stick around more than seven years. (Since ARM rates can change, refinancing from a fixed-rate loan to an ARM is more problematic.)

Consider refinancing anytime there's a difference of two percentage points or more between your fixed-loan rate and current rates.

Figuring the Cost

In the work sheet (right), first add up the cost of points and other fees, which can average 2% to 5% of the mortgage amount. To figure how long it would take to pay this back, calculate your new monthly payment, using the table on page 162. Subtract that amount from your current principal and interest payment to get your monthly pretax savings. Then, because the interest is tax-deductible, subtract 28% of the savings—or 15% or 31%, depending on your top tax rate—to get your approximate after-tax savings. Divide the total cost of obtaining the mortgage by those savings. The result is how long it will take to recoup refinancing expenses. The longer you expect to keep the loan beyond that point, the stronger the argument for refinancing.

What If You Have an ARM?

The problem with ARMs is that your current rate probably is below today's 30-year fixed rate. Should you keep it, trade to a fixed rate or take advantage of low teaser rates on new ARMs?

Switching to a fixed rate

If you plan to stay in your house, it could make sense to lock in a fixed rate. You wouldn't necessarily save a lot of money compared with the ARM you trade in, but you'd get peace of mind knowing you wouldn't lose if rates rose.

An ARM for an ARM

When first year "teaser" rates are two to three percentage points lower than your current ARM, it's tempting to consider switching an old ARM for a new one. First-year payments would drop substantially. But after that, the interest rate would reach about what it would have been on your old ARM, assuming the index and margin were the same. You come out ahead only if your first-year savings exceed the cost of refinancing.

Your Refinancing Work Sheet

This work sheet lets you figure out how long it will take to pay yourself back if you refinance. Figures for the example, based on a $100,000 loan, are typical. To compute your new monthly payments for the second step of the Payback section, refer to the table on page 162.

	Example	Your Loan
The Cost of Refinancing		
Add the following:		
Points	$ 1,000	$_____
Application fee	35	_____
Title search and insurance	500	_____
Inspections	200	_____
Survey	150	_____
Lender's underwriting fee	200	_____
Credit report	50	_____
Appraisal	250	_____
Attorney fees	250	_____
Recording fees	50	_____
Transfer taxes	1,000	_____
Other (prepayment penalty, and so on)	+ 0	+ _____
Equals Total Cost of Refinancing	**$ 3,685**	**$_____**
The Payback		
Current monthly mortgage payment (principal and interest; based on 30-year fixed-rate at 10%)	$ 878	$_____
Subtract new mortgage payment (P&I; 30-year fixed-rate at 8%)	- 734	- _____
Equals pretax savings per month	$ 144	$_____
Multiply your tax rate (eg., 28%) by pretax savings and subtract result	- 40	- _____
Equals your after-tax savings per month	$ 104	$_____
Divide total cost of refinancing	$ 3,685	$_____
by monthly savings	÷ 104	÷ _____
Equals Number of Months to Break Even	**35**	_____

Switching from a fixed-rate to an ARM

If you plan to sell within one to three years, you could cut your monthly principal and interest payments dramatically by switching to an ARM. Assume you have a 9.5%, fixed-rate 30-year loan. You can refinance with a 5% ARM, cutting monthly payments in the first year from $841 to $536. If you paid $3,000 in closing costs, you'd be ahead by nearly $650 without taking taxes into account. Even if the ARM rate jumped to 7% (because of a two-point annual cap), you'd pocket an additional savings of $2,143 in year two.

Comparing Points and Rates

A point, which is 1% of the mortgage amount, is prepaid interest—you pay it up front. Paying more points lowers the note rate by some fraction of a percentage point, so you have to decide between a higher rate and fewer points or a lower rate and more points.

The longer you'll be in the home, the better off you'll be paying more points to get the lower rate. A three-step calculation can help you choose the best combination of rates and points.

1. Estimate the number of years you think you'll keep the loan.

2. Divide the years into the number of points.

3. Add that to the interest rate.

To see how this works out, see the examples in the accompanying box.

The Difference Points Make

• •

The examples below assume that you'll keep your loan five years. In the first case, the interest rate is 8% with three points. Three points divided by five years equals 0.6. Add that to the interest rate for an effective rate—reflecting the points—of about 8.6%.

Interest Rate	Number of Points	Effective Rate
8%	3	8.6%
8.25	2	8.65
8.375	1.5	8.675

Tax Concerns

When you're refinancing just the balance of your mortgage, interest on the entire amount is tax-deductible. If you borrow additional money, the interest on up to $100,000 extra is deductible as home-equity debt. Unlike points for the original mortgage, points for refinancing must be deducted over the life of the loan, whether you pay in cash or add them to the loan, unless you use the funds for improvements to your home.

You can keep money in your pocket by folding the closing costs into the loan. This also has the effect of adding otherwise nondeductible charges, such as an appraisal fee, to the amount on which you pay deductible interest.

Shopping Tips

Check first with your current lender to see whether it offers lower rates to its customers. To compare fixed-rate loans, look at the APR, even though it has limitations—it assumes you'll hold the loan to maturity, for instance. Some lenders include the application fee, while others do not. Ask for the rate apart from the fees, and note which fees are nonrefundable.

Property values can be a sticking point because refinancing takes more equity than buying a house. Some lenders won't lend more than 75% of a home's value when you refinance for more than the balance on your current mortgage.

About one in four loan applications doesn't go through, and applicants lose hundreds of dollars in nonrefundable fees. Avoid that kind of disappointment and hassle by getting yourself prequalified. Check with local real estate agents to get an estimate of your property's value.

In 1989, the Federal National Mortgage Association (Fannie Mae), the biggest investor in home mortgages, eased refinancing rules for homeowners and lenders under certain circumstances. Unfortunately, the rules won't work for you if you are considering refinancing as a means of tapping your equity rather than as a means of getting a more favorable interest rate. Borrowers are allowed to take no more than 1% of the loan amount out as cash.

If you refinance with your current loan servicer, streamlined rules mean you could save $250 to $300 on the typical 3% to 5% of loan principal charged in refinancings, and possibly get your request processed and closed in weeks rather than months.

Because lenders want to sell the loans they originate, most now have policies that conform to Fannie Mae's guidelines.

You don't need a new home appraisal when refinancing into a fixed-rate loan with the same lender —provided the lender vouches that the property hasn't lost value since the original loan was made.

A full-blown credit report isn't necessary—just a check of your existing electronic credit file and a simplified income verification. Your mortgage payment record must be good but not necessarily perfect.

You can roll up-front refinancing costs into the new loan, and you need not wait any minimum time before refinancing.

Refinancing points—unlike points paid to buy a principal residence—are not necessarily deductible all at once in the year you pay them. If you're refinancing for home-improvement money, you can deduct the points immediately; otherwise, this expense is considered prepaid interest to be written off over the life of the loan (see Chapter 3 for details).

New Protections

For the first time, mortgage lenders must provide refinancers with "good faith" estimates of settlement costs and other fees associated with the loan. You must be given these estimates within three business days after applying for a loan, whether you have applied directly to a lender or used a mortgage broker. If you request the information, the lender must show you a completed "HUD-1" statement setting out actual charges one business day before settlement. (These changes bring refinancings under the Real Estate Settlement Procedures Act, RESPA, along with new home loans.)

Lenders don't have to give the HUD-1 form to you if you are taking out a second mortgage or home-equity loan. That right should be extended to home-equity borrowers some time in 1993.

Other changes that took effect as part of a package of consumer-protection laws loosen the prohibition against real estate agents' receiving fees for referring buyers to lenders. Agents can now charge you for mortgage advice or for accepting a loan application. The agent must tell you about fees up front and are forbidden to require the use of a particular lender. He or she must also give you a special HUD form telling you in plain language that you might save money by contacting lenders on your own. It's still a felony for real estate agents to accept cash or other rewards from a lender or title company just for sending business their way.

Special Help for Senior Citizens

If you find yourself in the awkward position of having too little income for a comfortable lifestyle, but plenty of equity in your paid-up home, you aren't alone. Three out of four Americans age 65 and older own their homes, and more than 80% of those people have paid off the mortgage. Total home equity held by America's senior citizens may be as much as $2 trillion.

But many of these elderly people have only modest incomes; they wouldn't benefit from conventional means of tapping home equity because they couldn't handle the monthly repayment schedule for a new mortgage or home-equity loan. If you face such a dilemma, you may want to look into ways to unlock that equity and convert it to monthly income (see the accompanying box).

Many elderly people have only modest incomes; they wouldn't benefit from conventional means of tapping home equity because they couldn't handle the monthly repayment schedule for a new mortgage or home-equity loan.

Special-Purpose Loans

A far simpler option is to take advantage of special- purpose loans available from many local government agencies, nonprofit organizations and a few state governments. These loans are usually restricted to homeowners with limited incomes. The loans most often carry low or no interest, and can be used for property taxes or to pay for home repair, health-related modifications or in-home services. They need not be repaid until the house is sold or you die or move away permanently.

The "loans" don't always involve cash. You might be able to defer paying your property tax by setting up a special account with a government agency. When you defer the tax, the account establishes a lien against your property for the amount of the tax, which will be payable when you sell the house or die.

More on Equity Conversion

● ●

The Home Equity Kit, by Andrew McLean (John Wiley & Sons), evaluates the income-producing benefits of various home-equity conversion options. McLean analyzes how much surplus income (additional yearly income from equity conversion, minus annual housing costs) would result from: a cash sale and purchase of a replacement home; cash sale and rental; installment sale and purchase of a replacement home; installment sale and rental; reverse mortgage; sale-leaseback; and renting out a room.

Though this book is currently out of print, it's worth looking for at your public library.

Reverse Mortgages

These special mortgages allow you to live off your nest egg and in it, too. Reverse mortgages mirror the cash flow of a regular mortgage: Instead of making monthly payments, you receive monthly increments as the loan is advanced to you. You pay nothing back until the term is up, when the advances plus interest must be repaid, presumably from the proceeds from the sale of your home. Monthly income is tax-free. Federally insured reverse mortgages are available from approved lenders in 43 states. In addition, noninsured loans can be obtained from some state and local government agencies, nonprofit organizations, and private lenders.

Insured loans

A program run by the Federal Housing Administration (FHA) provides government-backed insurance to local, private and public lenders who make approved reverse mortgages to older home-owners. You are eligible if you own your home and are at least 62. If you are married, your spouse must also be at least 62.

The FHA sets the initial maximum payout that can be made through the reverse mortgage, basing its calculation on your life expectancy, interest rates and equity in the home—up to the limit set by the agency in your area.

Using that figure as a starting point and assuming a certain rate of appreciation on your home, the lender then calculates what you could take out in a lump sum at settlement and what you could obtain as regular monthly income or withdraw periodically as needed. As you receive payments from the lender, you create a debt of principal and interest that you must eventually repay. When the house is sold or when you move, your equity pays off the loan. (There are ways to structure the mortgage to ensure that you will always have some equity if you have to move in the future.)

The FHA pools the insurance premiums it collects on each reverse mortgage. The pooled funds can be tapped by lenders who lose money on their loans. This could occur when a borrower outlives his equity—that is, he lives so long or the home appreciates so little that the final loan balance exceeds the value of the house. Whatever happens, you or your heirs would never owe more than the proceeds from the sale of the home, minus sales expenses.

FHA-insured loans offer three payment options:

- **Tenure.** With this option, you get equal monthly checks as long as the house is your principal residence.

- **Term.** You receive equal monthly payments for a fixed term. You choose the term.

- **Line of credit.** You determine when you need to borrow money and the amount. You may borrow up to the permitted limit.

Whichever option you choose, you can alter the pattern in the future should circumstances change. If you select a loan with a tenure or term-payment option, you may want to combine it with an agreed-upon line of credit that will permit you to tap a portion of the loan for unanticipated needs. Say you sign on for a tenure loan that pays $300 a month. A year later, you find you need to add a bath on the ground floor of your home for your husband, who has become too frail to use the only existing bath, on the second floor. You could contact your lender and request a lump-sum payment to make the improvement—so long as your request would

For More Information About Reverse Mortgages

- **Capital Holding Co.,** of Louisville, Ky., is currently the major private lender offering reverse mortgages. The company makes reverse mortgages in California, Florida, Kentucky, Maryland, Virginia and parts of Illinois. New programs are expected to become available sometime in 1993; you should be able to obtain information from the AARP or the National Center for Home Equity Conversion (addresses below).

- *Reverse Mortgage Locator* is a free publication with information about these loans and who is making them. Send a stamped, self-addressed envelope to the National Center for Home Equity Conversion (Suite 115, 7373 147th St.

West, Apple Valley, Minn. 55124). The center also publishes a book, *Retirement Income on the House* ($24.95, plus $4.50 shipping and handling).

- **For a list of reverse-mortgage lenders and an information booklet,** *Home-Made Money,* send a postcard to the American Association of Retired Persons, Home Equity Information Center, 601 E Street, N.W., Washington, D.C. 20049.

- **If you'd like to discuss this type of mortgage with someone,** call a Department of Housing and Urban Development automated hotline (800-733-3238) for help in locating a mortgage counseling center near you.

not exceed the maximum claim amount.

FHA-insured reverse mortgages can be fixed- or adjustable-rate loans. Lenders are permitted to offer reverse adjustable-rate mortgages with no monthly interest-rate adjustments and no annual limitation on interest increases, providing they also offer capped loans, which must carry a lifetime interest-rate cap of no more than five percentage points and an annual limit on rate increases or decreases of no more than two points.

With a reverse ARM, the payments don't change when interest-rate adjustments are made to the loan, but adjustments have the effect of increasing or decreasing the rate at which your equity is used up.

Sale and Leaseback

In a sale-leaseback, a homeowner gives up title to become a renter. Typically, parents sell their house to a son or daughter, who immediately leases it back to them for life. The parents, assuming they are 55 or older, can qualify to treat up to $125,000 of profit from the sale as tax-free income. Because the child owns the house and rents it out, he or she can depreciate it and deduct the expenses that go with being a landlord.

Most sale-leasebacks are seller-financed. The parents receive a down payment and take back a note for the remainder of the sales price. Things can be arranged so that the buyer makes monthly payments, providing a steady income stream to the parents. Some advisers suggest that the parents use the down payment to purchase a deferred annuity, which ensures that the parents will continue to receive the same amount of income if they outlive the payments on the note.

Sale-leasebacks are designed for people who want to spend the rest of their lives in the house, and they can work when the primary objective is to keep the house in the family. The main drawback is that these arrangements are complicated. Four separate contracts may be involved: a sales contract, a rental contract, a

Whichever reverse-mortgage option you choose, you can alter the pattern in the future should circumstances change.

mortgage contract and, usually, an annuity contract. Moreover, the terms of each contract are interrelated and open to negotiation.

Tax considerations should figure in choosing between a sale-leaseback and other options such as a reverse mortgage. The IRS requires that the landlord charge a market rate of rent, or it could decide the deal is a tax dodge and nullify some of the tax advantages. Charging the same rent for 12 years, for example, won't meet the test. It's advisable to put an inflation clause in the rental agreement—raising the rent annually according to a specified index.

Parents also generally want some assurance they can rent "their house" for as long as they live. You must accomplish this indirectly or the Internal Revenue Service may decide that no sale took place. A lease term that exceeds the parents' life expectancies and a clause that guarantees the seller the right to renew the lease each year may fit the bill.

For More Information

• •

If you believe a sale-leaseback may meet your needs, consult a knowledgeable real estate attorney in your state.

The National Center for Home Equity Conversion has a sale-leaseback guide and model documents that can be used to make sure you've examined the important financial and legal issues. The package is available ($39, including postage and handling) from the NCHEC (see address in box on page 282). Model documents may have to be adapted for use in your state.

Tax Angles of Selling a Home

You weighed the alternatives to selling your home and decided it's the right thing to do. Now take a closer look at the tax ramifications.

You didn't have to file forms with the IRS when you bought your home or report improvements that hiked your basis. But when you sell, the government wants the details. After all, there may be a tax to collect. There's a good chance, though, that the sale won't add a dime to your tax bill.

Determine Your Basis

When you sell, you'll realize how clever you were to keep meticulous records of every improvement made to your home. To determine the tax consequences of the sale, you have to know the *adjusted basis* of your home, a figure you can compute easily with the information in your well-kept files.

The adjusted basis is calculated by adding what you paid for the house plus the cost of all improvements, minus any casualty losses on the property you claimed while living there—for fire or storm damage, for example. The basis is also reduced by any gain from

To determine the tax consequences of the sale, you have to know your home's adjusted basis, computed easily with information in your well-kept files.

To defer the tax bill, you must buy a new principal residence —costing at least as much as you get from the sale of the old one—within two years.

a previous home that you rolled over into the house you're selling now.

Your profit or loss on the sale is the difference between that adjusted basis and the amount you realize on the sale. Since nothing concerning taxes is easy, the *amount realized* is not simply the selling price. That's the beginning point. From the selling price, you subtract costs connected with the sale, such as real estate commissions, points paid for the buyer, advertising, legal fees and termite inspection. You don't, however, subtract amounts you spend for repairs or other efforts to make the place more attractive to buyers.

If your adjusted basis is more than the amount realized, your loss is not deductible. (Note that this may change. Congress has shown interest in offering a tax break to homebuyers who lose money when they sell.) In the more likely event that your home sale produces a profit, the gain may be taxable in the year of the sale, sometime in the future, or perhaps never. The opportunity to put off or completely avoid tax on the profit has long been one of the most valuable tax benefits enjoyed by homeowners.

Deferring the Tax Bill

It's easy to defer the tax bill almost indefinitely. To do so, all you have to do is buy a new principal residence—costing at least as much as you get from the sale of the old one—within a specified time period.

To qualify, you must buy or build *and* occupy the new home within two years—before or after—the sale of the old one. (If you are in the armed forces or living outside the U.S. when your home is sold, you may qualify for a longer replacement period that gives you up to four years after the sale to buy and occupy a new principal residence.)

Be forewarned that the IRS is inflexible about the replacement period. In one case in which a serious illness prevented a taxpayer from occupying the new home before the deadline, the IRS prohibited the rollover of profit. What if you're building a new home and it burns down just before you're planning to move in? Again, the IRS says you forfeit the rollover privilege.

To defer the tax on all the gain on the sale of one home, the replacement home must cost at least as much as you realized from the sale of the old one.

An example: Assume that the adjusted basis of your home is $70,000 and you sell it for $100,000. Within the replacement period, you buy and move into a new home that costs $125,000. The tax bill on your $30,000 profit is deferred. Rather than report it as income in the year of the sale, you reduce the basis of the new home by that amount. The basis of the new home becomes $95,000—the $125,000 purchase price minus the $30,000 of deferred gain.

If you later sell that house for $150,000, in the eyes of the IRS the profit would be $55,000—the combination of the $30,000 gain from the first house and $25,000 from the second. Of course, you could put off the tax bill again by buying a replacement home within two years that costs $150,000 or more. Its basis would be reduced by the $55,000 of rolled-over gain.

You don't have to invest the actual proceeds of the sale in the new residence in order to qualify to defer tax on the gain.

An example: Say you sold a house for $200,000 and bought a new one for $210,000. You can roll over all the profit from the first house, even if you made a minimum down payment on the new house and used the remaining proceeds for some other purpose. The key is not how you pay for the new house, but that it costs at least as much as the one you sold.

Marrying or Divorcing?

What if you and your fiancé each own a home, sell both of them and together buy a new home? You can defer the gain on both the old homes if the price of the new house exceeds the combined sales prices of the old ones. Any profit left out of the rollover, though, would

Fix-up costs come into play for tax purposes only if your replacement home costs less than the one you sold.

be taxable in the year of sale. However, if you sell a home to move in with a new spouse in a home he or she already owns, you cannot defer tax on the gain. But if you're over age 55, you might qualify for the exclusion discussed on page 291.

The law does provide for a situation in which a jointly owned home is sold in connection with a divorce and each spouse buys a separate home. If each spouse invests his or her share of the proceeds of the sale in a new principal residence—within the rollover period—the tax bill on the profit is deferred.

An example: Say you and your spouse divorce and sell your jointly owned home for $150,000, including $40,000 profit. Assuming each of you is entitled to half the proceeds of the sale, each has a $20,000 gain. Each of you can defer tax on the gain by buying a new home that costs at least $75,000, your half of the amount realized on the sale.

If You Want to Spend Less

In any situation, if you choose a replacement home that costs less than the one you sold, you will owe tax on the profit to the extent that the *adjusted sales price* of the old home exceeds the cost of the new one.

The adjusted sales price is usually the same as the amount realized on the sale, but it can be less if prior to the sale you incurred qualifying fix-up expenses, such as the cost of painting or repairs to make the home more attractive to buyers. Those are costs that can't qualify as improvements to boost your basis. They come into play for tax purposes *only* if your replacement home costs less than the one you sold. (Although real estate agents encouraging you to spruce up your place may suggest that such costs are deductible, they are not. If you don't buy a replacement home, or if you buy one that costs enough that you can roll over all your profit, fix-up costs have no tax power.)

To qualify for this limited tax benefit, fix-up expenses must be for work done during the 90 days before you sign a contract to sell your house and must be paid for within 30 days afterward.

Trading down without tripping up

It is possible to buy a less expensive home without incurring a taxable profit in the year of the sale. Anything you spend on the new place that qualifies as an improvement—such as the cost of renovation or adding an addition or a garage—can serve to raise the new home's "price" for rollover purposes. The key here is that the expense must be incurred and the bill paid within the two-year replacement period.

This provision can prove especially rewarding if you move from an area of the country with high home prices to an area of more modestly priced homes.

An example: Say the "adjusted basis" of your old house is $100,000. You sell it for $150,000, after expenses. Thanks to a transfer to a less expensive part of the country, your new home costs just $120,000—the amount that sets the ceiling for rolling over the proceeds of your home sale. That leaves $30,000 of profit out in the cold, taxable in the year of the sale. In the 28% bracket, the bill is $8,400.

You can hold down or eliminate that tax bill, though, by investing more in the new place. If you spend $30,000 or more on improvements within two years after the sale of the first house, the entire profit could be rolled over.

Other Aspects of Rolling Over

- **The rollover provision applies only to your principal residence,** not to a second home, for example, or rental property.

- **And if you use part of your principal home for business**—by renting out a room, say, or having a home office for which you claim deductions—part of the profit from the sale will not qualify for rollover treatment. If you claim 10% of your home as a home

Because each sale will affect the basis of your next home, you'll want to hang on to a copy of every Form 2119 you file throughout your homeowning career.

office, for example, 10% of the gain on the sale won't be eligible for the deferral.

- **There is no limit on the number of times or the amount of profit you can roll over from one home to the next.** In fact, the profit from the first home you own is likely to affect the tax basis of the last place you live, a point that emphasizes the importance of detailed record keeping.

- **There is a restriction, however, that generally prevents you from using the rollover provision more than once every two years.** If during the replacement period you buy or build more than one new principal residence, only the last one can be treated as your new home for figuring the rollover. That restriction does not apply if the sale of your home is connected with a job-related move that qualifies you to deduct moving expenses. (Congress is considering eliminating this restriction.)

Reporting Home Sales

For the year of the sale, you must file a Form 2119, *Sale or Exchange of Principal Residence,* with your tax return. The form must be filed whether or not you owe tax on the sale. It's a relatively simple form, and it includes a section for determining the adjusted basis of your new home by subtracting from its cost any rolled-over profit from the sale. Because each sale will affect the basis of your next home, you'll want to hang on to a copy of every Form 2119 you file throughout your homeowning career.

What if you plan to buy a replacement home but haven't closed the deal by the time your tax return is due for the year of the sale? You can still postpone the gain. Just file a Form 2119—reporting only the date your old home was sold—with your return.

If the replacement home you buy costs enough to defer all of your gain, just notify the IRS Service Center with which you filed your return and file a completed Form 2119 at that time. If the new house doesn't cost enough to permit a rollover of all the profit—or if the replacement period expires before you buy—you'll have to file an amended tax return for the year of the sale. In addition to the tax on the profit, you'll have to pay interest on the tax due.

You handle things the same way if you follow the "trading down without tripping up" strategy discussed above. You report the sale of the first home for the year of the sale and, after you complete your major improvements on the new place, file a completed Form 2119.

You will have to file an amended return if you report the profit from the home sale—under the assumption that you won't replace the house—and later decide to buy a new home. If you occupy the new place within the replacement period, you can retroactively defer the gain and reclaim the tax that you paid on the original return.

The $125,000 Exclusion

So over the years you keep packing your profit with you from one home to another, holding the IRS at bay by purchasing more and more costly homes. But what happens when you finally decide to cash in on all that profit that has built up? When you retire or for some other reason decide not to buy another house, is the IRS going to swoop down and demand a hefty share of your nest egg?

Not if you qualify for the homeowner's protective shell: the right to escape tax entirely on up to $125,000 of profit. The same $125,000 exclusion is available whether you're married and filing a joint return or single and filing an individual one. If you are married but you both file separate returns, the limit is $62,500 for each spouse.

The value of this tax break is enhanced by the fact that it usually occurs around retirement time, when extra cash often comes in particularly handy. If you're

When you retire or decide not to buy another house, is the IRS going to demand a share of your nest egg? Not if you qualify for the right to escape tax entirely on up to $125,000 of profit.

in the 31% tax bracket, sheltering $125,000 of gain will save you $38,750!

With such a rich reward at stake, it's essential that you know how to claim it.

How You Qualify

To qualify, you must be at least 55 years old when you sell your home and you must have owned and lived in the home for at least three of the five years leading up to the sale. If you are married and the house is jointly owned, you can qualify as long as either you or your spouse meets all three requirements: age, ownership and residency.

Unlike the rollover rule, which applies only if the house sold is your principal residence at the time of the sale, you don't have to be living in the house when it is sold to qualify for the exclusion. You can still dodge tax on the profit as long as the sale occurs before so much time has passed that you no longer meet the three-out-of-five-year residency test.

An example: Assume that you are at least age 55 and have owned and lived in your home for at least three years. You retire and move to an apartment. As long as your home is sold within two years of the move, you will meet the three-out-of-five-year test and qualify for the exclusion. That applies whether you rent out your old home or leave it vacant prior to the sale.

More Marrying or Divorcing

Married couples are limited to a single $125,000 exclusion, and if one spouse used the exclusion before marriage, that scotches the other spouse's right to it as long as they are married.

An example: Say you own a home and plan to marry someone who also owns a home. Assume, too, that both of you meet the age, ownership and residency tests. If each of you sells your house before marriage, you each qualify for an exclusion up to $125,000. Wait until after the ceremony, though, and together you can exclude only $125,000. Similarly, if you plan to marry someone who has already used the exclusion, selling your home before the wedding can protect your right to the exclusion.

The exclusion can also come into play in divorce. If you're planning a divorce, in some circumstances it may make sense to hold off selling the family home until after the split. If the profit will exceed $125,000, postponing the sale until you are both single co-owners of the place can permit each ex-spouse to exclude up to $125,000 of gain.

Don't Use It Up

You don't necessarily want to use the exclusion the first time it is available to you. In fact, that can be a costly mistake. This is a once-in-a-lifetime opportunity. You can't use part of the exclusion to shelter $50,000 of profit on one home, for example, and later use the rest of it to avoid tax on the sale of another. Use any part of the exclusion and you use it all.

Your best bet will usually be to hold off using the exclusion until you sell what you expect to be your last home or until you can take advantage of the full $125,000. Don't worry about shortchanging your heirs by forfeiting the tax break if you die before using it; the tax on all profit that builds up during your life is excused when you die.

You have to claim the exclusion on Form 2119, the same form you use to report home sales and the deferral of gain.

Owner Financing

Sometimes, when mortgage rates are high or institutional lenders are very strict, the sale of a home goes through only because the seller helps finance the deal. If you wind up holding a note of some sort, your tax picture is sure to be complicated.

This is a once-in-a-lifetime opportunity. Use any part of the $125,000 exclusion and you use it all.

The selling price of your home—for purposes of determining the gain to be rolled over, excluded or taxed—includes the face value of any mortgage or note you receive, as well as cash. If you are deferring tax on the gain or using the exclusion to shelter it from the IRS, however, you basically report the sale just as you would if you received all cash.

Payments you receive on the note may be a combination of return of your basis (nontaxable), part of your gain (deferred or excluded) and interest on the loan (taxable). You should report the interest as income on Schedule B, the same form you use to report interest on a bank account. You will find there's even a special line for reporting interest on seller-financed mortgages and listing the payer's social security number.

If gain is taxable in the year of the sale and you help finance the deal, you may report the profit on an installment basis. That permits you to pay tax on the profit as you receive it over the years. Special rules apply, including those demanding that you charge a reasonable interest rate on the loan.

Renting Out a Slow Seller

This move can lead you into a maze of tax complications. The part of the tax law that permits homeowners to defer the tax on the profit from one house by rolling it over into a new home applies only to your principal residence. Can a house that's being rented to someone else when you finally sell it qualify as *your* home? If it doesn't, the vagaries of the housing market could force you to pay tax on the profit rather than roll it over.

If you can show the rental was temporary, the house still qualifies as your principal residence and the gain can be rolled over—as long as you sell the old house within two years of the time you buy the new home. If the old home hasn't sold within the rollover-replacement period, you're out of luck.

The IRS demands that you treat the rent you receive as income, assuming you rent the place for more than 14 days during the year (income from shorter rentals is tax-free). Temporary or not, you become a landlord in the eyes of the IRS. You may be able to completely offset the tax bill on the rental income, however, with deductions for rental expenses, including the continued mortgage interest and tax payments on the house, the cost of repairs and even depreciation.

The big question is whether the arrangement can produce a tax loss if expenses exceed rental income, as they often will. Such a loss, of course, could shelter other income—such as part of your salary—from tax, assuming you actively manage the rental and don't run afoul of the passive-loss rules explained in Chapter 23.

But the IRS says you can't have it both ways—you can't treat the house as a principal residence for rollover purposes and as a rental property for tax-loss purposes. According to the IRS position, you can deduct rental expenses up to the amount of your rental income, but no more.

The issue is up in the air, however, because courts have disagreed. In a key case in which the taxpayers beat the IRS, a federal circuit court ruled that because the taxpayers charged fair-market rent for their home they deserved the same write-offs available to other landlords, even if that meant they had a tax loss to shelter other income. At the same time, because the taxpayers continued their efforts to sell the place—and in fact did sell it before the replacement period ran out—the rollover provision also applied.

The IRS is sticking to its position, though. If you find yourself in this situation and claim a rental loss, the IRS may challenge your deductions if your return is ever audited.

Permanent Rental

If you make the conversion from home to rental property permanent, once the two-year replacement

The IRS says you can't have it both ways—you can't treat the house as a principal residence for rollover purposes and as a rental property for tax-loss purposes.

Promoters say home-sale losses can be deducted if, prior to the sale, you convert your house to a rental. That's true, but the tactic is worthless.

period ends, any profit on a sale—including any gain from previous homes that had been rolled over into the house—will be taxed. Neither the rollover nor the $125,000 exclusion provision will protect you.

Homeowners who plan from the outset to turn their old homes into rentals will find it an easy—though not always profitable—route to becoming a real estate investor. Turn to Chapter 23 for more discussion of the pros and cons of landlording.

There's a big catch to converting your home to a rental property, however, beyond forfeiting the chance to roll over the profit into a new home. The value of the house for figuring depreciation deductions—a key write-off for real estate investors—is your adjusted basis or the fair market value of the house, whichever is less. The basis may be far less than what the house is worth when you convert it, particularly if you have pushed it down by rolling over profit from previous homes.

An example: Assume that your house is worth $150,000. You bought it for $100,000 several years ago and at that time rolled over $30,000 in profit from your previous home. If you convert the house to a rental property, your basis for depreciation purposes is a skimpy $70,000. Because you cannot depreciate the value of land, you must subtract its value to determine the amount on which to base your depreciation write-offs. (If someone else bought your home for $150,000 and turned it into a rental property, the new owner's basis for depreciation purposes would be $150,000—minus the value of the land—and he or she would enjoy depreciation deductions more than twice as large as you are allowed.)

Selling Your Home for a Loss

Although profits from the sale of your home are taxable—except to the extent that you can defer or exclude the gain—losses are not deductible. You may have heard, however, that there's a way to write off such losses. Promoters say home-sale losses can be deducted if, prior to the sale, you convert your house to a rental.

That's true, but the tactic is worthless. The basis for figuring your loss begins as the *lower* of the adjusted basis or fair market value at the time of the conversion. (The basis is increased for any improvements after the conversion and reduced for any depreciation claimed.) In other words, any loss in fair market value that occurs while you're living in the house can't be deducted.

Congress may change the rules in this area to help homeowners who are hurt by falling home prices. One possibility, for example, would be to allow homeowners to "bank" a loss on the sale of a home to offset the profit on a future home. Keep an eye on this area.

If your purchase is connected with a job switch, you can rack up additional benefits; some of the cost of selling your old place and buying the new house may be deductible.

House-Hunting and Moving Expenses

Buying a new house is often part of a move to take a new job. If your purchase is connected with a job switch, you can rack up additional benefits; some of the cost of selling your old place and buying the new house may be deductible. In order to qualify for writing off moving expenses:

- **Your new job must be at least 35 miles farther from your old home than your old job was.** If your former job was ten miles away from your old home, for example, the new job has to be at least 45 miles away from that old home. It doesn't matter how far the new home is away from your new job. (If you are moving to take your first job, then the 35-mile test applies to the distance from your old home to your new job location.)

- **You also must work full-time for at least 39 weeks during the 12 months after the move.** If you are self-employed, in addition to working 39 weeks in the first 12 months, you also have to work full time at the new location for at least 78 weeks out of the first 24 months. (To pass these tests you must work in the same area, not necessarily at the same job for the required time.) You claim the deductions on your tax return for the year of the move even if you haven't yet met the 39- or 78-week test by the time you file. If it turns out you weren't eligible, you should either file an amended return for the year or report as income on your next tax return the amount previously deducted as moving expenses.

(See the accompanying box for a list of what you can deduct when you qualify.)

There is a dollar limit on the amount you can deduct for certain expenses. The cap for house-hunting trips and temporary living expenses is $1,500, and those costs plus expenses of buying and selling can't exceed $3,000. There is no limit to how much you can deduct for the cost of shipping household goods or for

Deductible Moving Expenses

If you meet the IRS's definition of a qualifying move, described in the accompanying text, you can deduct these items:

- **The cost of trips to the area of the new job** to look for a new house. There's no requirement that the house-hunting expedition be successful for the cost to be deductible.

- **The cost of having your furniture and other household goods shipped,** including the cost of packing, insurance and storage for up to 30 days.

- **The cost of getting yourself and your family to the new hometown,** including food and lodging expenses on the trip.

- **The cost of lodging and 80% of food expenses for up to 30 days in the new hometown,** if these temporary living expenses are necessary because you have not yet found a new home or it is not ready when you arrive.

- **Certain costs associated with the sale of your old house and purchase of the new one.** Alternatively, these expenses— including real estate commissions, legal fees, state transfer taxes, and appraisal and title fees—could be used either to reduce the gain on the sale of the previous residence or to boost the basis of the new one. But it's usually beneficial to count them as moving expenses up to the allowable dollar limits, because that gives you an immediate tax benefit.

travel expenses for yourself and your family. Any reasonable amount you pay can be deducted. (During 1993, Congress is likely to consider slapping a dollar limit on overall expenses. It's expected to eliminate deductions for meal expenses as of 1994.) You report expenses on Form 3903.

If your employer reimburses you for moving expenses, the amount should show up on your W-2 form for the year. You include the amount with your income and then offset it by claiming your moving-expense deductions.

Polishing the Merchandise

Nothing can help a sale more than a spit-and-polish campaign and below-the-surface attention.

Before you make any decision on how to sell your home—through an agent or by yourself—or even what price to ask for it, put your property in the finest possible condition to impress buyers, agents, appraisers and inspectors.

The way your house looks and functions will affect your bargaining power as a seller. Nothing can help a sale more than a thorough spit-and-polish campaign and below-the-surface attention, so now is the time for cleaning, touch-ups and postponed maintenance. Replace the torn screen in the basement window, reset the loose tile in the bathroom, repair leaking faucets, and repaint the scratched front door.

Any real estate agent can tell you that a well-maintained, nicely decorated home "shows well." Other things being equal, this kind of home will sell faster and for a higher price than a comparable house that isn't as attractive.

Do not, however, undertake a major redecorating or remodeling of your house just to prepare it for selling. Why? Your tastes may not coincide with those of the buyer. Rather than crediting you with work already done, a would-be buyer is going to factor in the estimated cost of redecorating the premises his or her way when figuring how much to offer you.

So stay away from such things as expensive new

curtains and wallpaper, and don't install wall-to-wall carpeting over otherwise good floors, such as plank hardwood or parquet.

Concentrate instead on the decorating you believe is needed to make your home look good—painting, replacing worn linoleum or placing wall-to-wall carpet over unfinished flooring. Choose neutral colors and simple patterns that are likely to harmonize with the tastes of most prospective buyers; they'll view these improvements as savings to them in both money and time.

Also consider the ideas for faster ways to sell presented in Chapter 20.

First Impressions Count

For More Information

● ●

Packaging Your Home for Profit, by Bruce Percelay and Peter Arnold (Little, Brown and Co.), provides comprehensive advice on what you can do, both inside and outside your home, to enhance its value and make it easier to sell. It includes tips on using color and aroma, and suggests which improvements will yield the highest returns on your money.

- **Start with a curb-to-door cleanup.** Prune shrubs and tree branches, edge the lawn and keep it mowed, and, if the season permits, add a show of color with annual bedding plants. Paint the front door and put out a new welcome mat.

- **Inside, make your home look as spacious as possible.** Get rid of everything extraneous, admit as much daylight as possible, and keep things shipshape. Inventory what you want to sell, give away or throw away when you move. Then do so before you begin showing your home. Clutter turns buyers off, so empty out crammed closets, pack away extra books and rarely used china, and sort out attic and basement storage spaces to avoid the flea-market look. Put things in commercial storage if that's what it takes.

- **Depersonalize your space.** Reduce distractions, and help would-be buyers visualize making themselves at

During your inspection, jot down problems and note what can be done to make each room attractive.

home. Tuck away the family pictures covering your bedroom wall. The display of family roots may fascinate some shoppers and embarrass others. A home that appears to be stamped indelibly with your personality and style can be harder to sell.

- **Remove obvious clues to your political, religious and social sentiments.** Store away banners, bumper stickers and partisan literature, including magazines.

Get the Place in Shape

As you begin, walk through your home making a list of everything that needs to be done. During your inspection, jot down problems and note what can be done to make each room attractive. Taking down dark curtains and opening a room to sunlight may change its character completely. So can repainting.

You can't anticipate what will catch the attention of a prospective buyer. Plaster walls and a new furnace may hardly elicit a comment—but the cracked toilet-tank top, that's another story. A buyer may spend hours assessing the heating and plumbing systems and apparently ignore the fresh paint, refinished floors and brand-new windows.

Use the following inspection guide to see your home as buyers might.

Do Your Homework

Be prepared to answer questions. Get out heating, cooling and water bills, and figure annual totals and monthly averages. Pull together appliance receipts, service records and information on when major systems, such as the furnace, were installed. Collect warranties on siding, roof shingles, and so forth. Organize them in a folder for easy reference.

Are Disclosures Needed?

The Radon Question

Radon wasn't a household word until a Pennsylvania nuclear-power-plant worker set off radiation alarms at work because he had been exposed to extraordinarily high levels of radon at home. A colorless, odorless radioactive gas produced by decaying uranium, radon exists naturally in soil and rock. But when it seeps into homes where it cannot diffuse as quickly as in open air, the gas can accumulate to unhealthy levels.

The Environmental Protection Agency (EPA) and private testing companies have detected unsafe levels of radon in nearly every state. But the EPA found unsafe levels in only about 20% of the homes tested in ten states, and of those, just 1% registered levels above 20 picocuries per liter, defined by the EPA as the equivalent of smoking two packs of cigarettes a day. The link between indoor radon and lung cancer hasn't been conclusively proven.

But once you decide to sell your home, you may want to test for it, anyway. In some areas home buyers are including contingency clauses in sales contracts that require a test for, and sometimes correction of, radon problems before they will buy. In most cases, unacceptable levels of indoor radon are handled by improving ventilation.

Check with your real estate agent about radon disclosure requirements and with your state or local

> ## *More on Radon*
>
> •
>
> You can request a free copy of the Environmental Protection Agency's *Home Buyer's and Seller's Guide to Radon* from your state's radon, radiation control or radiological health office, or write to request it from the EPA (Public Information Center, 401 M St., S.W., PM-211B, Washington, D.C. 20460; stock # 055-000-00428-5).
>
> Your state's radon office can also provide an EPA report that includes a list of radon-testing companies, as well as: *Citizen's Guide to Protecting Yourself and Your Family From Radon, Consumer's Guide to Radon Reduction,* and, for do-it-yourselfers, *Radon Reduction Techniques for Detached Houses—Technical Guidance.*

Preparing to Sell

Use this checklist to identify areas of your home that need work prior to putting it on the market.

INSIDE

Attic

- Check underside of roof for leaks, stains or dampness.
- Look around chimney for condensation or signs of water.
- Clean and clear ventilation openings if necessary.
- Clean out stored junk.

Walls and Ceilings

- Check condition of paint and wallpaper.
- Repair cracks, holes or damage to plaster or wallboard.

Windows and Doors

- Check for smooth operation.
- Replace broken or cracked panes.
- Repair glazing.
- Check condition of weather stripping and caulking.
- Examine paint.
- Test doorbell or chimes.
- Test burglar alarms.
- Wash windows and even woodwork, if necessary.

Floors

- Inspect for creaking boards, loose or missing tiles, worn areas.
- Check baseboards and moldings.

- Test the staircases for loose handrails, posts, treads.

Bathrooms

- Check tile joints, grouting and caulking.
- Remove mildew.
- Repair faucets and shower heads that are dripping.
- Check the condition of painted or papered walls.
- Test operation of toilet.

Kitchen

- Wash all appliances.
- Clean ventilator or exhaust fan.
- Remove accumulation of grease or dust from tiles, walls, floors.

Basement

- Remove clutter.
- Check for signs of dampness, cracked walls or damaged floors.
- Inspect structural beams.
- Check pipes for leaks.

Electrical System

- Check exposed wiring and outlets for signs of wear or damage.
- Repair broken switches and outlets.
- Label each circuit or fuse.

Plumbing System

- Check water pressure when taps in bathroom(s) and kitchen are turned on.
- Look for leaks at faucets and sink traps.
- Clear slow-running or clogged drains.

- Bleed air off radiators if needed, and check for leaking valves.

Heating and Cooling Systems
- Change or clean furnace and air-conditioning filters.
- Have equipment serviced if needed.
- Clear and clean area around heating and cooling equipment.

OUTSIDE

Roof and Gutters
- Repair or replace loose, damaged or blistered shingles.
- Clean gutters and downspout strainers.
- Check gutters for leaks and proper alignment.
- Inspect flashings around roof stacks, vents, skylights and chimneys.
- Clear obstructions from vents, louvers and chimneys.
- Check fascias and soffits for decay and peeling paint.
- Inspect chimney for any loose or missing mortar.

Exterior Walls
- Renail loose siding and check for warping or decay.
- Paint siding if necessary.
- Check masonry walls for cracks or any other damage.
- Replace loose or missing caulking.

Driveway
- Repair concrete or blacktop if necessary.

Garage
- Lubricate hinges and other hardware on your garage door.
- Inspect doors and windows for any peeling paint.
- Check condition of glazing around all windows.
- Test electrical outlets.

Foundation
- Check walls, steps, retaining walls, walkways and patios for cracks, heaving or crumbling.

Yard
- Mow lawn, reseed or sod if necessary.
- Trim hedges, prune trees and shrubs.
- Weed and mulch flowerbeds.

environmental office about testing methods. If you're concerned, you may want to get a test done by an approved professional.

Lead Paint

Eight states currently have lead-based paint disclosures as part of their mandatory property-condition reports. They are Alaska, California, Maine, New Hampshire, Ohio, Rhode Island, Virginia and Wisconsin. In addition, beginning on October 28, 1995, when you sell a home built before 1978, federal law will require you to tell all prospective buyers about known lead-based paint used in and around the property.

And More...

Many states require that owners who sell residential real estate disclose to all prospective buyers *any* material defect that the owner is aware of. Depending on the law in your state, you may be required to reveal known problems and defects in your home's roof, walls, foundation, basement, plumbing, heating and electrical systems, as well as past pest problems and the presence of hazardous materials such as radon, lead-based paint, and asbestos.

Protect Yourself

Shift as much liability as you can from your shoulders to those of the professionals you are paying to assist you with the sale. If you are using an agent to help you sell your home, ask to be informed of your responsibilities. Make it clear you want your agent to fully assume his or hers, as well. Use a home inspector who carries errors-and-omissions insurance. Discuss potential liability with your lawyer.

CHAPTER

18

Sell Through an Agent or Go It Alone?

The vast majority of homes are sold through a listing contract with a real estate agent, with the seller paying the typical 6% commission on the sales price. But what about the rest? Their owners apparently asked themselves, "Why pay someone thousands of dollars for doing something I can do myself, with the help of a few professionals whom I can compensate on a flat-fee or hourly basis?"

Saving $9,000 on a $150,000 home sale is plenty of motivation for a "fizzbo," or FSBO (For Sale by Owner)—a term real estate agents use somewhat disdainfully. The urge to try selling one's own home is especially strong in a seller's market, when qualified buyers are plentiful, listings are relatively few and everything that's fairly priced gets snapped up.

Agents can reel off a dozen or more arguments against trying to sell your own home, among them that you could set the wrong price, accept an unqualified buyer or lose the help of agents, who won't bring their clients by to see your home. Sure, all of those things can happen—but some of them might happen even if you list your home with an agent.

Saving $9,000 on a $150,000 home sale is plenty of motivation for a "fizzbo" (For Sale by Owner).

The tasks involved in selling a house can be accomplished by an organized, determined seller aided by key professionals.

An Agent's Strengths

The fact that most people do use an agent to sell their homes suggests that a lot of homeowners believe they get good value for the 6% commission. Selling a house by oneself is hard work, and it requires time, savvy and a knack for selling.

Good sales agents offer many benefits. They are experienced at the proper pricing of a property and writing of effective ads. They will advise you on sprucing up your home for an easy sale. In a slow market, they will beat the bushes for buyers. They can help screen buyers on financial qualifications. They'll review the buyers' offers and negotiate the best deal they can get for you. They'll help locate financing for your buyer and shepherd both parties through the twisting maze toward settlement.

Another important benefit of selling through an agent is getting your home listed in a multiple listing service (MLS)—the computerized clearinghouse of properties listed with professional brokers. You can't use the agent's MLS on your own, and you'll have to make up for this with your own advertising efforts.

Finally, if the agent can get you a price at least 6% higher than you could get selling your home yourself without paying a commission, then the agent's skills cost your nothing, theoretically (see Chapter 20).

Going It Alone

Without denying real estate agents their due, the tasks involved in selling a house can be accomplished by an organized, determined seller aided by key professionals—appraiser, inspector and real estate attorney—who will charge on an hourly or flat-fee basis rather than on commission.

You don't need a license or official permission to sell your own property. But you will need the following resources:

Time

Finding a buyer will take time, even in a feverish market. A house or condominium unit may not move quickly if it is unusual in some way, in disrepair, in a deteriorating neighborhood or equipped with expensive extras not every buyer wants, such as a swimming pool or tennis court.

Going it alone is risky if you must sell in a hurry. You might speed things up by telling prospects that you will cut the price by a percentage of the amount of a sales commission. Still, the odds are an agent with access to a multiple listing service and other contacts would get faster action.

Flexibility

You will need plenty of time to show your home during the day, as well as at night and on weekends. You can decide to show it by appointment only, but you probably can't afford to be too rigid about that, either. If you can't be at home, arrange for a responsible, interested adult to be there. It's not enough to make your home accessible by having a painter, babysitter or teenager open the door. That may be okay if an agent is coming to show it, but it's not good enough for a fizzbo. You have to *show* your home to prospects, not just allow them to wander about.

If you have any concerns about personal safety, you may want to reconsider selling your home yourself. Unlike a real estate agent, you probably won't have had the opportunity to meet and assess a prospective buyer in a business setting first.

Patience

Unless you are used to dealing with the public, it is easy to underestimate the amount of patience you will need to handle telephone calls, answer questions, give directions to your home and show the property—over and over again.

You will need plenty of time to show your home—days and evenings. You can decide to show it by appointment only, but you probably can't afford to be too rigid.

Information

You will need to know all about your neighborhood, your property, your appliances, furnace, roof, plumbing and electrical systems. You must be willing to get the facts you need to assist prospects with financing. You should be thoroughly familiar with all comparable properties in your area.

Knack for selling

If the prospect of displaying the merchandise, fielding questions, overcoming objections and solving problems in order to make the sale impresses you as indelicate or undignified, reconsider handling this project without a real estate agent.

Intuition

Will you be able to tell a genuine candidate from a window-shopper? Time spent with individuals or couples who haven't really decided to buy is time not spent with those who have—and who only need to be sold on your home.

A little money

You will need to pay up front for advertising, the copying of fact sheets, and hiring a lawyer to draw up a contract and buyer qualification forms. An appraisal isn't required but could be well worth the $175 to $350.

Elbow grease

Make your place gleam, even if it means hiring a cleaning crew. Paint and make other improvements. Everything said in Chapter 17 about getting your home ready goes double if you're selling it yourself. A glib agent can talk a client past a plaster crack or dirty wallpaper, but you'll have a much harder time of it.

Keep track of what you spend in getting the place in shape. If you buy a replacement home that costs less than the one you sell, fixing-up expenses incurred in the 90 days before the sale can be used to shave the tax on any profit.

Steps to Success for the Fizzbo

Price It Right.

The single most important task in the selling of a house is the pricing it—right at the market value, neither too low nor too high. This requires either your own careful study of comparable transactions in your neighborhood or the services of a professional appraiser, who will do the same thing for you.

The owner must decide whether to price the house at full market value and try to pocket the commission savings, or to share these savings with the buyer, settling for a little less than the full asking price but more than he or she would get from an agent sale at asking price minus commission. For a full discussion of pricing, see Chapter 20.

Prepare Fact Sheets.

Prospects seldom take notes as they are being shown around. They may be reluctant to appear too interested, or they may find writing distracts them from looking. But they rarely refuse a printed fact sheet.

These fact sheets are important; they tell at a glance what you're selling, highlight the best points, and can later refresh the memories of lookers who may have seen a dozen other offerings. See the accompanying box for a list of what to include.

In addition, inform potential buyers orally about known problems or defects. You're legally obliged to, and failing to do so could cause you to lose a sale or become entangled in a lawsuit. Find out what disclosures and forms are required from sellers in your state. Make sure you know your responsibilities with regard to lead-based paint, radon and asbestos. Make sure that professionals you hire, such as a home inspector or attorney, carry errors-and-omissions or professional liability insurance.

Get Contract and Buyer-Qualification Forms.

Preprinted contract forms, which vary from state to state, can be obtained from office-supply stores, stationers, real estate boards or lawyers. Alternatively, you can ask the attorney who will represent you to draw up a contract to meet your requirements and protect your interests while conforming to state and local laws—particularly with regard to disclosures about your property's physical and structural condition. Some real estate lawyers may help clients negotiate a deal and assess the creditworthiness and financial abilities of prospective purchasers.

Qualification forms, which you can draw up yourself or with your attorney's assistance, will help you decide whether a prospective buyer is financially able to follow through on his or her offer. When an offer is submitted, have the person fill out the form, listing annual income, debts, assets, place and length of

Just the Facts, Ma'am

When preparing a fact sheet for prospective buyers, include the items described below and type it, preferably on a single page. Add a statement that the "information is not guaranteed but deemed accurate to the best of my knowledge." You may want to include the appraised value and a drawing of the layout. For added impact, attach a snapshot of the place—one that shows it to advantage in its best season of the year. Make copies of your fact sheet so you can give one to each prospect.

Relevant Information About the Property
- age,
- construction,
- square footage,
- room dimensions,
- mechanical systems (heat, air-conditioning, and so on),
- appliances that go with the home,
- amenities,
- lot size,
- and proximity to schools, public transportation, shopping and such.

Financial Information
- the price,
- annual taxes,
- annual maintenance and utility costs,
- and any relevant information about the current mortgage, if assumable, and seller financing help, if any.

employment, credit references, and any other relevant information.

Gather Documents You May Need.

Questions may come up that could be answered by a site plan or surveyor's report. If you're selling a condominium unit, have handy the declaration or plan of condominium ownership (also called the declaration of covenants or the master deed), the bylaws of the owners association, and the rules governing property use. Have handy your actual stubs or photocopies of utility bills and recent tax bills.

Bone Up on Mortgage Financing.

VA and FHA Answers

● ●

Be prepared to answer questions about VA and FHA loans if your home is likely to attract veterans and first-time buyers. One reference is *The Mortgage Manual: Questions & Answers for FHA, VA & Conventional Loans,* by Albert Santi (Probus Publishing Co.). This book is currently out-of-print, but public libraries are likely to have it.

Offers usually are made contingent on the buyer's ability to get financing. It is in your interest to be helpful to buyers who find the prospect of getting a mortgage more intimidating than finding a home. Remember, this is the sort of service that a real estate agent provides to prospective buyers, and you must do the same if you are really serious about selling your house yourself.

Draw up a list of lenders and check weekly on financing rates and terms. Your local newspaper may publish such information, or you can subscribe to a mortgage reporting service (see Chapter 11 for names and addresses of some of the larger services). Keep an interest-rate table and calculator handy so you can help a prospect calculate on the spot what monthly principal and interest payments would be.

You may be asked by some prospective buyers whether you are willing to assist them by taking back a second trust on your house. Before the issue arises, discuss the risks with your attorney. Familiarize yourself with the various kinds of "creative financing" discussed in Chapter 10 and consider whether you'd want to get involved with it. See Chapter 21 for mistakes to avoid when offering seller financing.

Generally, when interest rates are not too high and there are many qualified buyers, you don't have to help the purchaser with financing. A sale that gives you cash for your property sets you free to invest as you wish, whether in your next house or in some other investment.

Put Up an Attractive Sign.

Create a good impression by putting up a bright new sign in the front. Look in a hardware or sign shop for a "For Sale by Owner" sign that has a place below the main message for an add-on sign (or have one made professionally). During the week, you can hang out a phone number. And if you have an open house, you can remove that portion and hang an "Open" sign.

Signs are effective sources of clients for both amateur sellers and real estate firms. A response to a sign is a more valuable inquiry than a response to a newspaper ad. The sign caller is already in the neighborhood. He or she probably knows and likes the area and obviously likes the look of your home well enough to want to see the inside. You are two selling steps ahead of a classified-ad caller. That person is responding to general

---

What Makes an Effective Real Estate Ad

• •

Read the Sunday paper and study the ads written by the professionals. You'll find that the best ads have full descriptions of the house, not sketchy write-ups with so much abbreviation that they're hard to decipher. The strong points are played up, the weak points omitted or put in the best possible light. A small house, for example, becomes "cozy" in a good ad. Avoid exaggeration and overly cute writing. In addition:

- Always put in the price.
- If it's an ad for an open house, list the address and some general directions.
- Otherwise, you may wish to list only your phone number, to get calls for appointments.
- Run the ad in the Sunday paper.
- To ensure the most accurate ad, deliver ad copy to the newspaper rather than calling it in by phone.

information, and may or may not like your area or the external appearance of your home when and if a viewing appointment is made and the prospect arrives.

Give Good Directions.

All the good advertising money can buy won't get people into your home if they get lost trying to get there. Prepare maps and directions. Anticipate where prospects will be coming from, and route them along the simplest, most direct and most attractive route you can devise. Put up a large map near your telephone to help you answer questions and redirect turned-about buyers who care enough to call.

Hold an Open House.

Sunday open houses are a ritual among house hunters. You'll get a lot of serious buyers, a lot of lookers who are just curious and a few neighbors who like to keep abreast of the local market. Any of these could lead to a successful contract, sooner or later.

Have a visitor register handy—a simple pad of paper will suffice—so you can get names and phone numbers. Some people will gladly sign it, while others will decline, preferring anonymity; be careful not to press the point.

Most buyers like to go through a house by themselves, so that they can discuss its strengths and weaknesses without embarrassing the owner. Station yourself in the front hall or the dining room, greet visitors warmly, and hand them a fact sheet that they can take through the house with them. But don't escort them unless they ask you to. (If you're worried about security, make sure any small objects of value are locked up or stashed out of sight.) Before they leave, ask them if they have any additional questions. Remember you're selling your house; try to engage visitors in conversation so you can make your best points.

Most buyers like to go through a house by themselves, so that they can discuss its strengths and weaknesses without embarrassing the owner.

If you're lucky enough to have a "live wire" buyer in your midst, be ready to deal.

If both spouses of a couple feel comfortable showing the house together, that's a good idea. If one gets into a deep discussion (or even an unexpected negotiation) with a serious prospect—in a private place, out of earshot of other visitors—the other spouse can continue to greet new visitors.

Be Ready to Negotiate.

Some interested buyers will want to sleep on their first impressions and return to your house one or more times, ideally getting more comfortable with it each time they come.

But the highly prepared buyer—who knows just what he wants and thinks he has found it in your property—may want to get right into a negotiation, especially if the market is tight and he's afraid your house will go fast.

It isn't unheard of for a visitor to an open house to take one of your prepared contract forms, go home and fill it out, and then come back to submit it before the day is out.

If you have a "live wire" buyer in your midst, be ready to deal. There are some questions about your acceptable contract terms that are fine to discuss orally, such as an ideal settlement date, occupancy date (if different from settlement) and your willingness to finance part of the deal yourself.

But the most important element—price—should not be negotiated orally, nor your intentions telegraphed. While still in your home, some buyers will ask questions like, "Is your price firm?" or "What are you really willing to accept?".

Don't answer directly, but try to deflect these questions in a courteous, noncommittal way that keeps the buyer interested, with an answer like, "The house is fairly priced for the market right now, but all offers will be considered," or "The price, like other aspects of your offer, can be negotiated; please feel free to make us your best offer."

For a fuller discussion of seller negotiating strategies, see Chapter 21.

Anticipate Agents.

As soon as you start advertising or hold your first open house, you'll get calls from agents asking for a listing. They will often tell you that your home is priced way too low, and if they help you sell it, they'll get you enough to more than cover the commission and net you more than you'll get selling by yourself.

They might be right; but then, their judgment isn't exactly objective. If you've proceeded on your course with care and have priced your house according to comparable values in the market, stand your ground—at least for a while. Tell inquiring agents you intend to try it yourself first.

Be wary of anyone who attempts to get a sales listing on your house by claiming to have a hot prospect who is looking for a home just like yours. If the agent's prospect is truly motivated, he or she probably checks out the Sunday real estate ads and will see your ad; at that point, you will get a direct inquiry from the buyer. (The main exception to this assumption, which makes the agent's claim more valid, is the out-of-town buyer who is relying totally on the agent to find houses.)

While you're holding firm to your own sales effort, don't allow agents to visit your property with prospects. If you allow the agent to bring a prospect without a written agreement, you may have in effect granted an open listing to the agent. And if the prospect buys, you may end up paying a commission, even without a written agreement. (Some states have tried to avoid misunderstandings—and suits—between fizzbo sellers and agents by enacting laws that effectively bar an agent from collecting a commission unless there was some sort of written agreement with the seller.)

While holding eager agents at bay, set a time limit

Set a time limit on your own brokering. Give yourself 30, 60 or 90 days, depending on the current selling climate and how quickly you must sell your house.

on your own brokering, exactly as you would with a professional broker. Give yourself 30, 60 or 90 days, depending on the current selling climate and how quickly you must sell your house. Then, during your time period, be clear and firm with agents seeking a listing: "No listings until I've taken a crack at it myself." Do your best to sell the home, but if you don't succeed within your time limit, back off and turn the job over to an agent of your choice.

Getting Help

You don't have to go it entirely alone to bring off a sale. There are a number of ways to get professional help and still pay less than full commission.

Temporary Listing Contract

If you think a particular agent has a buyer who might not see or buy your house without the agent's cooperation, you might be persuaded to give the agent a shot at selling your house, but for less than a 6% commission. This calls for a short-term, custom-tailored listing agreement.

Tell the agent to come *alone* to your house (even if the prospective buyer just waits in the car at the curb) and sign a temporary listing agreement that contains the name of the agent, the amount of the commission (generally just 2% or 3%, since you've done most of the work yourself), the name of the prospective buyer and the asking price for this particular transaction. To cover the commission you're going to pay if the deal goes through, the price will probably be higher than what you've been asking for a fizzbo transaction.

Be professional and direct: You should limit the time an agent has to bring you a purchase offer from this buyer, so the agreement—covering only the particular named buyer—should be valid for only one or two days at most.

Open Listing: 3% Deal for All Agents

Because many house hunters do their searching with agents, who get compensated for those efforts only by sharing in the sales commissions, it's understandable that the agents will try to steer their clients away from fizzbo listings. A fizzbo who refuses to pay any commission will, in effect, be trying to split house hunters away from the agents who may have given them considerable help in the search.

If, as described above, you are willing to pay 3% to an agent who brings in the final buyer, you should let other agents know. They will probably be more than willing to cooperate—a 3% commission is about as much as they make on most home sales, because the 6% commission is usually split between the listing broker and the broker's agent. Agents will ask you to draw up a listing agreement—called an open listing—that guarantees them their commission if the deal goes through.

You should be willing to sign such a listing, one for each agent. Unlike the agreement above, it need not identify a particular buyer. It can cover as long a period as you wish, but writing in a finite expiration date is essential, because you may not legally sign an exclusive listing agreement with any agent while you have valid listings like these still floating around open.

If you decide to try this partial fizzbo method, make sure you put the words "sale by owner; brokers welcome at 3%" in your ads.

Discount Agents and Counselors

Some real estate brokers offer bare-bones service, charging flat fees or lower commissions in exchange for specific services that can run the gamut from the most basic—renting a sign—to service barely distinguishable from full-service brokerages. Most offer something in between. WHY USA, a real estate company based in Phoenix, for example, charges sellers a flat fee of $990—$495 when a seller lists the home and the rest

A fizzbo who refuses to pay any commission will, in effect, be trying to split house hunters away from the agents who may have given them considerable help.

when the sale is closed. The $495 paid up front covers setting the price, signs and advertising. Prospective buyers are directed to the seller, who answers questions and shows the home. WHY USA agents will assist sellers with contract preparation and will help buyers locate financing. They also represent the seller at settlement.

If you are considering a discount broker, apply all the same standards you would if you were selecting a full-service broker (see the next chapter). One service you probably shouldn't pass up is having your home advertised to other agents through the multiple listing service in your area. Make sure any discount broker you're considering can list your home with the service.

There also may be real estate counselors or broker-consultants in your community who help owner-sellers for 1% or 2% of the selling price or work on an hourly basis. For names, check with large real estate firms in your area and watch for advertisements in the real estate section of the paper. In some communities, title companies will help you close the deal once you have a contract with a buyer.

Picking a Broker, Listing Your Home

If you're like most Americans, your home is your principal asset. If you want to turn the work of selling your home over to a broker, try to choose one who will help get the highest price (or the best deal) for you and perform the task honestly and effectively.

While any broker can list, advertise and show your home, brokers and agents—like lawyers, doctors and car dealers—come in every variety, bringing with them different economic backgrounds, personalities, resources, and levels of skill and integrity. Regardless of whom you hire, you're going to end up paying a broker and her agent thousands of dollars for their services. Despite the importance of the job, two out of three sellers hire the first agent they contact. Needless to say, that's not the best way to do it.

Identify one or two brokerage firms in your area with a reputation for integrity and a proven track record selling homes comparable to yours. Then interview at least three of those firms' successful agents whose personalities and selling styles are compatible with yours.

Consider hiring a discount broker—a firm that will help you sell your house for less than a full 6% commission, in exchange for your doing some of the

Two out of three sellers hire the first real estate agent they contact. Needless to say, there's a more effective way.

work that the listing agent normally does (see the discussion in Chapter 18).

Selecting the Firm

- **Find out how intensely the firm works your area.** How many listings does it carry, both in and out of season? What percentage of those listings is sold by the firm's agents? One indicator is the frequency of the firm's name in the by-neighborhood listings in the Sunday paper and the number of the firm's signs you see in your area.

- **Check with lenders, lawyers and former clients about the company's reputation and experience.** When you sign a listing agreement, you are employing a firm or a broker to find a buyer for your property. If you pick a brokerage firm because you want to work with a particular agent, keep in mind that you are still relying on the firm's experience, contacts and reputation. While most of your contact may be with the agent, satisfy yourself that behind that agent is strong supervision and plenty of expertise. To whom will the agent turn for advice should problems arise? In most firms the managing broker is responsible for resolving financial problems, supervising complex contract preparation and counseling agents.

- **In your initial telephone contact, ask whether the 6% commission could be reduced under special circumstances**—for example, if the buyer is found by the listing broker, with no sharing of commission with another firm. While brokerage commissions are officially negotiable, in practice most firms hold tight to their stated commission. Review each firm's standard listing contract.

- **Find out how the firm is staffed.** How many agents are full-time? How many are part-time? How experienced is the group as a whole? Do most agents concentrate on selling homes, or do they dabble in commercial real estate and property management as well? Do agents have access to administrative and secretarial help?

- **How will telephone queries about your property be handled?** Call the firm as though you were a prospective buyer, and ask a few friends to do the same. When you call as a seller, you're almost assured of a warm welcome; the reception could be less enthusiastic for purchasers, especially in a seller's market when agents are busy. Does a would-be buyer get an alert and enthusiastic response? How long does it take to get a call returned? How carefully are messages and phone numbers taken? Does the answering agent have listing information available, and is he or she able to tell you what you want to know about the property?

- **Does the firm participate in the local multiple listing service?** An MLS provides a computerized master list of all the homes for sale in a marketplace through its member real estate companies. Agents use this information extensively to match up buyers and sellers.

- **Is the firm hooked into a nationwide referral system?** If your home could be attractive to corporate transferees, find out how many referrals the office received during the past 12 months. How many of those referrals resulted in sales and what was the average selling price?

Finding the Best Agent

Ask the head of the firm you select to give you the names of the agents in the office who have the most experience in your neighborhood and price range. An agent who does a lot of business with sellers in the area may work at developing a list of interested buyers or may maintain close contact with agents who have such clients. Select one who knows the community's price history and who has weathered bad years as well as profited during good ones. Look for an agent who can not only answer a buyer's questions about recently sold homes, but who can also frequently say, "We made those sales."

As always, ask for referrals, especially from your former neighbors. Track down at least two who sold within the past six months to a year; ask them about the agent they used and those they chose not to use. See the accompanying box for a list of suggested questions.

Assessing a Referral

Use this list of questions to help you assess the experience of your neighbors, friends and co-workers with the agents they've worked with.

- **How long was the house on the market?**

- **Did it sell for the original price,** or did you have to reduce the price substantially?

- **With how many agents** did you have your home listed? If more than one, what happened to the other one(s)?

- **Did you refuse to renew the listing,** or did the agent withdraw voluntarily? Either way, why?

- **Do you think your agent got you the best available deal** in both price and terms, or did you accept the offer because you had to make a decision without any more delay?

- **Did the entire office push your home,** or did the job fall almost entirely to the listing agent?

- **Did your agent and her firm make it easy or hard** for other firms to cooperate?

- **Did the firm maintain a strong selling push,** or did you have to keep prodding?

- **Do you think the property could have been sold faster?** For more money?

- **Did the agent see you through closing?**

- **Were the people you dealt with courteous** and pleasant to work with?

- **Did they call for appointments** to show your home and call to cancel when they had a change of plans?

- **Knowing what you know now,** would you use the same agent again?

Interviewing the Agents

To save time, you may wish to hold an informal open house for agents, during which several will come to tour your home at the same time. Select two or three to give you a full "listing presentation" (see the accompanying box for what the presentation should include).

After all the presentations, select the one agent you want to do business with first. Your decision should be based on everything from professionalism and knowledge to personality.

After your interviews, you may find yourself looking at a pretty wide range of suggested asking prices. What then? Don't automatically jump to list your home with the agent who so confidently suggested the highest asking price. Make a couple of phone calls to other agents whose presentations impressed you. Ask for their reactions. Compare the high suggested price with comparable recent transactions.

Elements of a Listing Presentation

A prospective agent's listing presentation should include:

- **Information about the agent's** experience, education and background.

- **Advice on repairs** and other improvements that would make your home more appealing.

- **Information about the housing market** in general and current activity in your neighborhood.

- **Market analysis** showing all recent comparable sales in your area and properties currently on the market. It should specify the selling price and date of sale for the sold homes, and date of listing for the unsold ones, along with detailed descriptions of each property.

- **Suggested asking price,** based on how quickly you wish to sell your home.

- **Discussion of the kind of advertising** and promotion to expect.

- **"Net proceeds" sheet,** illustrating what you might realize on the sale under varying financing arrangements and with various levels of commission.

- **Explanation of various kinds of listings** and listing agreements.

Just as some agents will try to talk you into a low asking price to assure themselves a quick, easy sale, others will give you an inflated estimate of your house's value to get the initial listing.

Just as some agents will try to talk you into a low asking price to assure themselves a quick, easy sale (and sure commission), others will give you an inflated estimate of your house's value to get the initial listing. Only later, after your home has sat unsold for too long, will they suggest a price reduction.

Kinds of Listings

Once you've selected an agent, you'll need to work out an employment contract—called a real estate listing—with the agent's broker. The listing contract appoints the broker (and his agents) as your agent for the specific purpose of locating a buyer for your home who meets the conditions set out in the listing. The agreement, whether oral or written, exclusive or nonexclusive, is a legally enforceable contract.

As you work through the listing contract with your chosen agent, keep in mind that the standard contract can be modified to suit your needs. With any kind of listing, if the agent brings you the deal that the listing calls for (full price and exact terms offered by a buyer who is ready, willing and able to buy), you are obliged to pay a commission *whether you accept the deal—or not.*

These are the most frequently used arrangements:

Exclusive Right to Sell

This is the most common agreement. The listing agent is entitled to a commission no matter who sells the property, including you. If another agent produces the buyer, you still owe only the one commission, which will be split between the listing broker and the broker who found the buyer. This type of agreement usually assures you the most service. The agent is guaranteed a commission if he produces a sale, and you have an agent to hold responsible for making all "reasonable" or "diligent" efforts to find a purchaser.

If your employer has guaranteed to buy your home at a discount if you can't get a better offer on the open market (usually in cases of a transfer), be sure to amend an exclusive-right-to-sell agreement to prevent an agent from claiming a commission on your company's purchase.

Exclusive, or Exclusive Agency

You don't pay a commission if you find your own buyer without help from the agent. If you sign an agreement like this, you're in effect competing with your own listing agent; if you get direct queries about your property, handle them yourself and don't refer callers to your agent.

If you have a good prospect who expressed an interest in your home before you listed it with an agent, use this kind of agreement and add a clause that says you may sell the house to this named party—and any other whom you find yourself—without paying a commission to the agent.

Open

You agree to pay a commission to any agent as long as he or she is the first to produce an acceptable buyer. Again, you don't owe any commission if you are the first one to find a buyer.

This type of listing is most common when there is no multiple listing service. It's also the kind of listing often used by sellers who want to do most of the selling work themselves but want the cooperation of agents in finding buyers.

The commission is typically half of the standard rate—say, 3%. The seller should notify agents of such an offer by putting the words "Brokers welcome at 3%" in newspaper ads and even on the "For Sale" sign. Then the seller signs a simple open-listing agreement with each agent who expresses an interest in bringing a buyer to see the home.

Make sure you specify an expiration date (not too distant) on every open listing, because you can't sign

*Generally, the
shorter the listing
the better, but it isn't
reasonable to insist
on 30 days when
homes like yours are
taking three to six
months to sell.*

an exclusive listing with one agent if you have open listings still in force.

Elements of the Listing Contract

Expiration Date

Knowing the average and median length of time it takes for homes to sell in your neighborhood should influence your choice of a listing expiration date. A period of 30 to 90 days is common. Generally, the shorter the better, but it isn't reasonable to insist on a 30-day listing when homes like yours are taking three to six months to sell.

A relatively short listing will give you the option of switching agents if friction develops with your first agent, or if you feel he or she isn't working hard enough to sell your home.

You can extend a listing beyond its original life, but don't inadvertently sign an agreement containing an automatic extension. If you wish, substitute a provision that extends the listing as much as 60 days if a buyer reneges on a signed sales contract.

You also may want to add a clause reinforcing your right to cancel the contract should the agent fail to do a good job. If you exercise that option, however, you may find that you are still liable for certain expenses that were incurred by the agent. Moreover, some listing contracts may even require you to pay a penalty for having canceled.

Protection Period

If, after the listing expires, you sell your home to someone your former agent had a hand in finding, there may be a clause in the contract that entitles the agent to a commission. Naturally, no agent wants to lose a commission because the listing agreement expires while he or she is still working with a prospective buyer.

Typically, protection clauses give commission rights to agents for 30 to 60 days after a contract ends. If a listing agreement contains such a provision, it also should provide, in fairness to the seller, that the agent give the seller the names of prospective buyers *before* the listing expires—and require written purchase offers from any such buyers within a reasonable time *after* the listing expires.

Commission

Commissions are negotiable. They are not set by law or by industry rules—something most sellers don't realize. A listing agent usually gets a commission based on a percentage of the final sales price of the property—typically 6% to 7%.

As a practical matter you won't get very far negotiating a lower rate unless you have special circumstances that make your property more economical to sell than others. You can make a strong argument for a lower commission or other concessions in the following cases:

Easy sale

The property is fairly priced, and it's in a good location. Or, the mortgage carries an attractive interest rate and is assumable, and the house is already in immaculate condition.

Volume discount

You have other properties to put on the block along with your home.

Double score

Another agent from the firm listing your property delivers a buyer, so the commission won't be shared with another broker.

Scaled-back service

You take on some of the burden of selling and lower the commission accordingly. You also may be able

If you have special needs or just want your home sold quickly, consider offering a bonus or additional commission to the agent who brings in a buyer within 30 days.

to find a "discount" real estate broker. In either case, be sure the listing contract is clear about what will be done for you in the way of advertising and promotion. Keep in mind that if the commission cut is too deep, cooperating brokers may not be interested in working for a share of an already small commission.

Agent has a buyer at hand

You pay less because the agent won't have to advertise, hold open houses at the property or split the commission.

The purchase contract or settlement is at risk

An agent may be willing to make concessions to hold on to a piece of a deal that's on the verge of getting away. Suppose the seller is dealing directly with a buyer he found himself; if that buyer's offer—which might net more for the seller—is accepted, the seller's listing agent won't get any commission on the sale. To compete, the agent may have to present a considerably higher contract from another buyer and also shave the sales commission, to make the second contract net at least as much as the first one.

Another reason for a shaved commission might be a problem that develops on the way to settlement—say, the seller finds out he has to pay more mortgage discount points than he expected. If the deal is at stake, the agent might offer to make up the difference out of his or her own commission.

Condition of Property and What's for Sale

The listing agreement should describe the general condition of the property. It should show what is being sold "as is" and what, if anything, will be repaired, removed, substituted or altered prior to settlement. The agreement should list every fixture that will be sold with the house, and those that will not.

Make the agent aware of problems or defects in the property. If the listing agreement doesn't adequately spell out the current condition of the structure, the appliances and the electrical, mechanical and plumbing systems, have it corrected or write a letter to the agent setting out the information.

Marketing Plan

Get the proposed marketing plan in writing as an addendum to the listing contract. It can serve as documentation should you feel that your agent is not fulfilling his or her commitments. Also arrange for weekly progress reports.

Know your target market. Ask the listing agent to give you a profile of your home's most likely buyer or buyers. Will they be first-time buyers, retirees or corporate transferees? What kind of income will they have?

The marketing strategy your agent proposes should be designed to reach those potential buyers. A comprehensive plan should include these elements:

Advertising

How often and where will your home be advertised? When your home is not being advertised, will the firm be advertising a comparable home so that interested buyers can also be referred to your property?

Open houses

What efforts will the agent make to bring interested buyers to your home? For example, will agents who deal with likely clients be sent an information sheet describing the property and date of the open house? Will ads and signs be used?

Multiple listing service

How promptly will your property be placed in the MLS? Ideally, it should go into the computer very quickly, and you should specify a deadline in the listing contract; some multiple listing services require their members to enter new listings within 24 hours of the signing of the contract.

Ask the listing agent to give you a profile of your home's most likely buyers. The proposed marketing strategy should be designed to reach them.

Some brokers will try to keep a new listing out of the MLS computer for several days or more; that gives their own agents a shot at selling the property "in house," so that the whole 6% commission is kept within the firm. Once agents at other firms see the listing in the computer and bring prospective buyers in to see the home, the odds increase that the listing broker will have to split the eventual commission with another broker (called the "co-op" broker or agent). You'll pay only the full commission in any event, and your interests are served by a fast sale.

Agent tours

An organized tour for other agents in the office should be arranged soon after you sign the listing. An open house for agents from other firms is another useful sales tool.

Spreading the word

Will your agent inform your neighbors that you are selling? What other networks will he or she use?

Financing

Will your agent be able to work with interested buyers to locate financing?

Get Ready to Sell

Your agent will set about the task of selling your house as soon as the ink is dry on a listing contract, so you had better be ready, too.

Ideally, your home will be ready to show immediately, but if it isn't, do all the last-minute touch-ups and cleanups described in Chapter 17.

From now until a sales contract is accepted, your home has to be in tip-top condition and ready to show on a moment's notice. It's difficult and sometimes stressful living in a home that's for sale, but its tidiness during an appointment or open house will have a lot of bearing on how fast it sells and for how much.

Try to have everyone out of the house when your agent brings a prospect to inspect it, even if that means gathering up kids and parents on short notice. When you aren't there, the agent and house hunter can talk more candidly and the buyer can more easily imagine his or her own family living there comfortably.

Most important, you should be emotionally ready to deal with serious buyers. The signing of the listing contract and presentation of the first buyer's contract is not the time to discover that you have misgivings about selling or qualms about the asking price.

CHAPTER

20

Setting the Right Price

Setting a fair price from the outset and including a little room for negotiation is always the best strategy.

To set the right price on a home, you should combine an objective evaluation of your property with a realistic assessment of market conditions.

In good markets and bad, you are more likely to benefit by determining a fair value and sticking close to it than you are by asking an unrealistic figure and waiting for buyer response to sift out the "right" price. And in a buyer's market, setting the right price from the outset may be the only effective strategy.

Underpricing can deprive you of money that's rightfully yours. Unless you are in a frightful hurry, aim for full market value. Avoid overeager or unethical agents who suggest a price that will assure them a quick and easy sale—one that won't require an investment of time, effort or money on their part.

The Dangers of Overpricing

You could set a fair price and then refuse to bargain. But that would deter all those people who hate to pay full price for anything and like to feel they're "getting a deal."

Better to leave a little room for negotiation by asking slightly more than you expect to get. How much more? Asking 5% to 10% above appraised value could be a good starting point. If sales are brisk in your area, you might just end up getting top dollar.

What many sellers don't realize is that overpricing can result in their getting *less* for their house than if they priced it right to begin with. The reason: Knowledgeable agents and buyers often won't bid on a severely overpriced house. By the time the seller wises up, many of his best prospects will have bought other houses, decreasing demand for the now properly priced property. An overpriced house can end up being sold for less than it would have a few months earlier.

Occasionally, an agent may agree to list a property for far more than it is worth—usually at the owner's insistence. The agent knows that, if the owner is serious about selling, the price will have to come down sooner or later. But sometimes an agent who is competing against other agents for a listing will give a seller an unrealistically high estimate of value, to ensure getting the listing. After the house sits on the market awhile, the agent will suggest a new, lower price more in line with what other agents suggested in the first place.

Some sellers who don't have a deadline for selling ("unmotivated sellers," they're called) will cling for a long time to their overly high asking price—say, 20% higher than it should be. They probably won't get their asking price, and even if they do manage to sell a year later for the original price, it will be because a rising market finally caught up with their price.

They might think they were smart to hold firm, but in fact they were naive, ignoring the time value of money. In the year (or even six months) they clung to their high price, the rest of the real estate market probably wasn't standing still. The next home they buy may have gone up in value by at least the same margin, and possibly more. Even if they don't buy a replacement home, they have lost the earnings they would have received on the invested proceeds of an earlier sale—say, 5% per year if conservatively invested and possibly much more if invested in tax-free bonds or a rising stock market.

What many sellers don't realize is that overpricing can result in their getting less for their house than if they priced it right to begin with.

Study the Comparables

You run the risk of either overpricing or underpricing if you settle on a price based on less-than-solid information. Shop your competition. Whether you are using an agent or not, learn the offering and selling prices of similar properties. Find out how long each took to sell.

To be comparable, a house that sold has to be close to yours in age, style, size, condition and location. You should also know the terms under which a house was sold. A $100,000 all-cash-to-the-seller sale is very different from a $100,000 sale with $10,000 down and a $20,000 second mortgage taken back by the owner.

Timing is all-important, too. If you are offering your home when sales are brisk and demand is high, you should be able to add something to the price.

Try to find at least three comparables no more than six months old. Sales prices of homes are published in local or regional sections of newspapers. Information on home sales is available at the courthouse or city real estate tax office (see the accompanying box). You won't learn anything at the tax office about the terms of the sale, the style of the house or how long it was on the market. If you are going it alone, your best bet is to copy the names and contact the buyers and sellers yourself.

If you are listing your home with an agent, this kind of market research should be prepared and presented to you. Nevertheless, ask questions. You owe it to yourself to be sure that properties being described as comparable to yours really are.

Converting Tax to Sales Price

• •

In jurisdictions where there is a tax on the transfer of property, you can determine the sales price of a house by the tax paid. For example, if the tax or fee is 0.1% of the sales price and the transfer fee is $88, then the price paid was $88 divided by .001, or $88,000. You'll find the information you need at the courthouse or city real estate tax office.

Seller Financing?

The market for mortgage money will play a major role in what you can ask—and get—for your home.

In the short run, mortgage interest rates and home prices usually move in opposite directions; when mortgage rates soar, it dampens demand for homes, and real estate prices level off or even decline. (But not always: In the late '70s, inflation and interest rates headed up at a furious pace, but so did home prices—until the recession of 1981–'82.)

The less a buyer has to pay in interest each month, the more house he or she can afford to buy—or to state it another way, the more the buyer will be able to pay for your property.

Conversely, when interest rates zoom up, not only are there fewer people out looking for houses, but also those qualified buyers will be able to drive hard bargains on price.

As a seller, getting the price you want when interest rates are high could depend on whether you've got something to offer in the way of financing help.

Do you have a low-rate assumable mortgage? That would be a big plus for the buyer and might justify a somewhat higher sales price. Look at your mortgage contract, or ask your lender if you're not sure. (Loans backed by the Federal Housing Administration and Department of Veterans Affairs are assumable.)

Are you willing to offer take-back financing to assist the buyer in making a deal? If so, you should be able to command a higher price.

Most seller financing is, in effect, a discount on the sales price, so if you're offering a second mortgage (which would have to be discounted even further in order to be sold), you've got to get more from the buyer to make up for it. (For more on seller financing, see the next chapter.)

An appraisal prepared by an experienced, licensed professional comes as close to an objective evaluation as you can get.

Get an Appraisal?

If your idea of what your property is worth and the listing broker's recommendation don't coincide, an appraisal may be in order. An appraisal is an especially good idea if you are attempting to sell your home yourself. The $200 or so it will cost is money well spent.

Real estate appraising is part art, part experience and part science. As a result, opinions are subject to honest dispute. Nonetheless, an appraisal prepared by an experienced, licensed professional comes as close to an objective evaluation as you can get. Names of good appraisers should be available from real estate agents, mortgage lenders and professional associations.

The value of your home falls within a range of prices. An appraiser uses education and judgment to determine that range, and should give you a market-value figure based on the most probable price which a property will bring. Appraisers should adjust the value of properties being used as comparables to reflect creative financing, sales concessions, and seller contributions or buy-downs.

If your home is in the low-to-moderate price range, you might want to consider a VA or FHA appraisal. Cost varies with the locality, but a typical charge for a single-family home is about $200; a condominium report is slightly more. What you get with this type of appraisal is a certificate of reasonable value from the VA or a conditional commitment from the FHA, rather than the more detailed report you'd expect from a private residential appraiser.

A VA or FHA appraisal doesn't lock you into selling under that agency's auspices. VA and FHA appraisals are interchangeable, so if you have a VA appraisal and a buyer appears who wants an FHA loan, the FHA will accept your existing appraisal.

With an appraisal report in hand, you and the listing agent should be able to come to an agreement. The asking price you ultimately choose may well be higher than the appraised value, but in most cases, it shouldn't be substantially higher. There's the rub. What is "substantially" higher in one community may be an accepted markup in another.

Go back to the comparables. How much of a spread was there between the original asking price and the actual selling price in each case? Is that the normal differential? Has anything occurred to warrant setting a higher margin?

Once you've done your analysis of all the variables that could justify your price, make your decision with confidence.

Special Advice for Fizzbos

If you plan to sell your house yourself, then setting the right price becomes imperative. Study your comparables closely. Get an appraisal. Use it to bolster your sales pitch when necessary.

Some fizzbo sellers solicit pricing opinions from real estate agents, even though they don't intend to list the house with an agent. That may strike you as a bit shady, but look at it this way: If you don't make a sale within your time frame, you'll probably turn the job over to a professional. Agents may be willing to prepare market analyses for fizzbo sellers because it gives them a chance to introduce themselves and an opportunity to persuade sellers to use their services for a commission.

At the heart of any fizzbo pricing decision is motivation. Do you want a fast, easy sale? Then set the price lower than you would if you were selling it through an agent. Do you want to sell for top dollar and still keep the saved commission for yourself? Then be prepared to bargain on other aspects of the deal.

In most cases, the best deal is one that's good for both parties. You keep some of the saved commission, but you don't hog it all. Aim to show a prospective buyer that:

1) the asking price is consistent with the market,
2) he'll save because there's no commission involved,
3) and you'll net more for the same reason.

The key to success is to start with inexpensive and risk-free enticements, then follow up as you need to with more complex strategies.

Faster Ways to Sell

You need to sell your home and you know it's not the best of times. Cheer up. There are more steps you can take to add luster to your home.

In a slow market, sellers often list their houses at what they believe is a realistic price but assume they'll have to lop off several thousand dollars. Would you do better by lopping that money off the top and listing your home for less? Probably not. Price cuts may be taken for granted in bad markets, and the buyer will probably offer you less than your asking price, anyway.

Instead, look for ways to help the buyer. Don't automatically shy away from unconventional deals. Perhaps you can get your new dream house by selling your home to the builder, or save a hurried buyer time by having your home inspected and repaired before putting it on the market.

The key to success is to start with inexpensive and risk-free enticements, then follow up as you need to with more complex strategies to custom-design an approach that will sell your house. Get your house really ready. Go beyond fresh paint, spotless floors and a well-groomed yard (see Chapter 17) by offering warranties, inspections and, in some cases, fix-ups.

Get Your Home Inspected.

Having your property inspected before you list it can pay off because you have time to decide what to do about a problem before a buyer finds it. Ask the home inspector for repair recommendations on these big-ticket items: roof structure, shingles, foundation, basement or crawl space, heating and air-conditioning systems, and electrical and plumbing systems. Should you fix the problem or cut the price? Find out what it would cost to do the repair. Compare that with the price cut a buyer might ask. Keep in mind that buyers often insist on a discount that's more than the cost of a fix-up. If you offer to pay for the repair, your motives may be suspect. You may get a green light, but with conditions if a buyer believes you'd have the work done on the cheap.

Your agent should be able to give you the names of home inspectors in your area, or you can look in the Yellow Pages under "Building Inspection Services," "Engineers (Inspection or Foundation)" or "Real Estate Inspectors." Inspectors who are members of the American Society of Home Inspectors (ASHI) have agreed to abide by a written code of ethics and by prescribed standards of practice. Others are certified by the National Institute of Building Inspectors, which requires, among other things, continuing education and adequate liability insurance.

Expect to pay $250 to $350. You may be able to defer payment until closing, even if you hire an inspector on your own. Some real estate firms can also arrange for deferred-payment inspections (see Chapter 9 for more information on home inspections).

More About Warranties

● ●

The National Home Warranty Association (NHWA), a trade group of eight warranty companies, offers a free publication, *Guide to Home Warranties for Consumers and Real Estate Professionals*. To receive a copy, send a self-addressed, stamped, business-size envelope to NHWA, 498 Thorndale Drive, #200, Buffalo Grove, Ill. 60089.

Offer a Decorating Allowance.

Say you've spruced up the place along the lines suggested in Chapter 17, but along comes a couple who love the house but hate the carpet and can't stand your wallpaper. Offer a decorating allowance—to be paid at settlement—covering agreed-on redecorating expenses.

Consider a Home Warranty Policy.

This protects the buyer by paying for certain repairs and costs of replacing heating and air-conditioning systems and major appliances—less deductibles—for up to a year as specified in the warranty contract. The cost: $300 to $400. Ask your agent for names of companies that offer home warranties.

Target Your Buyer.

Ordinary ads are of little use when buyers are scarce. So are fliers and the other scattershot approaches. What you need is something to catch the buyer's eye—something that makes your house stand out. That might be as simple as paying for a larger classified ad, for example (for more information about sales tools like signs and ads, see Chapter 18).

Offer Help With Financing

Here's where things get more complex. You'll want to consider how you can offer a financial package that appeals to more than one type of prospective buyer. Just make sure your choices work to your advantage by obtaining good advice from an agent and lawyer who represent you.

Buy Down the Mortgage Rate.

A buy-down, in which you pay to reduce the buyer's interest rate, can be a powerful selling tool. It isn't complicated, and it lets you avoid the risks of lending directly. It's also relatively cheap, and it could help maintain your sales price. Sellers who buy down the purchaser's rate by one percentage point for the full term of the mortgage get roughly 2% more for their homes than do homeowners who don't offer buy-downs, according to William Fox, president of Fox & Lazo, a Philadelphia-area real estate company.

The amount you pay to buy down the interest rate for the life of your purchaser's mortgage loan depends on the size of the loan. The lower the buyer's down payment, the bigger the loan and the higher your cost. Fox & Lazo's affiliated lender, for example, charges

4.75% of the loan amount for a one-point buy-down. Short-term buy-downs—two percentage points off the rate the first year and one point the second year, for example—are cheaper; they cost about 1% of the mortgage for each point you buy down. At closing, you write a check to the lender that covers the agreed-on portion of the interest charges. The lender holds the money in escrow and credits the interest monthly as the payments come due.

A buy-down can work better than a cut in your asking price because buyers get a double benefit: a cheaper mortgage and the ability to qualify for a larger loan. For example, on an 8.5% fixed-rate, $100,000 loan, a buyer would have to make monthly principal and interest payments of $769. A one-percentage-point buy-down—to 7.5%—would cut the monthly principal and interest payments by $70, to $699. And because lenders use the reduced interest rate to qualify the buyer, you make it possible for the buyer to afford about 8% to 10% more house.

Lowering your sales price—and the amount the buyer will need to borrow—by the cost of the buy-down ($4,750, or 4.75% of $100,000) won't accomplish the same thing for a buyer who is struggling to meet lender qualifications. At that amount ($95,250), the buyer would make principal and interest payments of $732 a month, $33 more than with the buy-down.

Treat the cost of the buy-down as a drop in sale price. This should reduce the commission you pay to the real estate agent (your contract should specify a fee based on the net sales price) and any taxable gain on the house.

Pick Up Some Payments.

You can draw buyers—especially first-timers strapped for cash—by offering to pay their principal and interest for several months.

Have the contract worded so that you write a check at closing for the amount you've agreed on.

A buy-down can work better than a cut in your asking price because buyers get a double benefit: a cheaper mortgage and the ability to qualify for a larger loan.

Specify that the money be put in an escrow account with the lender and applied monthly to pay for principal and interest. It helps the buyer's cash flow and, more important, it has tremendous psychological appeal. Buyers like the idea of getting to live for free while you pick up the tab. You treat it as a reduction in price for tax purposes.

Offer Help at Closing.

Maybe your buyer isn't concerned about the monthly payment. Maybe he or she has a good salary but not much in savings. In that case, during negotiations you can offer to pick up some closing expenses. But be aware that lenders place a limit on seller contributions. If you exceed that limit, the additional assistance will reduce the amount the lender is willing to finance.

A simple and effective tactic is to offer to pay one or more of the points the buyer would have to pay to get a mortgage. You may also offer to prepay taxes or, for a condo or townhouse, to pay the first year's common charges. As the seller, you treat these concessions as a reduction in price. Even prepaid taxes get taken off the price, except any prorated share for the time during the year that you still lived in the house.

Consider Becoming a Lender.

Helping the buyer at closing is attractive because you don't take on the risks of becoming a lender. But if your buyer can't qualify for an institutional mortgage (because she's self-employed, for example, or already owns a number of investment properties), offering financing is your next choice.

Becoming a lender is riskier to you, so read Chapters 10 and 21 for tips and traps. You should require one to two percentage points above the going rate on any loan you make and terms that meet your particular needs. Limit the length of any loan—three to eight years is typical. Have your agent check the borrower's credit, financial condition and employment status carefully. Work with an experienced and knowledgeable real estate lawyer (and perhaps a real estate agent as well) on contract terms and financial safeguards. Make final approval contingent on a legal review. Then record a lien to protect your interest.

Lend Part of the Down Payment.

The trade-off is more risk. Be very cautious about making a loan so large that it reduces the buyer's equity in the property below 20%. The lower the new owner's stake, the more likely a drop in property value could trigger a default on the loan. A second mortgage puts you second in line, behind the primary lender, if the buyer defaults. For your protection, include language in the note and the contract to the effect that should the buyer default on any mortgage lien against the property, you have the right to declare him in default on all of them.

Consider selling the borrower's note to a private investor and look into what you would be paid for it. Expect to accept a discount—it could be 20% or more—because investors want to be compensated for factors such as risk and the time value of money. If you intend to sell the note, make final acceptance of the purchase offer contingent on locating someone who will buy the note at closing. Your real estate agent should be able to help you locate an investor.

Hire a real estate attorney to draw up the loan documents. Use legally acceptable terminology and, whenever possible, standard mortgage documents and terms, advise Martin M. Shenkman and Warren Boroson in *How to Sell Your House in a Buyer's Market* (John Wiley & Sons).

Treat the discount as a capital loss, which can offset capital gains and up to $3,000 per year of other types of income for tax purposes.

Be very cautious about making a loan so large that it reduces the buyer's equity in the property below 20%.

Provide an Interim Mortgage.

You could also offer to become the primary or sole lender for a limited period of time. Say a couple has cash for the down payment but can't qualify for a mortgage while still paying on their old house. As a seller, you could offer a loan at 10% for one year, with interest-only payments due quarterly and the full principal due as a balloon payment either when the old home sells or at the end of the year, whichever occurs first. (You would treat the interest as taxable income.)

Get Creative.

In lousy markets, sellers must come up with innovative strategies custom-made for the deal.

Substitute the down payment.

Consider taking a note or equity in place of a cash down payment. You may have a buyer who has a note carried back on the sale of another property. He or she may be willing to assign this note to you in lieu of all or part of a down payment. A couple may have considerable equity in a property they want to keep and may be willing to write a note secured by a deed of trust or mortgage on their property in your favor. This could become part or all of the down payment on your home.

Look for a trade.

If you've found a home you like and your own place isn't selling, talk to the other owner about a trade. Trades can be tricky because there's seldom an even exchange. Builders, for example, often insist on taking a steep discount for the traded house. Get expert advice (for more on tax-deferred exchanges, see Chapter 23).

Propose a deal in which everyone wins.

The dream house one couple and their three children wanted was a new Cape Cod–style home with a bowed roof and details not often found in houses today. The builder had dropped the price by $50,000, to $225,000. But all offers for the couple's own house—listed originally for $149,900 and reduced to $144,900—fell through when prospective buyers couldn't sell their own houses.

Finally, the builder offered $131,600 (the equivalent of $140,000 minus the agent's commission) for their old house. That was a little less than they had hoped for, but "we figured we would trade the risk of losing a few thousand dollars of profit for the certainty of closing and getting the house we wanted." The builder ended up selling the old house six months later for $140,000.

Take the Lease-Option Route.

When home buyers are so scarce that cutting the price of the house isn't the answer, think about leasing instead, and turn the lease into a sale. The easiest but least-effective option does nothing more than give the renter the right of first refusal to buy the house. A better offer is a lease-option. This lets you tap into a wider pool of people: buyers who could handle the monthly mortgage payments but don't have enough cash for a down payment.

How a lease-option works:

A potential buyer agrees to two things: to lease your house for a specific monthly rent, and to pay you for an option that gives him or her the right to buy the place at a set price within the option period—typically six months to two years. Payment for the option—

Hire a Sitter

● ●

If you move into your new home before you can sell the old one, you're at a considerable disadvantage. You're saddled with two mortgages. An empty house is harder to market, and if it sits vacant for too long, your homeowners insurance could be canceled. You could rent the place, But that can have unhappy tax consequences. And the delay in selling could be costly if your market heads south.

In such a situation, consider hiring a sitter, or home manager. One option is:

Caretakers of America (303-233-2676), which operates in about 23 cities.

A one-time, up-front nonrefundable payment and an amount paid in addition to rent are credited toward the purchase price —a powerful incentive to buy.

called option consideration—generally comes in two parts. First is a one-time, up-front nonrefundable payment, which is often 3% to 5% of the price of the house. Second is an amount—typically $50 to $300 monthly—that is paid in addition to rent. Both are credited toward the purchase price when the option is exercised and should act as a powerful incentive to buy. If the renter chooses not to exercise the option, the money is yours to keep.

Lease-option sellers often get their sales price, even in slow markets. For example, a house in North Palm Beach recently stayed on the market for only 16 days before being lease-optioned for the asking price. Nearby houses were going at 15% discounts and averaged 160 days on the market. The lease-option buyer, who was waiting for an insurance settlement, bought the house outright in four months.

Is it better than renting?

Critics say lease-options are no better than renting because they take your house off the market. But proponents believe tenants who consider themselves potential owners are better caretakers. They are also financially strong enough to make the up-front option payment and write big monthly rental checks.

A greater concern is that if home values drop, your renters may not exercise the option. You can always renegotiate at the end of the option period. But even if your home appreciates, you can't be sure they'll buy—which can cause real problems if you've already bought a new, more expensive home: You must sell your old home within two years of the time you buy the new one or you'll owe tax on the profit when you finally sell the old home.

Check out the buyer.

You want to be certain your lease-option renter will qualify for a mortgage when the option term is up. Lenders will generally require that the buyer come up with a 5% down payment in addition to any part of the option consideration credited to the down payment. Your buyer must also have the income to qualify for the mortgage loan.

Consider the tax consequences.

The money you receive as option consideration is not taxable, at least not right away. If the option is exercised, that money is considered part of the purchase price; and that means it affects your gain or loss on the sale. If the option expires, however, you must report that amount as taxable income in the year the option expires.

The part of the monthly payments not attributed to the option is rental income. It's taxable, but you also get to deduct rental expenses (see Chapter 23 for more on the taxation of rental income).

Make sure the lease-option contract is properly drawn up by an attorney. Also check with your lender before you set up a lease-option arrangement. You don't want your lender to treat the arrangement as a sale during the lease period because that could prematurely force you to pay off your mortgage.

Boost the Incentives.

Real estate agents hit by hard times are sometimes more willing to negotiate lower commission fees. But in the same climate, others dare to ask for more—and get it, by arguing that homeowners need more help when buyers are scarce. At one point in 1991, Realty World Countrywide, in San Marcos, Cal., was charging up to 7%, with 4% going to the agent who found the buyer. Some commissions in New York City hit 10%.

Century 21 Dorchester Associates, in Boston, encouraged sellers to add $2,000 to the standard 6% as a bonus for the selling agent. Other firms used gimmicks such as the "10K" program: Home sellers were asked to kick in $250 at closing, part of which went for marketing. The rest went into a pot, which was awarded in $10,000 chunks to participating selling agents.

If you agree to pay a larger-than-normal commission, make sure you get a top-selling agent with a track record of moving homes even in a bad market.

When times are tough, you don't have to buy the argument that paying more is the way to go. But if you're willing to pay up and that's what it takes to sell, use the following guidelines:

- **Get the best.** If you agree to pay a larger-than-normal commission, make sure you get a top-selling agent with a track record of moving homes even in a bad market. Ask for extra services such as inspections, appraisals, warranties and decorating help.

- **Insist on a short listing period (60 to 90 days).** If the broker doesn't get the job done in that time, then find someone who will.

- **Get a written marketing plan,** including concrete commitments on when the agent will show the house and on the placement, type and frequency of ads. Look for innovative marketing, such as a no-cost, ten-day "red hot summer sale" with extra advertising.

- **Insist that your house be listed in the multiple listing service quickly,** usually within 24 or 48 hours.

- **Make sure the broker is knowledgeable about financing options,** including take-back mortgages.

Negotiating With Buyers

Tension between buyer and seller is inevitable. A buyer wants the most house for his money; a seller wants the most money for his house.

If you've employed an agent to represent only you, rely on this professional to direct events toward a satisfactory conclusion. If you are selling on your own, consider hiring an attorney or agent (acting as a real estate consultant) to help with negotiations; alternatively, brush up on basic aspects of the art when you hang out the "for sale" sign.

Read the chapters meant for buyers. They'll give you a sense of how an informed, well-prepared buyer might go about selecting a home, making an offer and negotiating the best deal.

Negotiating Through an Agent

Buyers and sellers usually find bargaining awkward and uncomfortable. Both are likely to be more frank and open when talking to a third party. For these reasons, an experienced agent often is successful when two-party, face-to-face negotiations fail. You should be comfortable being utterly frank with your agent. Agents know sellers sometimes take positions they don't mean to hold to the end. Let your agent know what is most

Get ready for a little give-and-take, and look forward to a deal everyone can live with.

Early contracts on a well-priced house are usually submitted by the most serious, well-qualified buyers.

important to you. Be precise about what is and isn't acceptable. Make sure the agent has satisfied himself—and you—that the buyer is financially qualified to fulfill the contract offer; this can be done only by checking all the facts the buyer has submitted on a written financial-qualifications form.

If a cooperating agent brings in a serious buyer, have your agent (usually the listing agent) brief him on your requirements as soon as possible. Cooperating agents should be firmly instructed not to reveal any confidential information about you or your situation to the buyer. If for some reason your agent cannot do this, impress it on the co-op agent yourself before sending him back to the would-be buyer.

As your agent should know, all negotiating should be done in writing, not orally. Be careful not to react to trial balloons the buyer sends up hoping to discover your bottom-line price and other terms. Ask for a written offer.

Don't feel you must commit to the first contract presented, particularly when it's below your expectations. Remain confident. You've priced your home properly and it's competitive with other houses on the market, so hang tight.

On the other hand, don't disregard a good offer just because it's the first or second one you receive. As experienced agents know, early contracts on a well-priced house are usually submitted by the most serious, well-qualified buyers—people who know their own needs and resources and who have studied the market carefully. A reasonable offer from such a prospect is worth serious consideration and probably a counteroffer from you.

Considering the Contract

Money, people and the law are primary elements in any real estate sales contract. A valid real estate contract must be in writing and must have been freely offered by the buyer and accepted by the seller. All parties to the contract must be legally competent to do business (for example, of legal age and mental competence). Money or other valuable consideration must be exchanged for title to the property.

Assuming you are using a specific-performance contract—the most common form of contract used in home sales—keep in mind that if things go wrong the buyer could *require* you to sell your home to him or pay damages. Obviously, you should be familiar with the terms of any contract form you give to a would-be purchaser. But when a buyer presents you with an offer set out in an unfamiliar document, take time to study it before responding.

Once a contract offer passes your preliminary review and becomes a candidate for acceptance, it should be reviewed by your attorney or be made contingent on that review. (See Chapter 8 for a discussion of contingencies that are commonly sought by purchasers; decide in advance how you want to respond to these conditions.)

Consider the contract as a whole. Is it slanted in favor of the buyer? If so, consult with your attorney about making changes. Analyze the document as a series of paragraphs or clauses, each written to benefit one party or the other. Evaluate them one by one.

Don't be overly impressed by a large earnest-money deposit—it doesn't automatically cement a contract. Most offers contain language that makes it likely such deposits will ultimately be returned to their offerers if a deal doesn't go through. Look for other signs—contractual and psychological—as evidence of a buyer's serious intentions.

Beware of the contract that binds only you. Getting a seller to accept an offer that nails down the price and terms but leaves the buyer free to escape through any number of clauses is a perennially favorite buyer strategy. Avoid such a pitfall by examining each contingency. Is each clear and precise? Is it reasonable?

Beware of the contract that binds only you. Examine each contingency. Is each clear and precise? Is it reasonable?

A first offer, even a low one, may reveal what's most important—price or terms—to this buyer and give you the key you need to begin bargaining.

Key Elements of the Contract

Price and Terms

The two are inextricably linked—something you may be inclined to overlook when you first see what you consider to be an insultingly low offering price. If that's what comes your way, remain cool about the offered price until you've examined the terms. Price always comes linked with a specified down payment, number and amount of payments, length of loan period, interest rate, and other terms that can have a dramatic impact on the *value* of the offer. Still, nothing evokes a more emotional response than a low bid. Be realistic and objective. Was the price based on an independent appraisal or a broker's market analysis? How long has the property been on the market? How many written offers have you received? Has the market changed?

Most properties don't bring full price, after all. Don't use price alone as a reason not to counter or negotiate. A first offer may reveal what's most important—price or terms—to this particular buyer and thus give you the key you need to begin the bargaining.

Condition of Home and Inspection

It is fair that the purchaser should have the opportunity to have your home inspected for soundness of construction and state of repair. Keep the process fair by insisting that the person or firm to be used is named in the contract by professional designation, and set a time limit for the removal of the contingency—five or so working days.

Include all mandatory and voluntary disclosure statements about the condition of the property and known defects in the body of the contract. If radon or lead-based paint is a problem in your area, having test results available will save everyone time. The same goes for other required or desired tests.

Watch what you guarantee. Occasionally, a purchaser asks a seller to guarantee that the roof won't leak, the heating system won't go out or any number of other such assurances. Don't do it. If you do, you are not making a sale, you are taking on a partner. Do not undertake to remain responsible for your property once you have sold it.

As a rule, contract language determines what must be in working order at settlement. Make sure everything is clearly spelled out; otherwise, local law and custom may prevail. Suppose that only three of the four burners on your stove work and you don't want to pay for repairs. Unless your contract specifically states that the stove is being sold with three working burners, not four, you may end up paying for the repair at the settlement table.

Buyers often are willing to negotiate on the condition of the house. For example, if your home is a candidate for extensive upgrading, a prospective buyer who is planning renovations that include installing central air-conditioning may be happy to bargain over the broken window unit because it would be discarded anyway once work begins.

Financing

If the contract is contingent on a buyer's ability to obtain an acceptable loan, does the clause spell out what actions are required by the buyer? What interest rate and number of discount points does the buyer consider "acceptable"? Is there a time limit? What will happen if no loan is secured by the agreed-on deadline? How will you know when the buyer gets a loan commitment? How can the contingency be removed? Generally, you'll want to leave the buyer as few escape hatches as possible.

Response Deadline

You'll be asked to respond to a contract offer within a specified period of time—say, one or two days. Try

When you accept a contract offer contingent on the sale of the buyer's house, you are shouldering a great deal of risk.

to get as long a response time as possible. If you are presented with a desirable contract containing a deadline you are unable to meet—perhaps because your attorney or spouse is out of town—counter promptly with a more suitable time frame—and an explanation.

If you think you'll have other offers coming in, you'll want to buy as much time as possible to review them and perhaps use one offer to jack up another. Tell other interested parties (or have your agent tell them) that you've got a good offer on the table and that if they want a shot at this purchase, they had better move fast with an attractive offer.

What if you receive multiple offers at the same time? You have two choices: Either respond in exactly the same manner and with exactly the same wording to each, or examine and respond to each in the precise order in which you received it.

While you are studying the offer, keep the buyer informed of your progress. A buyer left hanging for too long may have second thoughts and may even withdraw before you have a chance to accept or to produce a counteroffer.

Sale of Buyer's Home

Should you cooperate with a prospective purchaser who must sell a home before buying yours? Maybe. But when you accept a contract offer contingent on the sale of the buyer's house, you are linking the sale of a property you know—yours—to the sale of one you don't know—his. You'll be taking your house off the market until the buyer's house is sold and closed. If things go awry, you could end up weeks later just where you started—hanging up a "for sale" sign. You are shouldering a great deal of risk when you agree to this kind of contingent sale. George Rosenberg and Bill Broadbent, authors of *Sell Your Property Fast: How to Take Back a Mortgage Without Being Taken,* (see below), suggest it may be desirable to counter such an offer in the following way:

Inquire about equity in the buyer's house. If there is enough equity (in terms of loan to value) to safely create a note secured by the buyer's house, then you can complete the sale of your house. The note created by your prospective buyer is made payable to you, the seller, whose house he wants to buy. The note could be due in a year or so and bear interest at any mutually agreeable rate. You could agree to allow interest (if any) to accumulate and not be payable until the note is due or the buyer's home sells, whichever event occurs first. You could also agree to accept the created note in lieu of a downpayment. When the house sells, the note is paid off.

This kind of agreement works only when the buyer has substantial equity in her house. The combination of the new note plus old mortgage(s) should add up to no more than 80% of the current market value of the buyer's home. It puts buyer and seller on more equal footing and ensures that the buyer will be motivated to sell.

Nevertheless, if you believe accepting an offer contingent on the sale of the buyer's home is the best you can hope for under the circumstances, seek the advice of a broker familiar with the market in the area of your potential buyer's home. Assure yourself that the property is salable and reasonably priced. Get marketing plans set out in the contract. For example, it should be clear what the owner proposes to do if the home doesn't sell after one month, after two, and so on.

Consider asking for an up-front nonrefundable option (in lieu of an earnest-money deposit), which you will retain if the deal fails to close within a specified time. Have the contingency sale clause reviewed by your attorney. Better still, have her write it.

Settlement Date and Occupancy

If you're selling your home because you already have another house under contract, seek a settlement date that will enable you to take your sales proceeds to

If you need a temporary place to live after settlement, don't consider staying in your old home even one more night.

the next closing. Be realistic; the buyer of your home will probably need at least 30 to 50 days to arrange financing and come to closing.

Most sold homes are delivered to the buyer empty and clean on settlement day. If you need a temporary place to live after settlement, resist the path of least resistance. Don't consider staying in your old home even one night after closing. And don't accept the new owner's offer—no matter how friendly—to accommodate you with a short-term lease.

Other Conditions

Other contingencies address problems or events that may happen between the time the contract is signed and the time title is passed to the buyer. If your house burns down, what happens? Does the buyer have to buy and pay the agreed-on price? Can the whole deal be called off? Can a lower price be offered? What about insurance proceeds?

Take Back a Mortgage?

High interest rates and shortages of available mortgage money are always bad news for both home buyers and sellers. Be sure any solution suggested to you—by whatever name and by either buyer or agent—doesn't just shift the problem from their shoulders to yours.

First of all, do you really belong in the mortgage-lending business? If you need your equity to make a down payment on another home, you shouldn't take back a mortgage. And even if you can afford to help your buyer with financing, you may not want to. Mortgage lending is complicated. It involves both originating and servicing the loan. Origination is setting up the loan—screening applicants, appraising the property and drawing up papers. Servicing is collecting monthly payments, dunning for delinquencies, sending annual statements and foreclosing when necessary.

Tempted by the possibility of earning a high return from taking back a first or second mortgage?

A properly drawn and executed first deed of trust or first mortgage would put you in the most secure position, assuming you required a large down payment as an equity cushion should the value of the home drop. Once recorded, the house generally can't be sold without your permission. A second deed of trust or second mortgage, however, puts you second in line behind the lender holding the first. Should the buyer default, forcing the first-trust holder to foreclose, you could be wiped out unless there is enough equity left after paying off the first to pay you.

There are rewards, but they don't come easily or cheaply. Take-back financing is never without risk. Your biggest danger is ending up with a deadbeat buyer and a contract that doesn't give you the legal protection you need. Close behind is financial risk. Because seller take-back mortgages are usually worth less than sellers realize, they are the equivalent of cutting the price. And when interest rates and other terms of seller take-back mortgages are too generous to buyers, holding such paper can be distinctly inferior to alternative investments you could obtain with cash.

> ## *Take Back or Taken?*
>
> •
>
> For a discussion of what you'll go through—and *should* go through—to get a deal you can live with, get a copy of *Sell Your Property Fast: How to Take Back a Mortgage Without Being Taken!*, by Bill Broadbent and George Rosenberg (Who's Who in Creative Real Estate, P.O. Box 23275, Ventura, Cal. 93002; 800-729-5147; $25, plus $3 shipping and handling; readers who mention this Kiplinger book get a $5 discount).

How to Protect Yourself

Avoid making these all-too-common mistakes:

Amateur loan documents

Generally speaking, the best-drawn documents are the ones prepared by lawyers and used by professional lenders. Don't settle for less. Hire an agent who specializes in real estate loans and an attorney who has experience writing mortgage loan documents. Ask professional mortgage lenders, mortgage loan brokers and agents for names of the lawyers they use.

Too little down payment

By all means, don't take back a mortgage when a buyer wants to put down less than 20%. Professional mortgage lenders demand at least that much equity when there is no mortgage insurance, and so should you. This gives you an adequate buffer in the event of foreclosure because it increases the probability that the property can be sold for enough to cover your loan. It also gives the borrower a big incentive to avoid foreclosure in the first place.

Too low an interest rate

Sellers rarely ask enough, even on second mortgages. A lower-than-market interest rate reduces your return if you keep the note and reduces what you will be paid if you sell it. In addition, the Internal Revenue Service requires that a minimum interest rate be charged. Check with your attorney or tax accountant for information on how much or how little interest you can charge the buyer without running afoul of either state law or the IRS.

Too long a term

Keep the length of the loan as short as possible—one or two years, if you can get it. Resist going over three years. The longer the term, the deeper the discount when you sell the loan. (Since one to three years isn't a long loan term, find out how the buyer proposes to pay off the note. If it's by refinancing, you'd be wise to provide the buyer with a reasonable way to extend the note.)

Skimpy credit check

Too often, laymen tend to rely on appearances. If the buyer to whom they intend to extend a mortgage seems okay, they make the loan. Prospective buyers of that mortgage, however, are likely to ask for the credit report on the borrower. A credit report is inexpensive and relatively easy to obtain by sending your request along with the buyer's authorization, name, address and social security number to a national or local credit bureaus (see Chapter 2 for more information).

Allowing late payment

Pros have learned that failure to crack down on first-time delinquents often leads to costly problems. Make sure your loan documents include a late charge, and enforce it to the letter.

Avoid getting involved with anyone (buyer, broker, agent or investor) who proposes that you take back a note and deed of trust without recording it. It could happen like this: A buyer offers you $2,000 down on your $100,000 home. The buyer will obtain a bank loan for $80,000 and wants to give you, in lieu of cash, a note for $18,000 secured by a second deed of trust on the house—*providing* you agree that instructions to the escrow officer or settlement attorney will reflect only the new $80,000 loan and that you received $20,000 outside of escrow. You are asked to hold the $18,000 note for several months without recording it so that the bank won't be aware of the additional lien on the property.

This is illegal. If you go along with it, you are essentially participating in a scheme to defraud the lender. There is nothing to keep the new owner of your home from further encumbering the property without your knowledge. You also have no way of knowing whether any judgment was attached to the owner that would take first priority over your unrecorded second deed of trust.

Forging an Agreement

If you're selling through an agent, contracts will be presented to you through that agent, and you will

Avoid getting involved with anyone (buyer, broker, agent or investor) who proposes that you take back a note and deed of trust without recording it.

counter all offers through the same agent.

Everything in the offering contract is negotiable. Decide what you don't want to give in on and what doesn't matter that much to you. Changes can be inked in over or next to language on the contract, or a new contract can be drawn up from scratch. A draft contract can go back and forth between buyer and seller any number of times, but you'll both want to avoid an interminable negotiation, where fatigue and disgust could jeopardize the whole deal.

When everyone has agreed to the terms, initialed the changes and signed the contracts, you've got an agreement binding on all parties. All that remains is the removal of contingency clauses, arranging of financing, clearing of title, and other steps on the road to settlement.

Strategy for Negotiation

● ●

If you are a for-sale-by-owner seller, you will probably be doing your own negotiating with prospective buyers. In that case, a little book worth its weight in gold is *Getting Past No, Negotiating Your Way From Confrontation to Cooperation,* by William Ury (Bantam Books).

Selling on Your Own

If you're on your own—one on one with the buyer—keep your dealings as professional and courteous as possible. Don't take anything personally; remember, the buyer has a right to try to pay as little as possible and get the best terms, and you have a right to strive for the same. It's a business deal, so try not to be offended by a low initial offer or overly generous terms or any other initial offer the buyer may make.

If an offer is to be made, both parties must be willing to ask for what they want, voice their objections and offer alternatives. Begin negotiations by seeking out areas of agreement. Find out what is attractive about your property, and build on that. Move on to issues that don't involve anyone's ego, such as the desired date of possession. (Normally, that's not a touchy issue, but, like everything else in a real estate sale, it can be.) Get the buyer thinking about moving in; it makes the whole purchase seem more real.

You could hire an experienced real estate attorney to negotiate for you, paying the attorney a flat fee or hourly rate. When you consult an attorney to have your sample contract drawn up or to review a contract presented by a buyer, find out whether he or she would consider negotiating on your behalf.

Check the Buyer's Credentials.

If the buyer intends to assume your current mortgage, you must be even more careful than usual about verifying his or her financial stability and credit record. Under some circumstances, if the new owner defaults on the mortgage he assumes from you, you could be held liable.

All the legal fine print in the world can't make a good deal with a bad buyer. You could be back to square one if an impulsive or unprepared buyer is derailed by the first negative comment from a home inspector or mortgage lender. To repeat: Make a judgment about a prospective buyer's commitment and financial capability before proceeding into a nitty-gritty examination of the purchase offer. Ask your prospect for a net-worth statement and get answers to the questions outlined in the accompanying box.

Before a Buyer Assumes Your Mortgage

If a prospective buyer wants to assume your current mortgage, ask the following questions. You have the right to know:

- How does the buyer intend to pay for the property?

- Has he or she been prequalified by an agent or lender?

- Where will the down payment come from?

- How knowledgeable is the buyer about market value, the neighborhood and so forth?

- Are the terms of the sale understood?

- Has the property been examined thoroughly?

Keep Selling.

When you sense your prospect is getting close to the contract-writing stage, keep selling. Now is not the time suddenly to begin acting the role of pleasant host or hostess, assuming the buyer will take it upon herself to do the rest. Avoid these common mistakes:

Appearing too eager

If the buyer feels you are overly eager, or too anxious to make a deal, you may lose a sale. He may become suspicious, or he may pressure you into making major concessions.

Appearing too tough

A good deal can slip through your hands if you are too rigid or unpleasant to work with. Try to be flexible and objective. If you can't agree over one point, keep pushing toward agreement in areas where you do see eye to eye. Try not to close the door on any one point completely; just put the matter off until later.

Failing to empathize

Try to see the buyer's side of things. Never become defensive. Be ready with all the information needed; be confident and patient.

If you reach a point where you recognize you must compromise or concede, get everything else agreed on in writing. Then, when you do concede the point, the deal essentially is locked in.

Once you have an accepted contract—fully signed and with all changes initialed—stop talking! Stand up, shake hands and change the subject.

Now you have a contract and are on your way to the settlement table.

CHAPTER

22

Preparing for Settlement

Buyers may dread the arrival of closing day and the huge outlay of cash, yet still be eager to get on with it so they can move into their new home. Sellers look forward to collecting their bounty, but their anticipation may be tinged with anxiety and sadness about giving up their home for good.

The bulk of the work between contract signing and closing falls on the buyer, who must arrange for a home inspection, financing, and homeowners and title insurance policies.

As the seller, you have relatively little to do at this point. If you agreed to have something repaired, do it now. If a problem arises with the title, you could become involved with paperwork, legal bills and delicate diplomacy (see Chapter 12). If a title problem is so complicated it threatens to delay settlement, your buyer may want to void the contract. Your attorney may be able to smooth things over for a time, but if the deal seems headed for the rocks you'll need to determine what your rights and options are.

Keep Yourself Informed

Keep abreast of progress on both sides. If your buyer is having trouble getting a loan on the terms

Even though the bulk of the work falls on the seller, you need to keep abreast of progress on both sides. You can help avoid common glitches.

specified in the contract, you should know it; if she is turned down, it could jeopardize the whole deal, and you could end up putting the house back on the market. A day or so before closing, make sure all the necessary papers and documents have been gathered and are in the hands of the right players. The settlement agent was probably selected by the buyer, but you are free to bring your own attorney to the closing.

Nothing is more tedious than sitting around a settlement table while the escrow officer or settlement attorney telephones lenders, insurance companies, contractors and others for figures that should be at hand. A process that should take an hour instead drags on for half a day.

At this stage, there should be no arguing over who pays what because everything should have been spelled out in the contract. You don't want any surprises, either. Your agent should have kept you up to date on what you should expect to net from the transaction. You should have received an estimated-net sheet when you signed the listing agreement, and another along with each contract presentation. Prior to settlement, the escrow officer or settlement attorney should have provided you with a copy of the settlement sheet (see Chapter 13).

If you are handling your own settlement, you can get an estimate at the time you arrange for closing, or "open escrow," whether it is with a title or abstract company or an abstract attorney.

Can things go wrong? Sure. Documents can be misplaced, delayed or lost. Some of the common last-minute glitches can be avoided.

- **People who should be present at closing need to be kept informed of any change in the date, time or place.** They should be reminded a week before closing, and again the day before. If closing is being conducted by the buyer's attorney, and you want your attorney to be there, too, you should have cleared the initial date before signing the contract.

However, if closing is delayed or changed for any reason, you'll need to clear it with your attorney again. The same follow-through technique should be used for each individual you are depending on.

- **Anyone named on the deed under which you hold title must sign the new deed by which you grant title.** In many jurisdictions, if you have married since acquiring title, your spouse also will have to sign the deed. If a co-owner doesn't live nearby, allow time to have the deed signed and returned before settlement.

- **You should know when you will be paid.** Don't expect to walk away from the settlement table with a check in hand, but don't leave the question of when and how you will be paid undetermined. Most settlement attorneys do not disburse checks until all the necessary documents have been recorded. If that's the procedure, when will the recording take place, and how often are checks made up? Most likely, the buyer's lender will want to review settlement papers and wait for the deed to be recorded before disbursing any funds.

- **If you are buying another property, consider having both settlements at the same office, scheduled back-to-back.** That way, the timing of the disbursement is not a problem. You sign a paper authorizing the title company or attorney to assign the funds from your sale to your purchase.

The Papers You'll Need

For more detail on the settlement process, see Chapter 13, "Get Ready for Settlement." Here's a checklist of what will be needed for closing.

- **A copy of the sales contract and documentation showing that any contingencies have been removed or satisfied.**

- **All documents needed to complete the transfer of title.** These usually are handled by the title insurance or abstract company and your attorney or closing officer. They may include: certificate of title, deed, correcting affidavits, quitclaim deeds, survey, and title insurance policy or binder. Be sure the closing officer has the necessary papers showing that all judgments, liens and mortgages have been removed or satisfied.

If You Hold an FHA Loan

• •

Federal Housing Administration (FHA) rules permit mortgage lenders to charge sellers a month's worth of interest no matter how early in the month settlement occurs. A seller paying off an FHA loan who agrees to settle on June 5 will pay May interest on June 1, and then pay non-prorated interest for the month of June on June 5. This practice is allowed because these loans are pooled and sold to investors in the secondary market. Investors are promised a entire month of interest income no matter when in a month they buy Ginnie Mae mortgage securities. A lender who waives the right to charge sellers a full month's interest must pay the difference to investors out of it's own funds.

- **Homeowners insurance policy.** When the buyer plans to take over the unused portion of your hazard insurance, you'll need to make arrangements in advance so that all the paperwork will be completed on time.

- **Prorations for ongoing expenses** such as insurance premiums, property taxes, accrued interest on assumed loans, and utilities (if not shut off between owners). The proration date usually is determined by local cus-tom but can be different if the contract so specifies.

- **Receipts showing payment of the latest water, electric and gas bills.**

- **A certificate from your lender indicating the mortgage balance and the date to which interest has been prepaid.** The closing officer usually obtains these figures calculated to the day of settlement.

P A R T

T H R E E

For Investors

Are Investing and Managing for You?

The historic popularity of small-scale real estate investing is rooted in the record of home prices since World War II. A well-chosen residence in an economically stable area has been a pretty good investment, at least holding its value and often appreciating more than the rate of inflation.

When the 1980s boom fizzled, however, small investors found themselves pressed to make a financial go of it. Price run-ups made it hard to find homes generating enough cash flow from rents; tax benefits could no longer be counted on to turn pumpkins into carriages; appreciation leveled off or ceased altogether; and in some areas prices actually fell. Adding to their woes, small landlords too often found their dreams turning to nightmares as courts increasingly held them liable for damages on several fronts. But prices and rates are now low enough that investors are once again being tempted by prospects of rewarding returns. You may be able to find affordable properties—with good prospects for appreciation—capable of generating a positive cash flow (that is, monthly rent more than covers outlays for principal and interest on the mortgage and other operating expenses).

Assuming you have adequate savings, and invest-

Prices and rates are now low enough that investors are once again being tempted by prospects of rewarding returns.

ments in mutual funds or stocks and bonds, a rental house could be a reasonable addition to your portfolio.

So You Want to Be a Landlord?

This section is a guide for the small-scale, beginning investor who wants to buy one or more detached, single-family houses as rental property. Of course, you could find yourself labeled a landlord without making a deliberate decision to become one. It could happen when you decide to rent out rather than sell a former residence, or when you buy a vacation property to lease and use personally.

Keys to Success

Examine your goals.

No one should invest in something as illiquid as real estate without determining how it fits in with his or her long-term personal and financial goals. Would owning rental real estate help you meet those objectives? For example, if you need more portfolio diversification, would a Real Estate Investment Trust (REIT), a mutual fund that invests in real estate, or mortgage securities such as Ginnie Maes suit your purpose better than rental property?

Assess your situation.

Success at owning a rental property also depends on your expectations, skills and emotional makeup. Before you get too focused on finding property, ask yourself the following questions:

- Do you have the analytical and negotiating skills you need to locate and buy a good investment property, or the desire and time to acquire them?

- Do you have the money to make a downpayment of 20% or more?

- Can you tie up money for three to ten years?

- Are you temperamentally suited to being a landlord? Do you have time to manage the property, the patience and ability to do so?

- How would you react to landlord/tenant conflicts? A defiant tenant? A lawsuit?

Consider the possible consequences.

For example, you could be held responsible for the acts of people you hire. The Fourth U.S. Circuit Court of appeals recently ordered the owner of a Falls Church, Va., apartment to pay $5,000 in damages after his property manager refused to rent an apartment to a single woman, in violation of the federal Fair Housing Act. The owner did not know about the illegal actions of his property manager and had instructed her in a letter not to discriminate.

You could be held more accountable for tenant safety than you think. Your responsibilities and liability aren't clear now, and litigation is on the rise. What's more, acting on behalf of tenants could get you in hot water with employees. As John Reed put it in his newsletter, *Real Estate Investor's Monthly:* "Tenants' attorneys say you need to test [your employees] for drugs, but employees' attorneys say you'd better be careful how and when."

You could be responsible for damage if children ingest lead paint. The law is confusing and standards of care expected of landlords even more so. Measures passed in 1992 apply only to federally subsidized housing. How the law will be interpreted for landlords of private apartments and detached homes remains to be seen. You can expect the issue to be fought out in thousands of pending cases on the state and local level.

Get connected.

If after that you still want to go ahead, then join a

local real estate investment club, or start one yourself. You may want to make your first foray into real estate with others, via an equity-sharing deal, for example. Club members can help each other by sharing advice and horror stories. They may even tip you off to the right property for your needs.

Acquire the necessary analytical tools.

Whether residential real estate turns out to be good for you—or a costly ordeal—depends to a large degree on when you buy, what you pay, where the property is located and how long you hold it.

Join the Club

• •

The **National Real Estate Investors Association** (NREIA), based in Atlanta, is a nonprofit umbrella organization for more than 60 real estate investment clubs around the country. You can get the names of the clubs nearest you by writing NREIA, 4250 Perimeter Park South, Suite 123, Atlanta, Ga. 30341 (404-451-4900). The organization can also advise you on starting a club.

Going Prospecting

Use local newspapers, friends, co-workers, club members and local brokers to help you locate potential investment properties. Check out nearby possibilities first. Subject any property that comes to your attention to these three questions before you give it more serious consideration:

Is It in a Good Location?

Look for neighborhoods relatively free from crime and drugs, with good public schools and nearby stores, parks and recreational facilities. Is public transportation available and easily accessible? Rule out property more than a 30- to 45-minute drive away if you plan to be on call for emergencies and small maintenance and repair jobs.

Does It Have Desirable Amenities?

The house should appeal broadly to would-be tenants who can afford to rent it. It should be typical, not unique or suited only to those with special needs. A house with too steep an approach or too many stairs inside could turn away elderly renters or parents with infants. If it is located in an urban area, it should be near enough to public transportation that renting it doesn't depend on owning a car. Sometimes a house that at first glance doesn't appear suitable can be readily—and inexpensively—improved. You can charge more rent when you add a bedroom to a one-bedroom cottage by taking space from a large living/dining area, or when you upgrade the appearance with a fresh paint job and add one or two new appliances.

Can You Determine Its "Rental" Value?

It takes the right price to turn a house into a good *investment*. Single-family detached houses are often overpriced relative to the rent they can generate, particularly when they are close to a major city. The asking price doesn't have to be the selling price, of course, since that's what bargaining and negotiating are for. But you have to be able to figure what it would be worth to you as investment property.

We'd like to emphasize the word *investing* at this point. Some purchasers of real estate are really speculators. The speculator buys low-priced properties in decaying neighborhoods that appear poised for a rebound. Speculators also buy foreclosed houses in cities suffering from economic distress, betting that when things get better, they'll make a killing on appreciation. Most investors won't touch situations like this. As in every kind of financial challenge, the bigger the potential reward, the bigger the risk. The speculator who guesses right will make a heap of money, but if he's unlucky, he should be prepared to lose a lot, too.

Running the Numbers

Familiarize yourself with some of the analytical tools needed to evaluate the economics of owning and renting a property.

Start with several relatively simple methods for computing real estate gains and losses. Once you have developed your own estimates for inflation and real estate appreciation, the calculations require straightforward math applied to the data normally used to prepare an income-tax return. Once you gain experience and are comfortable, you can move on to more sophisticated analysis.

Your return on investment property involves the interaction of six elements: on the positive side, rental income and appreciation; on the debit side (in addition to maintenance expenses) interest payments and depreciation, which can be used to offset income from the property—and may be used to "shelter" other income as well.

Loan Payments

In general, a mortgage you get from an institutional lender will be a fully amortizing loan and, as such, monthly payments you make will consist of both principal and interest amortization. The entire payment reduces your cash flow from earnings, but only the interest is deductible for tax purposes. Amortization reduces the mortgage-loan principal, thereby increasing equity—your stake in the property.

During the first year of a loan, monthly payments consist mostly of interest. The proportion steadily declines thereafter. As a result, the tax break you get on mortgage interest drops off year by year until it disappears. Most investors sell or refinance their mortgages before that happens. Obtaining a new loan lets you draw money out of the property without selling it.

Depreciation

This is a noncash expense that can put money in your pocket. You must depreciate rental property by claiming deductions that are supposed to reflect how the building is being "used up." You depreciate your basis in the building (what you paid for the property minus the value of the land). Depreciation is key to many real estate investments because if rental income fails to cover all out-of-pocket expenses, tax savings generated from depreciation—by sheltering other income from the IRS—can make up much, if not all, of the difference, depending on your tax bracket.

You use straight-line depreciation, stretching write-offs over 27.5 years. Current rules apply to buildings put in service in 1987 and later. (Before '87, buildings could be depreciated over 19 years using the Accelerated Cost Recovery System (ACRS) method. It was "accelerated" because the write-off schedule bunched bigger deductions in the earlier years.)

The size of your first-year depreciation deduction depends on when you put the property in service. The deduction is calculated using what is called the mid-month convention. That is, no matter when during a month you actually began renting or trying to rent the house, you get a deduction for only the second half. It makes no difference for tax purposes whether you rented your house June 1 or June 29, your first-year depreciation write-off would be for 6½ months—half of June plus the rest of the year.

Figuring your depreciation write-off is fairly simple. Begin with the depreciable basis—the value of the building itself. (That's less than you paid when you bought the place because you must subtract the value of the land, which is not depreciable.) Divide the depreciable basis by 27.5 for the annual depreciation amount. Divide again by 12 to get a monthly figure, and multiply that by the number of months it was available for rent, whether or not you actually had a tenant. After the first year, a property with a $100,000 depreciable basis would get a deduction of $3,636 ($100,000 divided by 27.5), or 3.64% of your basis each year, until the final year, when the write-off would again be affected by the mid-month convention.

Depreciation cuts both ways, though. Each deduction reduces your adjusted basis in the property. When you sell, the reduced basis is subtracted from the sales proceeds to determine your profits. Thus, every dollar you deduct as depreciation results in a dollar of taxable profit when you sell.

When you improve rental property, the cost is

Tax-Saving Expenses

Be sure to subtract the following items when computing your net income from your rental property:

- **Mortgage interest.**

- **Property taxes.**

- **Insurance premiums** you pay.

- **Fees** paid to a management company.

- **Cost of advertising** the availability of the property.

- **Legal or accounting costs** connected with drafting a lease or evicting tenants.

- **Cost of repairs** to the property.

- **Utilities you pay** for tenants or while the place is vacant between renters.

- **Salary or wages paid to others for care of the property**—cleaning or gardening, for example. This includes what you pay a family member if he or she really works on the rental.

- **The cost of travel** to look after your properties. This can include driving across town to repair a leaky faucet, or expenses—including transportation, meals and lodging—you incur visiting out-of-town rental property. The key to including such costs is that the principal purpose of the trip be to inspect or work on your property. For example, taking a two-week vacation to Florida and spending an afternoon checking on a rental condo won't qualify. A week-long visit, five days of which are spent on painting and repairs to prepare the place for a new tenant, should.

added to your depreciable basis and trims the taxable profit when you sell. Major capital improvements, however, should be depreciated separately from the building. Say that four years after you begin renting a house you add a $20,000 addition. Depreciate that $20,000 over its own 27.5-year tax life rather than adding it to the current basis of the house.

Other Rental Expenses

Deduct the costs of producing rental income from the gross income generated from the property. Since Uncle Sam demands a share of only your net income, it's clearly in your best interest to tote up all the tax-saving expenses that can trim that figure (see the box on the preceding page).

Cash Flow from Rent

How much rent you can charge is a function of supply and demand in your area in general and rents on comparable properties in particular.

Look for a property that, when rented, will produce a positive annual cash flow, however slight. That means rental income should exceed payouts for mortgage, taxes, insurance and maintenance.

A simple rule of thumb, offered by real estate investor Sean McCarthy, is to aim for a monthly rent that is 1% or more of the fair market value of the house. On a $80,000 house, that's at least $800.

If you prefer something more technical, you have other options. John Reed suggests buying investment homes at the low end of the price spectrum. "The guys who have the positive cash flow buy at gross rent multipliers (GRM) of 90 to 110 times monthly rent." For example, a house that rents for $700 a month and sells for $80,000 has a gross rent multiplier of $80,000/$700, or 114. (This is also known as the price/rent ratio.)

Another simple but useful ratio is the income-to-expense ratio. If income is $950 and expenses are $850, the ratio is 1.12. You want a ratio of *at least* 1. The hard part, however, is figuring what the actual income and expenses will be, particularly on a house that is owner-occupied when you acquire it.

Appreciation Prospects

Time spent assessing economic and demographic trends that would affect the appreciation prospects of rental property is time well spent. Nice homes in good neighborhoods will remain good investments, as they have been for decades. Nevertheless, counting on appreciation to turn a negative return into a positive one will be, on the whole, riskier than it was in the past.

Tenants generally don't pay rent based on what a house *may* be worth to its owner down the road. They pay for its shelter value—a function of space, number of bedrooms, baths and amenities. Consequently, as you begin prospecting for houses to buy, you'll discover an ugly fact: Anticipated rents from most rental properties you look at won't cover holding costs. Once an owner, you will experience negative cash flow—an operating loss. Not only will you dig into your pocket every month, but also you must rely on a substantial increase in property value when you sell to offset your loss and provide a good return. And that means having a pool of prospective buyers seeking to purchase a home at the appropriate time (and willing to pay a price higher than would be justified by rents alone), as well as timing the sale to occur when mortgages are readily available and reasonably affordable.

When you buy a home, you may be willing to pay a premium for an unusual house in a good neighborhood. But as a cash-flow-conscious investor, be wary. Such property may not generate enough rent, relative to price, to give you a positive cash flow. That would leave you dependent on appreciation for your return—appreciation that may well occur more slowly on an unusual house than on a more typical one.

When you buy a rental house with negative cash flow that fails to appreciate, you are essentially *paying* for the privilege of managing tenants every month you own the house.

Figuring Rates of Return

There are numerous ways to figure your rate of return on small residential properties.

In the methods presented here, we'll work with two hypothetical properties, one (Property A) costing $120,000, the other (Property B) $80,000. Assume both are acquired with 30-year fixed-rate mortgages at 8% covering 70% of purchase price. (Expect to pay a higher rate of interest for a loan on an investment house than on a home—one to two percentage points is common. Institutional lenders also expect bigger down payments—usually 30% or so.)

Assume, too, that each property is sold after five years of ownership, and that both appreciated at a compounded rate of 4% a year. In addition, we'll say rents, property taxes and maintenance costs did not increase during the five years; in the real world they would, of course, but they could cancel out one another to some degree. Leaving them constant simplifies the example considerably.

We'll see that by the time the properties are sold five years later, the less expensive property (bought for $80,000 and sold for $97,332) generated an annualized total return of 13.6%. The $120,000 property, sold for $145,998, showed an annualized total return of 9.5%.

How Reality May Differ

There are many variables that would affect *your* rate of return. For example, you'll do better if your properties are located in high-growth regions where home prices (and possibly rents) appreciate faster than inflation. Also, our examples assumed the cost of agent-assisted sales with a 6% commission; property you

Expect to pay a higher rate of interest for a loan on an investment house than on a home. Institutional lenders also expect bigger down payments.

sell yourself or obtain with favorable owner financing would improve the bottom line.

On the other side, our example is calculated with continuous 12-month-a-year rental of the homes, with no rent lost between tenants; that's not likely. In addition, we assume owner management of the properties and very modest maintenance costs. Your return would be lower if you paid a professional property manager or if maintenance costs were higher.

Our examples beginning on page 384, use 30% down payments on each property—the amount many institutional mortgage lenders currently require from investors. A smaller down payment and a larger mortgage would increase the monthly out-of-pocket loss but could improve your eventual return.

Beyond Basics

Internal Rate of Return (IRR)

Most small-scale investors in single-family houses will find the above calculations adequate, but if you want to figure a more precise rate of return, use one of two calculations relied on by sophisticated investors in multifamily housing and commercial properties: the internal rate of return (IRR) or the adjusted rate of return (ARR). You'll need a financial calculator and computer spreadsheet—plus patience. The IRR assumes that cash flows are reinvested at the IRR rate, whereas the ARR allows you to choose a reinvestment rate—typically an after-tax rate. In general, the ARR will be lower than the IRR.

Using an IRR or ARR allows you to insert the time value of money into your analysis by taking into account the fact that money made on a sale is earned not in equal annual amounts (as an annual return assumes) but in a lump sum at the end of a holding period. The calculation factors in expenses, income,

beginning equity, tax savings from interest and depreciation deductions, appreciation, income taxes, and the
timing of payments and receipts.

This time-value factor is significant. It's not hard to
grasp that the after-tax cash flow you earned three years
ago counts more than the same amount earned one
year ago. After all, money invested three years ago will
earn more than the same sum
invested just one year ago. By
the same token, the reverse is
true of cash you won't receive
until next year: The same
amount would be worth more
to you today because you
could put it to work elsewhere. Both the IRR and ARR
account for these factors.

The IRR or ARR also
properly values appreciation.
Unlike the measures of
profitability used in the preceding examples, it doesn't
assume that money made on
the sale is earned in equal annual amounts. Instead,
the IRR or ARR assigns the after-tax sales proceeds to
the after-tax cash flow in the year of the sale, thus crediting earnings when they are actually received.

What the IRR or ARR really tells you is the percentage rate of return it would take to make your initial
cash investment equal to the present value of all the
benefits associated with the property, accounting as well
for the time value of all costs incurred and income
received along the way. A respectable IRR on major residential and commercial properties is thought to be
from 15% to 18%.

For More Help

If you're boggled by the complexity of the IRR
or ARR, an accountant should be able to run the
numbers for you. Members of the American
Society of Real Estate Counselors, an affiliate of
the National Association of Realtors, will advise
investors on all aspects of a deal, including the
IRR. You can get a free directory of members by
writing to or calling the society at 430 N.
Michigan Ave., Chicago, Illinois 60611
(312-329-8427).

Other Routes

So far we've looked at buying a house using the
most typical approach, that of putting up cash as a

continued on page 397

Cash Flow Before Taxes

This shows how much spendable cash the property yields for the year. Essentially, you match anticipated gross income against overall cash outlay. Expenses typically include taxes, insurance, maintenance and management fees.

The mortgage payment figure used for both properties in the illustration represents the first year's payments on an $84,000, 30-year mortgage at 8% for property A, and a $56,000 loan with the same terms for property B. It is assumed in both cases that tenants pay the utility bills, so they are not included as operating expenses.

Because you are measuring cash income and expenditures, include as an expense the part of the mortgage payment that reduces the loan principal, even though that item is not tax-deductible, and exclude depreciation, which is deductible but requires no cash outlay.

Note what would happen to before-tax cash flow in each example if you failed to rent the properties continuously: Rental income for 10 months instead of 12 would bring your return on Property A to 0.26% and on Property B to 4.43%.

THE PURCHASE			Property A	Property B
Purchase price			$ 120,000.00	$ 80,000.00
Plus settlement costs				
Two points				
(.02 x purchase price)	$ 2,400.00	$ 1,600.00		
Other costs	+ 1,200.00	+ 800.00		
			+ 3,600.00	+ 2,400.00
Equals Total Cost			**$ 123,600.00**	**$ 82,400.00**
Minus mortgage balance			84,000.00	- 56,000.00
Equals Cash Invested (30% down plus settlement costs)			**$ 39,600.00**	**$ 26,400.00**

GROSS ANNUAL INCOME				
Monthly rent			$ 1,000.00	$ 800.00
Multiplied by months of occupancy			x 12	x 12
Equals Gross Annual Income			**$ 12,000.00**	**$ 9,600.00**

Minus expenses:				
Mortgage payment				
(principal and interest)	$ 616.36	$ 410.91		
Multiplied by 12	x 12	x 12		
Equals annual payments	$ 7,396.32	$ 4,930.92		
Plus taxes	1,000.00	800.00		
Insurance	600.00	500.00		
Maintenance	+ 900.00	+ 600.00		
Minus total expenses			- 9,896.32	- 6,830.92
Equals Cash Flow Before Taxes			**$ 2,103.68**	**$ 2,769.08**

RETURN ON CASH FLOW BEFORE TAX

Property A

$$\frac{\text{Cash flow before tax}}{\text{Cash invested}} = \frac{\$ 2,103.68}{\$ 39,600.00} = 0.0531 \times 100 = 5.31\%$$

Property B

$$\frac{\text{Cash flow before tax}}{\text{Cash invested}} = \frac{\$ 2,769.08}{\$ 26,400.00} = 0.1049 \times 100 = 10.49\%$$

Cash Flow After Taxes

Here, you measure current return after taking depreciation and taxes into account. Because loan payments that reduce principal are not tax-deductible, adding principal payments on the mortgage back into cash flow before tax is a mechanical device for removing them. They were subtracted from gross income to arrive at cash flow before tax; adding them back merely cancels out the subtraction.

In the example, annual depreciation is computed by taking the depreciable tax basis and dividing it by 27.5. That figure is divided by 12 to arrive at a monthly figure, and multiplied by the number of months and half-months you held the property during the tax year. As mentioned earlier, the law considers your property to be "placed in service" at mid-month. Whether you become owner of a rental home on January 1 or January 31, you claim depreciation for 11.5 months of that year,

For the tax calculation, a marginal 28% income tax rate was assumed.

In the past, real estate purchases often were arranged to produce losses, which were then used to offset income the investor earned from other sources. An investor in the 50% marginal bracket paid $50 less in tax for every $100 removed from taxable income.

But beginning in 1987, all taxpayer income or loss was broken into active, passive and portfolio categories, and a taxpayer's ability to offset gains or losses in one category against gains or losses in another was severely limited. In general, your salary or the income you earn while actively involved in a business or trade on a regular and continuing basis is classified as active income. Money received from investing in a trade or business usually is passive income. Dividends on stock, interest from bank certificates of deposit, and income from bonds and annuities are counted as portfolio income.

Rental activity (other than very-short-term activity such as would occur in operating a hotel, motel or country inn) is specifically labeled a passive activity. That was a knockout blow for a lot of landlords who counted on claiming tax losses to make their real estate investments financially feasible. However, the law includes a major exception to the passive-loss rules that makes rental real estate an oasis in the otherwise barren tax-shelter landscape. If you qualify for this exception, you can continue to deduct up to $25,000 of rental real estate losses against other income, such as your salary or interest and dividends.

To qualify you must first actively participate in the management of the property. Fortunately, the demands for passing that test aren't particularly onerous. You don't have to be on call for middle-of-the-night repairs, cut the grass and collect rents. The IRS rules don't say exactly what you do have to do, but even if you hire a management firm to handle day-to-day matters, you can be actively involved as long as you approve tenants, set the rent and approve capital improvements.

The $25,000 exception isn't for fat cats, though, no matter how actively they're involved. It is phased out by 50 cents for every dollar of adjusted gross income (which is your income before subtracting itemized deductions, exemptions and rental losses) over $100,000, and is completely eliminated at $150,000.

The $25,000 allowance doesn't protect losses generated by a limited partnership or any rental property in which you own less than 10%, so keep that in mind if you are investing with others.

Passive losses that you can't deduct immediately are not useless. They are suspended rather than obliterated. You can store the losses for future years and deduct them when you have passive income to shelter. And when you ultimately sell the rental property that generated the passive losses, any unused losses are liberated to be deducted against any type of income, including your salary.

If investing in a property would increase your income for federal income tax purposes, estimate the tax liability and subtract it from the cash flow before tax.

continued

Cash Flow After Taxes, Cont'd.

PROPERTY A

TAXABLE INCOME (OR TAX LOSS)

Cash flow before tax	$	2,103.68
Add back principal payment	+	701.71
Equals Net Cash Flow Before Tax	**$**	**2,805.39**
Minus one year's amortized points ($2,400/30 years)	-	80.00
	$	2,725.39

Minus first year's depreciation:

Closing costs added to price paid	$	121,200.00	
Minus value of land	-	36,360.00	
Equals depreciable tax basis of property	$	84,840.00	
Annual depreciation (tax basis/27.5)		3,085.09	
Monthly depreciation (annual amount/12)		257.09	
Multiplied by length of ownership (adjusted for mid-month convention)	x	11.5	
Equals first year's depreciation			- 2,956.54
Equals Tax Loss		**$**	**- 231.15**

CASH FLOW OVER FIVE YEARS

(Note: Years 1 and 5 reflect the "mid-month convention," discussed above.)

Year 1

Net cash flow before tax	$	2,805.39
Plus tax saving (tax loss x tax rate; -231.15 x .28)	-	64.72
Equals Cash Flow After Tax	**$**	**2,740.67**

Years 2-4

Net cash flow before tax		$	2,805.39
Plus tax saving:			
Net cash flow before tax	$	2,805.39	
Minus annual depreciation	-	3,085.09	
	-	279.70	
Minus one year's amortized points	-	80.00	
Equals tax loss	-	359.70	
Multiplied by tax rate	x	.28	
Equals tax saving			- 100.72
Equals Cash Flow After Tax		**$**	**2,704.67**

Year 5

Equals Cash Flow After Tax (Same as Year 1, above.)	**$**	**2,740.67**

PROPERTY B

TAXABLE INCOME (OR TAX LOSS)

Cash flow before tax	$	2,769.08
Add back principal payment	+	467.80
Equals Net Cash Flow Before Tax	**$**	**3,236.88**
Minus one year's amortized points ($1,600/30 years)	-	53.33
	$	3,183.55

Minus first year's depreciation:

Closing costs added to price paid	$	80,800.00	
Minus value of land	-	24,000.00	
Equals depreciable tax basis of property	$	56,800.00	
Annual depreciation (tax basis/27.5)		2,065.45	
Monthly depreciation (annual amount/12)		172.12	
Multiplied by length of ownership (adjusted for mid-month convention)	x	11.5	
Equals first year's depreciation			- 1,979.38
Equals Taxable Income			**$ 1,204.17**

CASH FLOW OVER FIVE YEARS

(Note: Years 1 and 5 reflect the "mid-month convention," discussed above.)

Year 1

Net cash flow before tax	$	3,236.88
Plus tax liability (taxable income x tax rate; $1,204.17 x .28)	+	337.17
Equals Cash Flow After Tax	**$**	**3,574.05**

Years 2-4

Net cash flow before tax			$ 3,236.88
Plus tax liability:			
Net cash flow before tax	$	3,236.88	
Minus annual depreciation	-	2,065.45	
	$	1,171.43	
Minus one year's amortized points	-	53.33	
Equals taxable income	$	1,118.10	
Multiplied by tax rate	x	.28	
Equals tax liability			+ 313.07
Equals Cash Flow After Tax			**$ 3,549.95**

Year 5

Equals Cash Flow After Tax (Same as Year 1, above.)	**$**	**3,574.05**

Total Return After Sale

This calculation computes the overall return, after tax, from selling the property. In our examples, the sale takes place at the end of the fifth year of ownership.

Accumulated passive losses (those carried forward in any given year because they could not be used to offset passive income in that same year) are used to offset gains when a rental property is sold.

As we went to press, there was no special tax treatment on capital gains—profits from the sale of such assets as stocks and real estate owned more than six months. New rules have been proposed and are under consideration.

In our examples, gross income and costs—except for the interest deduction and annual income tax—did not change significantly during the five-year period. The selling price, though, rose 4% a year compounded—enough to produce a profit. In practice, your costs and income would increase or decrease annually.

Total Return After Sale of Property A

Sales price (reflects appreciation of 4% per year, compounded)	$ 145,998.35
Minus sales expenses (6% sales commission plus $800 costs)	- 9,559.90
Equals Gross Sales Proceeds	**$ 136,438.45**
Minus mortgage balance	- 79,859.00
Equals Net Sales Proceeds	**$ 56,579.45**
Cost (original price plus settlement costs excluding points)	$ 121,200.00
Minus total depreciation ($2,956.54 x 2 for years 1 and 5; $3,085.09 x 3 for years 2, 3, and 4)	- 15,168.35
Equals Adjusted Cost	**$ 106,031.65**
Gross sales proceeds	$ 131,438.45
Minus adjusted cost	- 106,031.65
Equals Taxable Gain	**$ 30,406.80**
Net sales proceeds	$ 56,579.45

Minus tax

Taxable gain	$ 30,406.80	
Multiplied by marginal tax rate	x .28	
Equals tax		- 8,513.90
Equals Net Sales Proceeds After Tax		**$ 48,065.55**

Plus annual cash flows after tax

Years 1 and 5 ($2,740.67 x 2)	$ 5,481.34	
Years 2, 3, 4 ($2,704.67 x 3)	+ 8,114.01	
Equals		+ 13,595.35
		$ 61,660.90
Minus cash invested		- 39,600.00
Equals Return		**$ 22,060.90**
Plus tax savings in year of sale from deduction of points not previously amortized ($2,000 x .28)		+ 560.00
Equals Total Return		**$ 22,620.90**

TOTAL RETURN

$$\frac{\text{Total return}}{\text{Cash invested}} \times 100 = \% \text{ Return} \qquad \frac{\$ 22,621}{\$ 39,600} \times 100 = 57.12\%$$

ANNUALIZED TOTAL RETURN	9.46%

continued

Total Return After Sale, Cont'd.

Total Return After Sale of Property B

Sales price (reflects appreciation of 4% per year, compounded)	$	97,332.23
Minus sales expenses (6% sales commission plus $800 costs)	-	6,639.93
Equals Gross Sales Proceeds	**$**	**90,692.30**
Minus mortgage balance	-	53,239.00
Equals Net Sales Proceeds	**$**	**37,453.30**
Cost (original price plus settlement costs excluding points)	$	80,800.00
Minus total depreciation ($1,979.38 x 2 for years 1 and 5; $2,065.45 x 3 for years 2, 3, and 4)		10,155.11
Equals Adjusted Cost	**-**	**70,644.89**
Gross sales proceeds	$	90,692.30
Minus adjusted cost	-	70,644.89
Equals Taxable Gain	**$**	**20,047.41**
Net sales proceeds	$	37,453.30

Minus tax

Taxable gain	$ 20,047.41		
Multiplied by marginal tax rate	x .28		
Equals tax		-	5,613.28

Equals Net Sales Proceeds After Tax	**$**	**31,840.02**

Plus annual cash flows after tax

Years 1 and 5 ($3,574.05 x 2)	$ 7,148.10		
Years 2, 3, 4 ($3,549.95 x 3)	+ 10,649.85		
Equals		+	17,797.95
		$	47,104.55
Minus cash invested		-	49,637.97

Equals Return	**$**	**23,237.97**
Plus tax savings in year of sale from deduction of points not previously amortized ($1,333.35 x .28)	+	373.34
Equals Total Return	**$**	**23,611.31**

TOTAL RETURN

Total return x 100 = % Return	$ 23,611 x 100 =	89.44%
Cash invested	$ 26,400	
ANNUALIZED TOTAL RETURN		13.63%

Overall Return on Total Capital

This measures operating income as a percentage of a property's worth and is calculated by dividing net operating income by current market value. Calculate net operating income by subtracting annual operating expenses, such as taxes, insurance and maintenance, from the property's total income, which, in our examples, comes exclusively from rents. Don't include annual mortgage payments in operating expenses.

Overall return on capital, however, doesn't give you perspective on whether the money you keep tied up in the property each year (the down payment, settlement costs, repayment of principal and appreciation) could be earning a higher return elsewhere. Return on equity will give you a better handle on making those kinds of comparisons.

$$\frac{\text{Net operating income}}{\text{Market value}} = \text{Overall return on capital}$$

Property A

$$\frac{\$12,000 - \$2,500}{\$120,000} = \frac{\$9,500}{\$120,000} = .0792 \,(100) = 7.9\%$$

Property B

$$\frac{\$9,600 - \$1,900}{\$80,000} = \frac{\$7,700}{\$80,000} = .0963 \,(100) = 9.6\%$$

Return on Equity

Many unsophisticated investors judge how well they are doing by return on investment. By investment they usually mean the down payment made when they bought the property in the first place. Calculated that way, return on investment typically goes up each year and our investor believes he or she is flourishing. In fact, real investment performance may be deteriorating gradually every year the property is held. Why? Because the value of the property may be increasing faster than the income that it is generating.

The down payment you make on the property when you buy becomes irrelevant after the purchase. What matters from that point on is equity—the difference between what the property is worth and what you owe on the mortgage. Equity represents your stake in the property, because it is capital you could realize as cash—and use for some other investment. Return on equity provides a more valid measure of investment performance than return on original investment. You can figure return on equity before taxes as follows:

$$\frac{\text{Cash flow before taxes}}{\text{Current equity}} = \text{Return on equity before taxes}$$

The following tables show how return on equity differs from return on investment. Say you buy a rental property for $100,000. After covering the mortgage payments and operating expenses, you have $2,000 left

continued

Return on Equity, Cont'd.

over at the end of the year—the before-tax cash flow. Your down payment was $30,000. Assume the before-tax cash flow and the value of the property both increase 10% per year and that you amortize the $70,000 mortgage over 30 years at 8%. The table demonstrates what your return on the $100,000 investment would look like, before taking selling costs into account.

Notice that return on investment increases each year. But look at return on equity. As you can see, it goes down, not up. In a rising real estate market, where equity in a property increases as fast or faster than income, returns will fall.

Return on Investment (assuming 10% increase in income each year)

	Years				
	1	2	3	4	5
Before-tax cash flow	$ 2,000	$ 2,200	$ 2,420	$ 2,662	$ 2,928
Investment (30% down)	30,000	30,000	30,000	30,000	30,000
Return on investment	6.7%	7.3%	8.1%	8.9%	9.8%

Return on Equity (assuming 10% price and income growth each year)

	Years				
	1	2	3	4	5
Before-tax cash flow	$ 2,000	$ 2,200	$ 2,420	$ 2,662	$ 2,928
Property value (year-end)	110,000	121,000	133,100	146,410	161,051
Loan balance	69,415	68,782	68,096	67,353	66,549
Equity	40,585	52,218	65,004	79,057	94,502
Return on equity	4.9%	4.2%	3.7%	3.4%	3.1%

Even if property values and rents increase only modestly, returns on equity still fall, but more gradually. In the example below, both cash flow and market value are increasing at 4% a year.

Return on Equity (assuming income up 4% a year, value up 4%)

	Years				
	1	2	3	4	5
Before-tax cash flow	$ 2,000	$ 2,080	$ 2,163	$ 2,250	$ 2,340
Property value (year-end)	104,000	108,160	112,486	116,986	121,665
Loan balance	69,415	68,732	68,096	67,353	66,549
Equity	34,585	39,428	44,390	49,633	55,116
Return on equity	5.8%	5.3%	4.9%	4.5%	4.3%

The Benefits of Improving a Rental Property

One way to improve return on equity is to renovate or otherwise improve your property, boosting its rental income and market value. The example below shows what happens if, in the third year of ownership, you refinance with a $90,000, 30-year mortgage at 8%.

Landlords, even more than homeowners, should investigate what improvements and additions yield the best returns and restrict improvements to those that give the biggest bang for the money. Adding a bedroom or turning a basement into another rental unit should enhance rental income; building a garage may not.

Don't over-improve rental property relative to other homes in the same neighborhood. You could end up with more negative cash flow each month and insufficient appreciation to offset your additional investment.

A program for improvement: If you decide to proceed, look into the FHA's Section 203(k) rehab loans. They can be used by investors who buy one- to four-family dwellings that need rehabilitation or renovation. Once loan proceeds are used to pay off the seller, remaining funds are placed in escrow and released as construction and rehab work are completed.

Return on Equity (reflects refinancing for improvements and to increase rent)

	Years				
	1	*2*	*3*	*4*	*5*
Before-tax cash flow	$ 1,000	$ 1,040	$ 2,500	$ 2,600	$ 2,704
Property value	100,000	104,000	130,000	135,200	140,608
Loan balance	69,415	68,732	89,248	88,434	87,552
Equity	30,585	35,218	40,752	46,766	53,056
Return on equity	3.3%	2.9%	6.1%	5.6%	5.1%

Pull Out Equity, Put It to Better Use

One way to deal with the decline in return on equity is to pull some out of the property through a full or partial refinancing. Loan proceeds can then be used for other investments—such as a down payment on another property, or stocks and bonds. That's how many small-scale real estate investors used inflation and leverage (borrowed money) to snowball their wealth

in the 1970s. It's harder to pull that off in a low-inflation environment, but the technique is the same.

Most investors realize their return can be magnified by borrowing a large part of the purchase price when they invest in real estate. But the same investors who eagerly use leverage when buying forget about its power after the purchase, often letting their

continued

Pull Out Equity, Put It to Better Use, Cont'd.

equity grow well beyond 20% or 30%. (In the first return-on-equity example, on page 394, investor equity over the five-year period rose from 37% to 59% of the property's value, and the return fell.)

The good reasons for using leverage when you buy apply to holding as well. You could make it a practice to set and maintain an equity target—say, 20% or 30% of property value. You could refinance, trade or sell the property as you think best.

The decline in return on equity and the difficulties and expense that may be encountered in refinancing create, in effect, a penalty for retaining property for long periods. But for now, the lack of special capital-gains tax treatment and relatively low tax rates counter the pressure to sell—at least for properties producing income on a before-tax basis.

Returning to properties A and B, described in the examples on the preceding pages, let's calculate the return on equity at the end of the first year, using before-tax and after-tax cash flows. We'll assume that each property appreciated 4% over its purchase price of, respectively, $120,000 and $80,000.

Return on Equity Before Tax (end of year 1)

	Property A	Property B
Before-tax cash flow	$ 2,104	$ 2,769
Property value	24,800	83,200
Loan balance	83,298	55,532
Equity	41,502	27,668
Return on equity	5.1%	10.0%

Equity Dividend After Tax

This illustration reflects the tax savings from mortgage interest and depreciation deductions that real estate investments provide.

Remember, these figures are projections, not results. Use them to assist you in making investment decisions, and then at least once each year to see where you stand.

Return on Equity After Tax (end of year 1)

	Property A	Property B
After-tax cash flow	$ 2,741	$ 3,574
Equity	41,502	27,668
Return on equity after tax	6.6%	11.8%

down payment and financing the remainder. There are other ways to do it.

Buying Default and Foreclosed Property

Two sources of income properties are "default" properties and "foreclosed" homes held by lenders. When you buy a house from an owner who hasn't been making mortgage payments—and has been informed that foreclosure procedures have been started—you are buying what is called a default property. Investors are always on the lookout for such situations, figuring the owner is desperate and may be willing to bargain rather than risk further damage to his or her credit rating.

Banks and s&l's end up with what are called real estate owned (REO) properties only after they have been auctioned off following foreclosure. An REO house, for example, belongs to an s&l because its bid was the highest-price offer at the trustee's sale or judicial foreclosure.

As you might suspect, lenders are eager to get rid of these properties. The price may be attractive and the financing terms hard to beat. Trouble is, lots of people know about these opportunities and prices can be overblown. In desirable locations these houses may be priced close to their market value—making them unattractive to investors.

Trustee- and court-ordered sales must be advertised in local papers of recognized general circulation and posted in public places, such as county courthouses.

Mortgage institutions such as Fannie Mae, Freddie Mac and Ginnie Mae, savings and loans and commercial banks acquire properties when borrowers default on their loans and force foreclosure. The Resolution Trust Corporation (RTC) also put auctions in the news as it divested itself of a huge inventory of homes, apartments, and commercial real estate.

Buying a foreclosed home involves a high degree of risk. You'll need to assure yourself that, among other things, the property can be mortgaged, the seller will be able to close in a timely manner and you'll be able to obtain good title.

But not all auctions are distress sales. In theory, an auction can work for both buyers and sellers. The situation is analogous to when a house is sold by an owner without help from an agent, and seller and buyer agree to split savings from the commission that would otherwise have been added to the price of the house. From a seller's perspective a quick sale at auction saves carrying costs; for an investor, it can mean more house for less money. It doesn't always work that way, of course, because good auctioneers earn their pay by getting bidders to pay as much as or more than they would in a conventional sale. Sit in on several auctions before you bid. Some auctioneers give seminars for prospective bidders, and there may be a short dry run given for newcomers on the day of the auction.

Locating Auctions

• •

How can you find out about auctions of properties in your area?

- Privately sponsored auctions are advertised in local newspapers, usually four to six weeks in advance. Call or write for the brochure that describes what's for sale and ask to be put on the mailing list.

- Inform local brokers of your interest.

- You can also ask the National Auctioneers Association for a free copy of its membership directory (8880 Ballentine, Overland Park, Kan. 66214; 913-541-8084).

Converting Your Home to a Rental Property

Conversion initially sounds like an easy route to becoming a real estate investor. After all, you know the property and the neighborhood, and you probably have a good idea of what would be a reasonable rent. Why not turn the old homestead into a rental property? That way you could enjoy the rental income and tax benefits, as well as the continued appreciation on the place.

Unfortunately, the government has a few special twists in store for homeowners-turned-landlords.

You *do* qualify to write off all the basic rental expenses, and if those expenses exceed your rental income, you may be able to use the loss to shelter up to $25,000 of other income. But once it comes to figuring depreciation and calculating the gain or loss when you sell the property, the picture may not be so appealing.

Although your home probably appreciated—perhaps quite significantly—while you lived in it, you don't get to use the higher value for depreciation purposes. Your tax basis in such a converted residence is the *lower* of the house's value when you convert it to rental property or your adjusted basis. That means you're usually stuck with adjusted basis, which is generally what you originally paid for the place, plus the cost of improvements. If you rolled over the profit from a previous home—as discussed in Chapter 16—your basis is reduced by the amount of the profit on which you deferred the tax.

This rule can make a big difference in your depreciation write-offs. Say you bought your home several years ago for $50,000, $40,000 of which was the value of the building. Although you've made no improvements, it's now worth $120,000, $100,000 of which is the value of the building. If you convert it to rental use, your depreciation is based on the $40,000 basis.

Special vacation-home tax rules apply to a property you rent part-time and use personally. You'll find a discussion of these rules in Chapter 14. Also remember this about converting a home to a rental property: Doing so means forfeiting the right to roll over profit on the ultimate sale of the house into a new home. That tax break applies only when the home sold is your principal residence.

Converting a home to a rental property means forfeiting the right to roll over profit on the ultimate sale of the house into a new home.

Equity Sharing

Equity sharing was one of the esoteric darlings of the late 1970s and early 1980s, when interest rates were sky high. Little companies sprang up around the country to help investors and other would-be owners with the reams of necessary paperwork. Those companies are gone now, along with most of the enthusiasm. Too many investors found equity sharing full of legal pitfalls and tax complications. What follows, then, is a description, not an endorsement of this form of investor ownership.

Basically, it works like this. You as the investor agree with an owner-occupant on who will pay how much of the down payment, mortgage interest, property taxes and other expenses such as insurance and repairs and on how the equity will be split when the property is sold. The owner-occupant also pays you fair-market rent for your part of the house.

Setting a fair rent for your share of the house is a key to whether a shared-equity arrangement will pass muster with the IRS. If you charge a bargain rent, the deal can fall under the vacation-home rules, which would prohibit you from deducting any expenses that exceed the rental income.

But remember that the owner-occupant has to pay rent only on the part of the house you own. For example, in a 50/50 deal, if similar homes in the area generally rent for around $1,000 a month, you wouldn't need to set the rent above $500. And you might be able to set it even lower if the owner-occupant can be considered to be a particularly good tenant. These arrangements are often used by parents and children (see Chapter 10), and the U.S. Tax Court said that "fair rent" for a relative can be as much as 20% lower than fair rent for a stranger.

As the owner-investor, you get all the tax advantages of owning rental real estate. You report the rent you receive as income and deduct the mortgage interest and property taxes paid as a rental expense. You also deduct your share of the insurance bills, for example, and the cost of repairs. In addition, you can claim depreciation deductions based on the cost of your half of the house. If your expenses outstrip the rent you receive, you may be able to qualify to deduct up to $25,000 of your losses against other income.

The owner-occupant of the house gets all the tax advantages of homeownership, on a scaled-down level. The portion of the mortgage interest and property taxes paid are deductible, just as if he owned the house outright. (Like any tenant, of course, he can't deduct the rent he pays you.)

When the house is sold, you and the owner-occupant will split the proceeds. As an investor, your profit may be taxable in the year of the sale. Since the house is the owner-occupant's principal residence, however, he or she may defer the tax bill by rolling the profit into a new home, as explained in Chapter 16.

The law requires that these arrangements be set up under a written "shared-equity financing agreement" that spells out the conditions of the deal, including each partner's share, which one will make the house a home, how expenses will be split and the fact that the owner-occupant will pay rent to the other owner. Because of the complexities, if you're interested in equity sharing, find a lawyer, real estate agent or mortgage-company official who is a specialist.

Property Management: Pay or Don't Play

Managing a rental property takes a lot of time, and novice investors nearly always underestimate how much—at least initially. Then they discover that collecting rents and getting repairs done at reasonable costs can become a big, never-ending headache. In fact, this scenario is played out so often that professional managers consider unseasoned "self-managers" a good source of business.

What can you do to avoid taking on a commitment you will end up despising? For starters, stick close to home. The first property you buy and manage should be located no more than 30 to 40 minutes away.

Even if time will not be a pressing factor, ask yourself whether you have the skills, toughness and

What can you do to avoid taking on a commitment you will end up despising? For starters, stick close to home. Your first property should be located no more than 30 to 40 minutes away.

perseverance to handle the job in a businesslike manner. Can you do a thorough job of screening prospective tenants? Can you handle phone calls? Would you respond calmly to emergencies? What kind of liability insurance will you need? Where will you get good contracts?

In addition to answering those questions, you should be prepared to tackle the following:

- **Setting the right rent:** Choose one that's neither too high nor too low.

- **Advertising:** A well-placed sign and classified newspaper advertising are effective ways to advertise your property to renters.

- **Showing prospects:** You can't rent a home without showing it to prospective tenants. Be prepared not only to take them through, but also to have the property cleaned, painted and in good repair. As you take tenants through, you may need to help them visualize what it will look like once they have moved in.

- **Screening:** Rejecting a potentially troublesome tenant can save you endless grief. Finding a tenant who will use the property as if he owned it is your goal. Use an application form that gives you all the information you need to check out the prospect thoroughly. Be sure to obtain written permission to check an applicant's credit history with the local credit bureau. Then follow through: Check all references, talk with former landlords, obtain current credit reports, and verify income and job history with employers.

- **Lease negotiations and renewals.**

- **Collecting security deposits:** You will need to find out what the law requires of landlords in your state and community.

- **Move-out and move-in inspections:** A major source of conflict between owners and tenants centers on property condition and what constitutes ordinary wear and tear.

- **Maintenance and repairs:** You will have to do them yourself or hire someone else to do them. Finding reliable, honest repair people willing to do small jobs on short notice is not easy.

- **Problem tenants:** Remain a landlord for long and, at some point, you will encounter a tenant who does not pay the rent. If you become too friendly with your tenants or sympathetic to their personal problems, you will have a harder time collecting and raising the rent.

- **Record keeping:** You may have an accountant, but you nevertheless will need to keep good records and detailed accounts.

Don't overlook liability insurance coverage that would protect you if a person you sent to repair a gutter or light switch got hurt or harmed a tenant.

Avoid These Traps

Many individual investors successfully manage their own properties. Many also get themselves tied up in legal squabbles or hobbled with horrible tenants. These traps could be particularly hazardous:

Failing to carry enough insurance

Professional property manager Ralph Tutor urges investor-owners to consult with their lawyer and insurance agent about liability protection. In many situations, owners can purchase substantial protection with a rider on their homeowner's policy. This coverage should be reviewed annually and increased in tandem with net worth.

Neglecting to protect your assets

How you own your home and other assets, including rental property, can affect the outcome of a lawsuit

Develop an inventory-and-condition report, which should be filled out in detail when your first tenant moves in.

brought against you. Ask an attorney or other individual who specializes in trust work about the benefits of putting rental property and your home in a land trust. (A land trust can be used only to own real estate and what issues directly from real estate, for example leases, options, mortgages, deeds of trust, and so forth. When you put property in a land trust, the title—or deed—is transferred to the name of a trustee. For example, if you were sued and a judgment was recorded against you, it would attach to you and to assets you own in your name. It generally would not attach to property owned by a land trust.)

Failing to keep up with relevant court cases and government mandates

Overlooking either one could put you out of business or cause you grievous loss. An individual who buys a single property and has a run of good tenants and no problems is most apt to stumble into this situation.

Neglecting to follow up on prospective tenants

You may ask for all the pertinent information on an application form and get the necessary written permission needed to verify creditworthiness and employment, but if you don't follow up with so much as a phone call, you're asking for trouble. If you can't do it, hire someone who will. A "lease only" company, for instance, could take on the job of advertising and screening your tenants. Service isn't cheap: The fee is commonly 50% of the first month's rent.

Overlooking recordkeeping

If you don't keep good records, you won't know how you are doing financially. Worse, you could end up tangling with the IRS.

Keep tabs on wear and tear. Ralph Tutor, author of *How to Make Big Money Managing Small Properties,* suggests landlords develop an inventory-and-condition report, which should be filled out in detail when your first tenant moves in. This report establishes a baseline with which future property inspection reports can be compared. Give a copy of this report to the first tenant when she moves in. Allow 48 hours for changes or additions. Then repeat this inspection process when the tenant moves out, using the report as a basis for determining whether all or part of the security deposit will be returned. Repeat with each tenant.

Hiring a Pro

Good professional management can be a boon to an investor. For example, if you are headed overseas or you own rental property in a distant resort area, trying to do without hands-on local management is just plain risky. Even investors with local properties decide they don't want the hassle of dealing with tenants. So weigh your options and be realistic about your capabilities. Remember that for tax purposes, even if you pay a management firm to handle day-to-day matters, you'll probably meet the IRS's definition of active management if you're involved in approving tenants, setting rents, and okaying repairs and capital improvements (as discussed on page 387).

If you decide to go with professional management, select carefully.

You will pay anywhere from 8% to 14% of your monthly rental income for the services of a property manager. On top of that, each time the property is leased or the lease is renewed, there will be a leasing fee of 20% to 50% of the first month's rent. On a home that brings in $900 a month in rent, that amounts to $1,350 each year, assuming a 10% monthly management fee and a 25% leasing fee. If you want the manager to handle mortgage or insurance payments, you also could pay a one-time set-up fee.

What should you expect in return? For starters, a property manager should be more than a rent collector (see the accompanying box). A good one will see that your property is rented and cared for in a way that max-

If you are headed overseas or you own rental property in a distant resort area, trying to do without hands-on local management is just plain risky.

Questions to Ask

When you look for a property manager, get answers to the following questions before you hire one:

What kind of experience does he or she have? Look for a manager with at least five years of full-time property-management experience. Look for experience with properties similar to yours.

Ask about educational background and professional affiliations. The Institute of Real Estate Management, for example, designates qualified individuals as certified property managers (CPMs) and accredited resident managers (ARMs).

What kind of properties does he or she manage? To whom do the properties belong? Can you look at them? Can you speak with the owners?

How many properties does he or she manage? What kind of support staff do they have, and how many? A property manager may be able to handle a large residential apartment building with very little help. That is not the case when managing dozens of single-family dwellings scattered over a metropolitan area. What's a good ratio of support staff to properties? Ideally, a manager should have one support staffer for every 50 to 75 properties under his or her management.

Are record keeping and bookkeeping handled on a computer? You wouldn't automatically reject a manager for not having this in place, but these days, it is a sign of efficiency and service capability. And better to have the system up and running before you come on board than to be involved in a "transition," with its inevitable glitches and gaps.

What kind of reports will you get, and how often? Monthly accounting statements and an annual property-condition report are minimal service. Look for routine property reports every six months and each time the lease changes. How often will drive-by inspections occur?

How will repairs and maintenance be handled? Does the firm have repair people under contract? On retainer? Are they licensed and bonded?

How does the manager handle vacancies? What about advertising? Tenant screening and credit checks?

What kind of insurance does he carry?

How does the fee structure work?

Under what circumstances can you be released from your contract?

Under what circumstances would the manager terminate your contract?

Will the contract be automatically renewed? If so, what action must you take to terminate the agreement?

Can you obtain references from the prospective manager?

imizes income and enhances value. That means selecting good tenants and keeping turnover low. It means
maintaining the property and charging the right
amount of rent.

The Management Contract

Ultimately, everything should be laid out clearly in
a management contract. You are appointing the property manager as your attorney-in-fact and giving him or
her the authority to negotiate leases, collect rents, hold
security deposits and, if necessary, evict tenants, on
your behalf.

On-the-ball property management firms already
have modified the language in their contracts to ensure
that investors will be treated as "active" managers for
tax purposes. But don't take it for granted. Discuss the
matter with prospective managers and double check
the contract wording. Remember, too, that should you
be audited, the IRS will look beyond the contract for
evidence of correspondence, telephone calls and the
like to verify your involvement.

Many management contracts commit you to using
the property manager as broker should you decide to
sell your property. That may suit you fine if you are satisfied with your property manager. The manager may
even be willing to charge you a lower-than-market commission if it appears that you may be able to sell to your
tenant or to another investor with properties under the
same management.

But where do you stand if you believe your investment has been badly managed and has been allowed to
run down? You don't want that manager handling the
sale. You can cancel your contract and manage the
property yourself for the next three months, then put it
on the market. But what if the current tenants are
uncooperative or destructive? Then you'll have to
decide which is worse: paying a sales commission to a
broker you think did you wrong or taking the risk that
the property will be worth considerably less by the time

*Ultimately,
everything should be
laid out clearly in a
management
contract. You are
appointing the
property manager as
your attorney-in-fact
and giving him or
her authority.*

you can sell it. And if you don't sell it yourself, you'll wind up paying a sales commission anyway.

Moving On, Selling Out

When you're ready to unload property, here are two strategies to consider:

Tax-Deferred Exchanges

You may have heard of a "tax-free exchange" of real estate, a concept that has definite appeal. This maneuver allows you to dispose of rental property without triggering an immediate tax bill on the gain. What it demands is that you find an amenable owner of similar property. Although that's not easy, some brokers specialize in real estate exchanges.

If you trade property for property of a "like kind," the IRS does not treat your disposal of your property as a sale. *Like kind* is liberally defined. Clearly, exchanging a rental house for another rental house is covered, but so is trading raw land for an apartment building. The advantage is that you hold off the tax bill on your profit from the first property.

Say you have a rental house with an adjusted basis of $50,000 and that it is now worth $150,000. You'd like to expand your rental activities by buying a duplex with a price tag of $250,000. If you sell the first house, you'll owe tax on $100,000 of profit. That will cost you $28,000 if you're in the 28% bracket. Instead, assume you persuade the owner of the duplex to trade—his $250,000 duplex for your $150,000 house plus $100,000 in cash. As long as the deal qualifies as a tax-free exchange, you avoid that $28,000 tax tab.

Avoid is really too strong a term. *Defer* is more accurate. Your basis in the new building would not be its $250,000 price but rather your old $50,000 basis plus the $100,000 in cash you had to put into the deal. When you later sell the duplex—assuming you don't work another tax-free exchange—the gain would be based on your $150,000 basis. That would give the IRS its delayed shot at the $100,000 of profit that built up in the first house.

Because, in this example, the owner of the duplex received cash as well as like-kind property, it would not be a totally tax-deferred exchange for him. Part or all of his profit—the difference between his basis in the property and the $250,000 value of your building plus cash—would be taxable. He would owe tax on the $100,000 (the amount of cash received). His basis on the rental house would be reduced by any part of the $100,000 that wasn't taxed in the year of the trade.

Like-kind exchanges have disadvantages. Your depreciation deductions on the new property will be held down because you carry over the basis from the old property. Also, if you use a like-kind exchange in a year you have suspended passive losses (see discussion in section, "Cash Flow After Taxes") you'll miss the chance to absorb some of those losses.

For an exchange to qualify as a simultaneous tax-deferred exchange, you must meet exacting IRS rules. You will want to obtain competent legal and tax guidance from individuals who specialize in handling such transactions, called 1031 exchanges for the section of the tax code that authorizes them.

> ### *For More Information*
> •
> Clark Boardman Callaghan publishes *Tax Free Exchanges Under § 1031,* an expensive but comprehensive book on the subject (CBC, 155 Pfingsten Road, Deerfield, Ill. 60015-4998; 800-221-9428; $95).

Installment Sales

Installment sales are a popular method for selling property, particularly rental real estate, because the seller can help grease the deal by providing at least part of the necessary financing for the buyer. Rather than demanding the full price up front, with an installment sale you agree to have the buyer pay at least part of the price in the future. And if you're lucky, the IRS may not tax your profit, depending on the guidelines in effect at the time of the sale.

If you will receive at least one payment in a year after the sale, you can use the installment method to report and pay tax on the profit as you receive it. Each year, the payments you receive will have three basic components:

- Return of your basis, which is nontaxable.

- Profit, which is fully taxable.

- Interest on the "loan" you made by financing the sale. This, too, is taxable.

Depreciation recapture

This is a complication—one of many—that may make you wonder whether the benefit of delaying the tax bill is worth the hassle. As mentioned earlier in this chapter, because depreciation reduces your basis, it translates into higher gain when you sell. The law demands that all depreciation recapture be taxed in the year of the sale, regardless of when the income is received. When considering an installment sale, consider the impact of depreciation recapture. You'll probably want to be certain that the down payment on the sale is at least enough to cover the tax bill that's due on the sale.

Minimum interest

The law requires that you charge an "adequate" amount of interest on the installment sale, and it's not because the IRS is worried that you'd otherwise have an unfair advantage over banks and other lenders. The IRS cares about the price of the sale because it affects the seller's gain or loss and the buyer's basis for depreciation in the building.

You can meet the IRS definition of *adequate* and still give the buyer a break on the interest rate. What

For More Information

In addition to sources cited elsewhere in this chapter, see the following materials for information on investing and managing residential real estate:

- *Investing in Residential Income Property,* by Douglas M. Temple (Contemporary Books, Chicago).

- The *Journal of Property Management,* published by the Institute of Real Estate Management, features articles on single-family property management. You can get single copies free by writing to the institute at 430 N. Michigan Ave., Chicago, Ill. 60611. Also inquire about the institute's seminar and book on how to manage single-family rental properties.

- *Creative Investment Advisor,* by M. Jane Garvey (P.O. Box 495, Glen Ellyn, Ill. 60138; 708-858-4663; $59 for 12 issues; free sample with self-addressed stamped envelope). Jane Garvey is an active real estate investor. In addition to her newsletter, she has written on the subject of rehabilitating houses.

- *How to Make Big Money Managing Small Properties,* by Ralph Tutor (Real Estate Software Co., 10622 Montwood, Suite D, El Paso, Tex. 79935; 800-327-9776). It covers important aspects of property management, including leases, credit investigation, tenant/manager relationships, property maintenance, rent collection, cost control and choosing a computer system. It also has an excellent selection of model contracts and forms that can be reproduced or adapted for use by individual owner/managers.

- *Sean McCarthy's Real Estate Report* (TAAS, P.O. Box 361, Triangle, Va. 22172; 703-659-5496; $35 for 12 issues; free sample copy available with self-addressed stamped envelope). Sean McCarthy is an active real estate investor. He also conducts seminars, consults in the area of land trusts, and writes on the subjects of real estate and asset protection.

- *The Home Equity Kit,* by Andrew James McLean (John Wiley & Sons). This book is out of print, but it may be available in public libraries.

- *How to Manage Residential Property for Maximum Cash Flow and Resale Value,* by John T. Reed (Reed Publishing, 342 Bryan Drive, Danville, Cal. 94526).

- *The Real Estate Investors Q&A Book,* by Hugh Holbert with Ron Tepper (John Wiley & Sons).

- *How to Find and Manage Profitable Properties,* by Robert Irwin (McGraw-Hill). This, too, is out of print, but worth looking for.

the agency demands is that you charge a rate at least equal to the "applicable federal rate" (AFR) in effect at the time of the sale. The AFR is set by the IRS.

If the contract fails to provide for adequate stated interest, the IRS will dictate what part of each payment is "imputed" interest—that is, what part will be treated as interest no matter what you call it. This affects not only your gain or loss and the buyer's basis but also the amount of interest income you report each year and the amount the buyer gets to deduct. It's much easier to check with the IRS before finalizing a deal to be sure you include an adequate interest rate.

Index

Profit From Our Experience

To order any Kiplinger product, call toll free, 1-800-544-0155 (ask for operator 25), or send your check to: Kiplinger Books and Tapes, 3401 East-West Highway, Hyattsville, MD 20782-1974.

Please send me:	Price		Quantity	Total
Books				
Kiplinger's Facing 40 (hardcover)	$19.95	R		
Kiplinger's Career Starter (paper)	$10.95	V		
Kiplinger's Working for Yourself (paper)	$14.95	N		
Kiplinger's Taming the Paper Tiger (paper)	$11.95	M		
Kiplinger's Invest Your Way to Wealth (hardcover)	$21.95	G		
Kiplinger's Make Your Money Grow (paper)	$14.95	S		
Kiplinger's Buying and Selling a Home (paper)	$13.95	T		
Kiplinger's Sure Ways to Cut Your Taxes (paper)	$13.95	Q		
Kiplinger's Take Charge of Your Career (paper)	$10.95	E		
Kiplinger's 12 Steps to a Worry-Free Retirement (paper)	$14.95	U		
Video Guides				
Kiplinger's Guide to Small Business Growth	$29.95	P		
Kiplinger's Guide to Retirement Security	$29.95	I		
Kiplinger's Guide to Personal Finance	$29.95	L		
Kiplinger's Guide to Family Finance	$29.95	J		
			Subtotal	
			Sales Tax	
			Shipping	$3.00
			Total	

SALES TAX: DC and FL residents add 6% sales tax; MD add 5%.

❑ My check payable to Kiplinger Books is enclosed for $_____.

❑ Charge my: ❑ VISA ❑ MasterCard

Card No. ❑❑❑❑❑❑❑❑❑❑❑❑❑❑❑❑

Signature _____

Exp. Date _____ Daytime Phone (_____) _____

Name _____

Company _____

Address _____ Apt. No. _____

City _____ State _____ Zip _____